THE LONGEST REBELLION

The Dunlavin Massacre, Michael Dwyer and West Wicklow 1797-1803

Chris

small world media

SMALL WORLD PUBLISHING
2 Great Strand Street
Dublin 1
Ireland
www.smallworldmedia.ie

First published by SMALL HISTORY as a trade paperback, October 2007

Trade enquiries to
00 353 [0]87 955 1504 (Ireland, Europe)

info@smallworldmedia.ie

ISBN: 978 0 9554634 2 6

The author gratefully acknowledges the generous support of the *Irish
Council for Research in the Humanities and Social Sciences* for his
ongoing research and work.

Cover and book design, typesetting: SMALL WORLD BOOK SERVICES

Cover photographs: Front (top): Commemorative stone erected on
Dunlavin Green in 1998; Front (bottom): The Dwyer-McAllister
cottage in Derrynamuck; Back: Michael Dwyer's headstone in Waverley
Cemetery, Sydney, New South Wales. All photographs by the author.

Printed by La Grafica Nuova S.C.R.L., Torino

Acknowledgements

I wish to thank the following people for their help and support.

Margaret, my wife.
Declan, Jason and Michael, my sons.
The staff of the National Archives, especially Mr. Brian Donnelly.
The staff of the National Library of Ireland, especially Ms. Joanne Finnegan
The staff of Naas library, especially Mrs. Ursula McManus.
The staff of the Leinster Leader archives in Basin Street, Naas.
Dr. James Kelly, Saint Patrick's College, Drumcondra, Dublin.
Dr. Raymond Gillespie, N.U.I. Maynooth, Co. Kildare.
Dr. Ruan O'Donnell, University of Limerick.
Dr. Elizabeth Malcolm, University of Melbourne.
Dr. Perry McIntyre, University of Western Sydney.
Dr. Philip Bull, La Trobe University, Melbourne.
Dr. Cindy McCreery, University of Sydney.
Mr. Philip Moore, Australian Irish Connections, Melbourne.
Mr. Derek Russell, TAFE Sydney Institute.
Ms. Penny Woods, Russell Library, N.U.I., Maynooth.
Mr. Shane Mawe, Trinity College Library.
Mr. Mario Corrigan, Kildare County Library, Newbridge.
Mrs. Margaret Birchall, Blessington Library.
Ms Maura Greene, Dunlavin Library.
Dr. David Craig, Director of the National Archives.
Mr. Paul Haycock, Wigton, Cumbria.
Mr. Harry Murphy, Glen of Imaal.
Mr. Jim Keogh, Dunlavin.
Mr. Gerard O'Dwyer, Dunlavin.
Mr. George Coleborn, Dunlavin.
Mr. Michael Deering, Lemonstown.
The management of Katie Lowe's, Kiltegan.
The Daynes family, Bluestone, Dunlavin.
Mairéad Evans, Edenderry Historical Society.
Mr. Patrick Power, Arklow.
Mr. Bill Walsh, Baltinglass.
Cllr. Tommy Cullen, Baltinglass.
Mr. Paul Gorry FSG, MAPGI, Baltinglass.
Mr. Donal McDonnell, West Wicklow Historical Society.
Fr. Patrick Finn, Donard.
Fr. Joe Whittle, Dunlavin
Mr. Joe O'Flynn, Rathsallagh House.

I would also like to express my gratitude to all the repositories, authors, publishers, companies and individuals who have allowed me to quote from their archive/works.

List of Abbreviations

A.A.	Anti Aircraft
A.D.C.	Aide de Campe
B.A.	Bachelor of Arts
C	Cavalry
Capt.	Captain
C.C.	Catholic curate
Co.	County
Dr.	Doctor
Esq.	Esquire
F.C.A.	Fórsa Cosanta Áitiuíl
Fr.	Father
G.A.A.	Gaelic Athletic Association
G.O.C.	General Officer Commanding
H.M.S.	His Majesty's Ship
I.	Infantry
J.P.	Justice of the Peace
L.D.F.	Local Defence Force
Lieut.	Lieutenant
L.S.F.	Local Security Force
Lt.	Light
M.A.	Master of Arts
M.C.C.	Member of the County Council
M.P.	Member of Parliament
MSS.	Manuscripts
N.A.I.	National Archive of Ireland
N.L.I.	National Library of Ireland
N.T.	National Teacher
N.U.I.	National University of Ireland
P.P.	Parish Priest
T.C.D.	Trinity College Dublin
U.D.C.	Urban District Council
U.I.	United Irishmen
V.F.	Vicar Forane

Picture Credits

Page 1:	Courtesy of the National Library of Ireland
Page 6-7:	Courtesy of the National Library of Ireland
Page 9:	Christy Lawlor
Page 15:	Chris Lawlor
Page 19:	Courtesy of Kevin Deering
Page 41:	Gerard O'Dwyer
Page 61:	Chris Lawlor
Page 81:	Aynia Brennan
Page 97:	Courtesy of the National Library of Ireland
Page 111:	Courtesy of the National Library of Ireland

There is one place in Ireland where the 1798 rebellion was not a mere flash in the pan. A huge event in Irish history, it can be argued that everything changed after 1798. Both Republicanism and Loyalism certainly changed. Despite this, the rebellion itself only lasted a few weeks in most areas of the country. Events in Wexford, Antrim, Down and Mayo were very significant, but in none of these places did the violence last beyond September 1798.

West Wicklow was different. The violence in this area continued until December 1803, making this area, with the parish of Dunlavin at its hub, the scene of the longest rebellion. There are a variety of reasons for this. The area had been deeply divided during the 17th century through a process of conquest, colonisation and settlement. The region was divided into 'haves' and 'have-nots', and the anger of the 'have-nots' seethed just underneath the surface throughout the 18th century. This polarisation worsened during the final decade of that century and on 24 May 1798 the whole area blazed into open rebellion, as the 'have-nots' made their bid to reclaim some of the status that their forefathers had once enjoyed. In West Wicklow, the response of the 'haves' was swift and terrible. For some time they had been conducting a reign of terror in the area with impunity. On 24 May that terror also reached a new high in the picturesque village of Dunlavin.

The execution of over forty men in Dunlavin that day [1] has been recorded in many studies of the 1798 rebellion. They had taken no part in the rebellion, because they were imprisoned before it broke out, and were not given any sort of trial. If it had happened in modern times, the Dunlavin massacre would probably have been referred to the War Crimes Tribunal in The Hague. This horrendous event ensured that resentment lingered long in the area and was the principal reason for the longevity of the violence in this region. The man who orchestrated the longest rebellion was the rebel leader Michael Dwyer.

The extraordinary life story of Michael Dwyer has endured in the psyche of people within County Wicklow. As well as being a historical figure, he is also a folk hero with a cult following. The mythic quality of Michael Dwyer is something that I have grown up with. In an article published in 1999, I stated that in the area covered by the parish of Dunlavin, Donard and Davidstown Dwyer's memory is almost tangible. [2] Some months later I received a letter from Co. Tipperary, part of which read: 'Dwyer's memory is almost tangible. Let me assure you that when I was growing up in the pre-television era it was actually tangible. My grandmother's accounts of the massacre in Dunlavin, Dwyer's stand at Doire na Muc and his many other daring deeds formed the patriotic philosophy and political opinions which I still hold to this very day.' This letter provides an excellent example of how powerful an influence the dramatic story of Dwyer's stout and prolonged resistance has had, in Wicklow and far beyond its boundaries.

At national level the name of Michael Dwyer ranks highly. A 19th century traditional ballad called The Three Flowers bears ample testimony to this fact. [3] In this ballad, Dwyer, the guerrilla leader of a tiny band of freedom fighters in the Wicklow Mountains is mentioned as an equal in the same breath as Wolfe Tone, the 'Father of Irish Republicanism' and Robert Emmet, the 'Darling of Erin'. The heroic aura that surrounded Dwyer's stubborn resistance in Wicklow was utilised to the full by Nationalist Ireland's agenda both during his lifetime and after his death. Dwyer probably never saw Wolfe Tone, let alone met him. While planning the abortive rising of 1803, Emmet and Dwyer only met twice. Unlike many of the leading figures within the United Irish organisation, Dwyer did not come from a well-to-do background. They moved in different social circles – and in different regions. Dwyer was at home in West Wicklow!

Dwyer's activities meant that West Wicklow, particularly the area centred on Dunlavin parish, remained a dangerous place for years, but eventually he ended his campaign and the authorities sent him to the penal colony of Australia. Dwyer's exile and eventual death in Australia meant that the 'Cult of Michael Dwyer' has also flourished there. Dwyer's Australian descendants describe themselves as 'political refugees'. [4] The longest rebellion has had long lasting consequences indeed.

NOTES

1: Some sources give the date of the massacre as the 25th of May, but the 24th is the correct date, as this study will explain.

2: Chris Lawlor, Unfinished Business, in Dunlavin-Donard-Davidstown Parish Link, Vol.V, No. 1, July 1999, p.6.

3: http://www.dwyerclan.com/Three_Flowers.htm (visited 1/7/2002). The ballad appears in appendix 3.

4: http://members.ozemail.com.au/~slaven01/mckeon/dwyer.html (visited 3/4/2002, this url is now closed).

Dunlavin Green circa 1910

PLACE

Dunlavin, a rural parish in the west of County Wicklow, is at the heart of this study. Any study of events in Dunlavin must begin with a description of the place itself. In 1926 one commentator wrote: [1] 'Geographically the parish of Dunlavin, entirely in West Wicklow, touches upon Hollywood, Ballymore-Eustace, Kilcullen and Narraghmore, and forms, to a great extent and for many miles, the north-western boundary of Wicklow. We run along the Kildare frontier from Tober to Colbinstown railway station ...' This description is very accurate, but it does not give us the full picture. The village of Dunlavin is only one mile from the Kildare border. This has numerous implications for life in the village. East Wicklow, with its major towns of Arklow, Wicklow and Bray, is a world away from Dunlavin. Each town in the east of the country is forty or more miles from Dunlavin. The two sides of County Wicklow are poles apart.

Coupled with distance, the great mass of the Wicklow Mountains forms a physical 'intervening obstacle' of the type referred to in the geographical Push-Pull model. Dunlaviners were much more likely to work in (or move into) neighbouring Kildare than East Wicklow, especially in the late 18th century, when transport was confined to horse power! Life then was much more static. The people of the area, villagers and tenant farmers alike, did not move around nearly as much as people in these more mobile times.

Wicklow's climate is another factor that hindered communications between the east and west of the county in the late 18th century. Snow and freezing conditions made the routeways through the mountains treacherous. We must also remember that the vast wilderness area of the mountains was much more exposed back then than it is nowadays. Most of the forest cover on the Wicklow range was not in existence in the latter half of the 18th century. The coniferous forests that dot the mountains nowadays are quite recent in origin.

This, however, is not to suggest that there were no routeways from West Wicklow across the mountains. There were roads (dirt tracks obviously) across both the Wicklow Gap and the Ballynabarnie gap (though not over the Sally Gap). The road system in the west of the county formed a good network, particularly below the 600-foot contour line or so. Robert Fraser's General View of the County Wicklow (1801) is quoted in Charles Dickson's study of Michael Dwyer stating that the roads in County Wicklow were 'uncommonly good'. [2] Good roads or not, topography, distance and climate ensured that Dunlaviners had more links to other towns in West Wicklow and in Kildare than to any settlements on the eastern side of the mountains. Dunlavin was 'about eleven miles from everywhere' — everywhere referring to the major towns of West Wicklow and Mid-Kildare! Baltinglass, Blessington, Naas and Newbridge all lay within a distance of ten to twelve miles from Dunlavin. Within this radius of twelve miles, with Dunlavin as the centre of the circle, lie places as diverse as Kilcullen (Kilcullenbridge in the 1790's), Hollywood Glen, the Quaker village of Ballitore and the Glen of Imaal. The village of Dunlavin, in fact, occupies a pivotal and strategic position. It is in the undulating land – or foothills – between the highland Wicklow wilderness and the great plains of Kildare and the central plain of Ireland. The strategic position of Dunlavin was highlighted in a letter from Mr. R. Nevill of Furness, Naas to Edward Cooke, the under-secretary, dated 10 December 1797. [3] Nevill was worried about the increasing number of robberies, especially those involving the theft of arms in the region.

There having been six robberies committed since last Sunday, vid. the widow Finnamore near Kilteel, where two blunderbusses were fired into the house and one man severely wounded. Peter Burchill's of Kilteel, where one blunderbuss was fired and both houses robbed of arms. Roberts and Byrne (Boyce) of Rathmore of arms and money, and Hill of Cromwellstown of money; also Adam Abraham and Slater at Beggar's Inn; we think it would be not only useful but necessary to have an officer and twenty men stationed at the village of Rathmore, it being the pass from the Blessington mountains to Dunlavin.

The letter brings up a number of points. Firstly, Nevill obviously saw Dunlavin as an area to be watched. The reasons for this will be examined in subsequent chapters. Secondly, Nevill shows a good understanding of the topography of the district. Indeed, the authorities knew full well that Dunlavin held a vital geographical position, and the village was one of the garrison towns of West Wicklow in the 1790's. Thirdly, the letter is the first example of a fact that I wish to draw on quite a lot. As I have already stated, East and West Wicklow were poles apart. Hence, material pertaining to Dunlavin is much more likely to be found in documents, correspondence etc. from nearby centres in County Kildare than in anything written in East Wicklow, even the county town itself. The village of Dunlavin is, in fact, a good example of why writing County histories may lead to omissions. Too peripheral to the county as a whole, Dunlavin often merits only a passing mention in any studies of County Wicklow. Historians in neighbouring Kildare, on the other hand, often feel that Dunlavin lies outside their terms of reference as it lies one mile into Wicklow. To date, the massacre on Dunlavin Green has been mentioned en passant in many works on 1798, but the histories of 1798 usually pay it little attention.

This is not to suggest that the massacre on Dunlavin Green is an event that should be studied in isolation. Far from it, in fact. However, the borderland position of Dunlavin does throw up the problem of where precisely the massacre fits into the scheme of things. I would suggest that the area to study to find out about the causes and consequences of this terrible event is the area around Dunlavin itself, not all of Co. Wicklow (or all of Co. Kildare, for that matter). The geographers refer nowadays to the concept of 'region' and this concept is a vital one in the case of Dunlavin. Using another geographical model, the Core-

Periphery model, the village of Dunlavin is peripheral to larger towns (higher order centres) like Baltinglass, Blessington, Naas and Newbridge. However, to get a true picture of the position of Dunlavin (even more so in the late 18th century, when settlements were much more self sufficient than is the case nowadays), I suggest that the core-periphery model be turned on its head. To Dunlaviners, Dunlavin is central. It would have been even more of a central place [4] in the 1790s. Neighbouring villages (Donard, Stratford, Ballymore-Eustace, Narraghmore and Ballitore) and outlying rural areas (Glen of Imaal, Crehelp, Tober, Merginstown) now become peripheral to Dunlavin, and events in this peripheral region undoubtedly had a huge bearing on the Dunlavin massacre.

The Glen of Imaal is particularly significant in the story of the events of 1798-1803 because it was the birthplace of rebel leader Michael Dwyer. Dwyer operated throughout the Wicklow Mountains, but there is no doubt that both the homeland and the heartland of the rebel leader centred on the Glen of Imaal. This glen is located in West Wicklow and runs roughly east-west from the present Blessington-Baltinglass road (N81) to the western and northern slopes of Lugnaquilla mountain. The glen is drained by the youthful river Slaney and its tributaries. On the eastern side of Lugnaquilla lies Glenmalure; the Glen of Imaal 'backs onto' this area. Both glens are very remote and both figured prominently as outposts of resistance to British rule in Ireland during different periods of history. During the late 16th century, for example, the Gaelic chieftain Fiach Mac Hugh O'Byrne carried out his military campaign from the fastnesses of Glenmalure, though he also used the Glen of Imaal as a channel of attack towards the plains of Kildare. This fact is referred to in stanza two of the song Follow Me Up To Carlow:

See the swords of Glen Imayle,
flashing o'er the English Pale,
see all the children of the Gael,
beneath O'Byrne's banners [5]

Possibly the best description of the Glen of Imaal as a distinct geographical region is to be found in the Shearman Papers. Referring to the eviction of a number of Catholic families in the glen, Father John Francis Shearman wrote: All this done in a remote glen of Wicklow in the year of grace 1862 – too remote to be reached by public opinion – a feeling well-nigh strangled in this region of serfdom. [6] This extract indicates that Shearman viewed the glen as a separate entity; a place which outside influence and public opinion found difficult to penetrate. A later writer also noted that the Glen of Imaal and the Glenspeople were perceived as 'different' even within their own parish. Rev. Samuel Russell McGee had asked a resident of Dunlavin village about some Glenspeople who were approaching and was told, They're mountainy men; they're not like us. [7] This indicated that the Glenspeople kept themselves to themselves. Their own perception of the upland-lowland divide within their parish only served to increase the social isolation of the upland parishioners. It was into this glen and its unique community that Michael Dwyer was born in 1772. [8] The long, narrow morphology of the glen – following, as it does, the upper valley of the River Slaney – makes the area inaccessible from three sides. The topography also makes the area difficult to negotiate and the terrain itself is often rough underfoot. This physical isolation led to social isolation also. Not alone were Glenspeople perceived as different; they also perceived themselves as different. Although within Dunlavin parish, the people of Imaal perceived Dunlavin village as a place apart.

Despite this, Dunlavin village served a wide hinterland. Possibly the closest description of Dunlavin as the nucleus of its own geographical region is to be found in a letter from another tragic time in Dunlavin's history. It is a letter from Mr. Boyle to Mr. Walker, dated 17 January 1847 (during the famine) and it refers to conditions in the village of 'Dunlaine, population 990, a comparatively good market town, the capital of a great district ...' [9] The position of Dunlavin in the 1790s, as a nucleus, was very similar to that quoted for 1847 – 'the capital of a great district.' Incidentally, Boyle's letter also gave a further indication of the links that existed between Dunlavin and neigh-bouring Kildare when it stated, 'It (Dunlavin) is chiefly supplied from Naas, seven miles distant.' [10] (Measurements were evidently in Irish miles).

One final fact worth noting about the position of Dunlavin is that it was on one of the main roads to the south-east (i.e. the Carlow-Wexford region) in the 1790s. Before 1829 the road to Tullow and Wexford diverged from the present Dublin road at Blessington and went through Ballymore-Eustace, Dunlavin and Stratford-on-Slaney, joining the road again at Saunder's Grove, where traces of it could recently be seen entering the demesne from Manger Bridge. [11] Thus Dunlavin, the nucleus of its district, controlled one of the main routeways from the south-east to the capital. It was this fact that made events in Dunlavin so vital and it was this fact that was partly responsible for the decision to shoot the prisoners in Dunlavin. Dunlavin, and its road, had to be held at all costs. Resistance to the authorities could not be, and was not, tolerated. Dunlavin is a village within a transitional zone. Two miles North of the village at Kennycourt (the last 'foothill') one has a magnificent, uninterrupted view across the plains of Kildare to the Hill of Allen. Two miles south-east of the village, at Tynte Park, the view is even more magnificent, this time a panoramic vista of the Wicklow Mountains with the summit of Lugnaquilla clearly visible. The best of both worlds then for Dunlavin – the plains of Kildare and the mountains of Wicklow – and events in both worlds were to play their part in contributing to the tragic episode that occurred on Dunlavin Green in 1798 and the protracted resistance of Michael Dwyer and his men in the Glen of Imaal until December 1803.

NOTES

1: O'Byrne, Patrick, West Wicklow, in Souvenir Guide and Programme of the Imaal Bazaar and Fete, Leinster Leader Ltd., Naas, 1926, p.56.

2: Dickson, Charles, The life of Michael Dwyer with some account of his companions, Browne & Nolan, Dublin, 1944, p.187.

3: N.A.I. 620/33/139.

4: I use the term Central Place in the geographical sense of Christaller's Theory.

5: Conway, Pat, A Pint of Irish ballads, Ossian Publications, Cork 1993, p.13.

6: N.U.I. Maynooth Library, Shearman Papers, XVII, p.169.

7: McGee, Samuel Russell, Dunlavin, County Wicklow – A Retrospect, Dublin 1935, p.14.

8: Dickson, p.22.

9: Letter quoted in Maeve Baker, The Famine in Wicklow 1846-1847, Journal of the West Wicklow Historical Society, No. 3 (December 1989), p.19.

10: Slater's Directory for Naas (1846) mentions a daily connection between Naas and Dunlavin: 'To Dunlavin, a caravan (from Dublin) every evening at 5.20, goes through Kilcullen.' This is further evidence of the link between this area of Kildare and West Wicklow, a link that also existed in the 1790s.

11: Chavasse, Claude, The Story of Baltinglass, Kilkenny Journal Ltd., 1970, p.62.

MICKLOW
COMMEMORATING
1798-1998

IN COMMEMORATION OF OVER 40 UNITED IRISHMEN
WHO WERE MASSACRED ON DUNLAVIN FAIRGREEN,
MAY 24TH 1798
COISTE CHILL MHANTAIN '98

Commemorative stone erected
on Dunlavin Green in 1998

TIME

Any event at local history level involves two variables –
place and time. It is local because it happened in a
particular place. It is history because it happened at a
particular time, and it is to this fact that we must turn our
attention in this chapter. The massacre on Dunlavin green
would never have happened without a build up of events
beforehand, both at local and national level. There is a local
history of national events, and the massacre on the green is one
example of how an event can have vast local significance and yet
be part of a much bigger national picture. To fully understand
what happened in Dunlavin, some knowledge of the general
background is essential.

This book does not give a general history of either Ireland in
the 1790s or of the 1798 rebellion itself. For the reader who
would wish to delve further into the overall picture of the
rebellion, there are many excellent books from which to choose.
[1] For readers with a more passing interest in the overall
picture, illustrated pamphlets are also available. [2] In many

places 1798 is remembered as the year of the great Irish rebellion. The revolt was not confined to parts of Ulster, Wexford and Mayo, though certainly these areas saw some of the heaviest fighting. However, many areas of the country were affected – Timahoe camp in Co. Kildare, for example, held out against the authorities after the Wexford rebels had been crushed.

The whole rebellion came as something of a shock to the British authorities, who knew of the activities of the United Irishmen and who thought that they had averted a United Irishmen's revolution. Indeed, many United leaders were arrested before the rebellion, and in many places it was local rebels – with local figures to lead them – who were involved in the rising (hence the British surprise).

The existence of the United Irishmen was central to events in 1798 – both nationally and in the Dunlavin region. The following extract from their 'catechism' makes their aims abundantly clear.

Question:	What have you got in your hand?
Answer:	A green bough.
Question:	Where did it first grow?
Answer:	In America.
Question:	Where did it bud?
Answer:	In France.
Question:	Where are you going to plant it?
Answer:	In the crown of Great Britain. [3]

Here, then, was an organisation that posed a threat to the British authorities, and all who were loyal to the British crown. It made reference to both the American War of Independence and the French Revolution. Both of these events were anathema to Great Britain and its monarchy. The American War of Independence threatened the very concepts of Empire and British 'superiority' in an age of imperialism. The loss of the American colonies was the first real blow suffered by the British Empire, and it cut deeply. The colonies were gone, but at least they were three thousand miles away. Now Ireland, the island on Britain's doorstep, was showing separatist tendencies. British Loyalists (in Ireland as well as in Britain) were horrified. The French Revolution did not affect Britain as directly as the American one, in that they lost no land as a result of it. However, in its own way, the French revolution had an even more profound effect on British Loyalists because it threatened the very concept of Monarchy. Europe's Ancien Regime and the idea of the Divine Right of Monarchs were swept aside. The French were guilty of possibly the worst possible crime in Loyalist eyes – regicide. After all, who were Loyalists loyal to, if not the Monarch? Coupled with this, in the British case, the monarch was the head of the Anglican Church (in both England and Ireland). In Ireland, where the overwhelming majority of the population was Catholic, religious fears grew and added to the Loyalist anxiety about Republicanism rearing its ugly head on the island that was Britain's neighbour -- in the form of the United Irishmen.

In fact, by the 1790s, there had been comparative peace in Ireland for a century. The last military action of any note to have taken place on the island was the Williamite War, which ended in victory for the Protestant House of Orange. The 18th century had seen the introduction of the anti-Catholic penal laws, an event that, by the 1790s, fuelled both Catholic resentment and Protestant fears. Generally the 18th century had been a peaceful one, although the odd violent incident did still occur, particularly in more remote areas like the Wicklow Mountains. A proclamation from 1715 informs us that:

> a barbarous and bloody murder was committed on the body of Mr. Abraham Coats, in his dwelling house at Killinure, in the county of Wicklow, on Wednesday the seventh of December last, between nine and ten of the clock at night, by shooting the said Abraham Coats with a pistol, whereof he instantly died. [4]

However, such actions were rare and were probably the work of individuals. Even the so-called Raparees (or Tories, from the Irish word Tóraíocht – Pursuit, as they were pursued by law) [5] usually worked for themselves and were not motivated by any great patriotic drive! Raparees appeared in the 1690s after the Jacobite defeat and they survived in mountainous areas well into the next century. Moreover, rural violence was rare in 1715, but by the 1790s the situation had changed. Agrarian unrest, Republican ideas and continuing religious problems contributed to the melting pot that was Ireland in the 1790s.

In October 1791, the society of United Irishmen was founded in Belfast and before its inaugural meeting on 18 October 1791, thirty-six members had already been secured; an additional six were elected on that occasion. Its objectives were to achieve a cordial union among all the people in Ireland, and to bring about a radical reform of parliamentary representation, and to secure the inclusion in that reform of Irishmen of every religious persuasion. [6] However, as the 1790s wore on the organisation became much more radical, seeking to break the link with Britain altogether. By 1796 Wolfe Tone was aboard a French ship, one of Admiral Hoche's expedition. Bad weather prevented any French landing at Bantry in 1796, but Tone had prepared an 'Address to the People of Ireland' for the occasion, part of which stated: 'The alternative which is now submitted to your choice, with regard to England, is, in one word, union or separation! You must determine, and that instantly, between slavery and independence; there is no third way.' [7] Strong words indeed, and no doubt as to the threat posed to Loyalists!

Predictably, Loyalists were uneasy. The Orange Order was founded in 1795, to counter the threat posed by a Catholic agrarian movement called the Defenders. The order, however, also opposed the United Irishmen. The appearance of a French fleet (albeit a fleet that never landed) at Bantry came as a real shock to Loyalists. The French, Republican threat was enough to ensure that Loyalists' attitudes hardened and after 1796 there was something of a hard-line Loyalist backlash against the Whigs (more liberal Loyalists). This led to a reign of terror being unleashed throughout Ulster and Leinster – including Dunlavin and the Glen of Imaal – in late 1797 and early 1798. This was crucial in the build up to the Dunlavin massacre. The men executed on the green were killed because they were suspected of being United Irishmen, and pressure was put on the liberal Morley Saunders shortly before the executions. Such, then, was the situation in the 1790s. At national level, the stage was set for revolt, and in the Dunlavin area and its hinterland the scene was set for tragedy.

NOTES

1: For example Thomas Pakenham, The Year of Liberty, Panther Books, 1972, remains an excellent overview of the period.

2: For example Michael Kenny, The 1798 Rebellion – photographs and memorabilia from the National Museum of Ireland, Country House Dublin in association with the National Museum of Ireland 1996.

3: Pakenham, op cit. title page.

4: Lawlor, Chris, The Massacre on Dunlavin Green – A Story of the 1798 Rebellion, Naas 1998, p.17.

5: I am indebted to the late Br. Labhrás O Muircheartaigh of Naas CBS for this piece of information.

6: Mac Dermot, Frank, Tone and his times, Revised edition, Anvil Books, 1968, p.73.

7: Cronin, Seán, and Roche, Richard, Freedom the Wolfe Tone Way, Anvil Books, 1973, p.196.

Martin Collins, Dunlavin's last blacksmith, makes pikes for an RTE series in the 1960s

MELTING POT

A popular 1798 ballad contains the words: 'The French are in the bay, They'll be here without delay, And the Orange will decay, Says the Sean Bhean Bhocht.' By 1796, the French had indeed been in the bay – Bantry Bay – and the Orange Order had been founded (but was hardly 'in decay'). The society of United Irishmen was also growing rapidly. In County Wicklow, as elsewhere, the society flourished. The organisation of the society was strictly intra-county. In fact, the basic unit used by the United Irishmen was that of the barony (a land area not much used in modern Ireland). To further complicate matters, Dunlavin parish is divided into two separate parts, one in the Barony of Talbotstown Lower and one in the Barony of Talbotstown Upper. Townlands as close together as Dunlavin Upper and Dunlavin Lower lie in different baronies. The village of Dunlavin itself can be taken to be in Talbotstown Lower. Although United Irish records exist at county and barony level, the most striking thing about United Irish records is the lack of them! By the late 1790s, the United Irishmen was a secret society, and many records were simply never written because the members did not want to commit dangerous information to paper. Also, it is fair to assume that many documents were destroyed at the time of the arrest of the leaders, and in the aftermath of a failed rebellion, when the fear of a vindictive military backlash was uppermost in the minds of many ex-rebels. Any records of the organisation that do survive do so by accident in a sense – i.e. either they fell into the hands of the authorities or failed to be destroyed by members for various reasons.

These facts notwithstanding, we do have the figures for the amount of United Irishmen in most areas of Leinster for the spring of 1798. [1] They make interesting reading, although the figure for Wicklow (the largest in a single county outside Dublin) would seem to have been rounded off and may be an estimate.

United Irish Strength in parts of Leinster

Wicklow	14,000
Kildare	11,919
Carlow	11,300
Meath	11,110
Dublin City	8,396
Dublin County	7,412
Kilkenny	6,700
King's County	6,500
Westmeath	5,250

Information about the society in Wicklow reached the authorities via a spy referred to as A.B. This man reported on the first meeting of the County Wicklow committee (held in Annacurra) and he referred to the delegates from Talbotstown as, 'Kavenagh, a yeoman in uniform and a lame man'. [2] Many of the delegates from baronies in the east of the county are named, so it is safe to conclude that A.B. was an easterner, who would not have known the West Wicklow delegates very well.

This is another manifestation of the fact that the two sides of the county are poles apart, and exist almost in separate worlds.

By 22 January 1798, the following breakdown was given for United Irish strength in the Wicklow baronies (in a document which has survived because it fell into the hands of Dublin Castle authorities). [3] Incidentally, as well as giving the United Irish strength and armaments for County Wicklow, this document also gives us some insight into their finances.

County Wicklow Committee

January 22nd 1798

Area	Strength	£ - Pounds s - Shillings d - Pence		
Talbotstown	2,974	£20.3s.4d	1st Pay	£12.10s.3d
Lr Talbotstown	700	£0.0s.0d	2 do	£22.15s.0d
Arklow	2,400	£59.8s.3d	3 do	£37.19s.3d
Roundwood	1,200	£17.0s.0d	No. 2	
Newcastle	1,000	£35.15s.0d	Advanced	£12.6s.5d
Upr Ballinacor	1,000	£13.15s.0d		
Lr Ballinacor	840	£0.2s.0d		£85.10s.11d
Shillelagh	1,000	£7.19s.3d		
Totals	12,794	£162.3s.4d	(Rest to Province)	

Return for arms

Talbotstown
181 guns
70 muskets
66 pistols
134 swords
321 pikes
3,331 musket balls
8,315 ball cotton
75 pounds of powder

Arklow
265 guns
85 muskets
60 pistols
87 swords
200 pikes
400 musket balls
8,050 ball cotton
500 pounds of powder

Roundwood
105 guns
94 muskets
62 pistols
75 swords
380 pikes
980 musket balls
500 ball cotton
17 pounds of powder

Newcastle
150 guns
41 muskets
20 pistols
30 swords
355 pikes
0 musket balls
5,965 ball cotton
169 pounds of powder

Total
789 guns,   298 muskets, 216 pistols, 326 swords, 1,256 pikes,
4,711 musket balls, 22,820 ball cotton, 761 pounds of powder

Arklow   210 guns, 75 muskets, 62 pistols
Roundwood   200 guns, 0 muskets, 0 pistols
Newcastle   100 guns,   0 muskets, 0 pistols

TOTALS   1,299 guns, 363 muskets, 278 pistols

Interestingly, the letter accompanying these figures made reference to the inmates of Wicklow Gaol, many of whom had been arrested as suspected United Irish sympathisers. The letter stated:

> Your committee feels with concern the apathy of their fellow citizens in the county Wicklow who refuse so small a pittance as one penny per man per month to alleviate in some degree the suffering of their fellow citizens and persecuted brethren in Wicklow Jail, where there are many deserving citizens in want of common necessities (much less comforts) of life, but who in extreme want, scorn to betray the trust reposed in them ... Your committee strongly recommends a subscription to be set on foot immediately for the express purpose of employing a law agent and of retaining counsel for defence of our persecuted brethren in Wicklow Jail and that the same be lodged in the hands of a treasurer appointed by this committee and brought forward to the next meeting.

In January 1798 Talbotstown Lower merited mention as a separate entity in the tables drawn up in this document. This indicates not only overall growth in the Society of United Irishmen, but also (more specifically) growth of the movement in and around the Dunlavin area, as the village was the major settlement in Talbotstown Lower. The United Irishmen were flourishing in Dunlavin as the year 1798 began. Further evidence of this fact is contained in a letter from John Smith to Edward Cooke, the under secretary, on 16 May 1797. [4] Part of the letter referred to events in a public house in Hollywood and Smith stated:

> I drank some punch at a public house in a mixed company. One man named Patrick Burke and who keeps a whiskey shop in Hollywood declared himself publicly to be up, i.e. An United Irish Man. There was likewise in company a person of the name Noble – a private in the Dunlavin Cavalry. Burke asked him was he 'up?' ... Noble replied that in the cause he was engaged in he would persevere even to death. Burke then said, 'Why, more than half the Dunlavin Corps are up and I am the lad that knows it.'

Smith was an Englishman, who spied on the United Irishmen in Belfast before he became active (also as a spy) in County Wicklow. In fact, Smith did not last long in Wicklow before his cover was blown, and the latter part of the letter gives us an indication that he was worried about being discovered, as he asked for weapons to defend himself. The letter continued:

> I had a great inclination to take Burke prisoner regardless of all
> hazards, but thought it fitter to write first. One thing I beg leave
> to observe is that if you are pleased to order to me to persevere
> in my enquires you will be pleased to let me have a brace of
> pocket and a brace of holster pistols to defend myself in case of
> necessity.

This letter raises a number of points. Firstly, Hollywood,
which is well within the Dunlavin hinterland, was a place where
men talked publicly about the United Irishmen. This would
indicate not only that the organisation was well established in
the area, but also that infiltration by spies (like Smith) might
not be too difficult! Secondly, the date of this letter – 16 May
1797 – tells us that the United Irishmen were thriving in the
region for at least a full year before the Dunlavin massacre.
However, the most relevant revelation contained in this letter
regarding the later executions on Dunlavin green must be
Smith's allegations against the Dunlavin yeomanry. Here, a full
year before they were shot on the fairgreen, was a testimony
that the local yeomen were not only disloyal, but active
members of the United Irish organisation. There is no doubt
that many Loyalists regarded the Saundersgrove Corps with
suspicion (and they were not the only yeomanry corps to be
suspected of Republican sympathies).

On the Kildare side of the Dunlavin hinterland too, the United
Irishmen grew in strength. Indeed, in Kildare the movement had
the leadership of some of the upper class – Lord Edward
Fitzgerald and Wogan Browne, for example – which was not the
case in County Wicklow. Thomas Kelly, the postmaster of
Kilcullen was described as a captain and swears in many on a
list of suspected persons. [5] One County Kildare source that has
great significance for events in the Dunlavin area is the record
kept by Mary Leadbeater, who lived in the neighbouring Quaker
village of Ballitore. She certainly saw the general air of change,
brought about by the influx of new ideas after the French
Revolution, and the Bantry Bay episode. In December 1796 she
wrote:

> Robinson, the minister of Bomba Hall, I suppose a curate for
> either Stratford or Dunlavin, an industrious intelligent little
> man, sometimes called upon us. He expressed very liberal
> sentiments, and rather more in the new way that one should

expect from his cloth. Republicanism, both in Church and State affairs, seemed now to be very prevalent; and serious divisions arose in our Society [of Friends]. [6]

The growth of the United Irishmen in County Wicklow (and in Wexford) owed much to the one-man crusade staged by William McCabe. By the beginning of 1798, however, the term 'United Irishmen' was something of a misnomer. This present work does not call for any in-depth analysis of internal society wrangling, but, to put it simplistically, there were now two wings within the movement. Both wings aspired to the idea of revolution against Britain, but the moderates felt that such a rising should only take place if there was French aid forthcoming, while the radicals felt that it was best to push ahead with plans for rebellion with or without the French and embarked on a policy of mass enrolment into the movement. Hence, in Wicklow as elsewhere, the United movement was actually divided.

On the other side of the coin, County Wicklow had quite a large Loyalist population. However, if the local United Irishmen were somewhat divided, the local Loyalists were, if anything, perhaps even more divided. This work does not go into detail regarding political divides with the local Loyalist population, but (and once again this is over-simplification) the basic division was between the hard-line Loyalists (Tories or Conservatives) on the one hand and the 'easier-going' liberals (Whigs) on the other. In County Wicklow (unlike other counties) the Whigs had the upper hand. In fact the two M.P.s returned for Co. Wicklow in the 1797 elections were both Whigs – William Hume of Humewood and Nicholas Westby of Highpark. Co. Wicklow and its Whig dominance was a talking point among Loyalists, but it became much more than this – it became a threat – once the United Irish organisation began to grow, and there was talk of a French invasion.

The dominant Loyalist power in West Wicklow however was not a Whig – far from it, in fact. The Earl of Aldborough is associated with Stratford-on-Slaney, [7] but the family also had a mansion called Belan in Co. Kildare. In fact, the Stratford parliamentary seat was actually in Kildare, hence Wicklow returned only Whig representatives in 1797. The Stratford Family, though, resided in Aldborough Castle as well as Belan, and they probably felt quite threatened in Stratford-on-Slaney as events became more violent in the surrounding area in the spring of 1798. The Stratfords had on one side of them the well-known Whig William Hume, and on the other they had a possibly even more liberal member of the gentry – Morley Saunders of Saundersgrove, a man who was to have a key part in the Dunlavin massacre. No wonder the hard-line Stratford family felt uneasy.

Proof of this unease is found in the letters written by Aldborough's younger brother, Benjamin O'Neale Stratford, (who succeeded to the title in 1823). Stratford was a regular correspondent to Dublin Castle, and to Cooke, the under-secretary in particular. However, when treating these letters as historical sources, some words of caution are advisable.

Firstly, as one would expect, these documents are biased, and it is probable that they contain exaggerations. This is not to say that O'Neale Stratford's veracity is in doubt in general matters, or in individual details, but the documents are coloured one way. (The colour that comes to mind is Orange – O'Neale Stratford was a member of Orange Lodge 176). [8]

Secondly, the sheer volume of his correspondence raises an interesting point. People writing letters to the Castle were doing so for a reason. O'Neale Stratford was alarmed at the events which were happening around him, and concerned with what he saw (probably correctly from a hard-line Loyalist viewpoint as things turned out) as lax Whig magistrates not doing enough to curb the growth of the United Irish movement. This alarm and concern probably clouded his judgement, and he failed to see the resentment that many of the measures that he called for would have stirred up in the mass of the local people.

Thirdly, and perhaps most importantly, there is a temptation to look upon O'Neale Stratford as a scared Orangeman writing to Cooke as a childish tell-tale behaves in the playground, and possibly also to boost his own sense of importance – i.e. 'I'm in the inner circle of the castle' syndrome. His letters, looked upon now, perhaps make us think of him as a fanatic whose lunatic rantings are to be taken with a pinch of salt. To think of him thus is however to fall into a dangerous trap.

We know now that the rebellion in his world – i.e. around the Dunlavin hinterland – did not have much chance of success. We have the benefit of hindsight, however – he did not. One must never forget that there was a very real threat to O'Neale Stratford and his ilk. There was in existence a United Irish plan to attack the garrison towns and to gain control of the route through Stratford and Dunlavin from Dublin to the south-east. When

Kildare rose, so did neighbouring West Wicklow. O'Neale Stratford was not totally wrong in his assessment of the dangers he faced in West Wicklow, either from the Society of United Irishmen or from his Whig neighbours who failed to control them. In short the letters of Benjamin O'Neale Stratford must be perused carefully, bearing in mind that they contain the truth as he, a hard-line Loyalist supporter, saw it; and that events around him coloured the way that he wrote the documents.

From the point of view of this present work, the Stratford letters are a very important source for the Dunlavin massacre. Not only was O'Neale Stratford a major player in West Wicklow, but he could also shed light on events in the area during the build up period before the day of the massacre. In addition to this, he knew personally the key people who were involved in the decision to shoot the prisoners at Dunlavin and his correspondence contains comments about them as well as about events in the village of Dunlavin and its hinterland, which he quite often refers to in his writing. His viewpoint is one that modern readers may not equate too readily to an inhabitant of West Wicklow, but we must remember that times were very different.

Just after the rising, in 1799, Co. Wicklow had Orange Lodges in Tinahely, Coolkenna, Rathdrum, Carnew, Newtownmount-kennedy, Wicklow town, Donard and probably Shillelagh. [9] Orangeism was part of Wicklow life in the 1790s and the area around Dunlavin was no exception, as demonstrated by the existence of a lodge in Donard, which is within Dunlavin Parish. On 9 June 1797, Benjamin O'Neale Stratford wrote to Cooke. [10] His letter stated:

> I hear that the contagion of the County Kildare is likely to creep into this part, to which I am sorry to say it is too near and that the Magistrates of the nearer part, have not been as strict as they should be is too visible. I will however engage with my life if sufficient powers be given any spirited person on whom Government may have reliance, with myself to put a stop to the growth of such principals here. My brother John who has been at my house some time went yesterday to Dunlavin to enquire into the state of that town and heard the United Irish Men were committing depredation and robbery within three miles of it and had wrote letters to the townspeople that they would be there in a few days to take away their arms. He saw in the town a field piece, which belonged to my late nephew Sir James Tynte, and he thinks it dangerous to have it there. I request to know if I shall send for it or if not that the government may ... Though I

trust I must not assure you that neither expense or risk of life shall ever deter me from showing my steady loyalty to the best of sovereigns.

This letter was written almost a year before the Dunlavin massacre, and perhaps Stratford was right to be worried about the state of the country in which he lived. There was evidently much unrest in and around Dunlavin as early a June 1797. The letter refers to 'depredation and robbery' within three miles of the village of Dunlavin itself; while the townsfolk were actually receiving letters from the United Irishmen, threatening to take away their arms. There is no doubt that such actions would have created a very volatile situation in Dunlavin in the summer of 1797; a situation that, logically, would have worsened as the fateful year of 1798 approached.

Indeed, Benjamin O'Neale Stratford was not the only one who felt apprehensive about the situation in Dunlavin that June. From over the Kildare border another letter confirmed Stratford's impressions of Dunlavin. Stratford's letter was written on 9 June, so John Ravell Walsh was in Dunlavin during that same week. He wrote to Cooke on 6 June 1797, and he too was worried about the arms in and around Dunlavin falling into the wrong hands. [11] O'Neale Stratford's letter mentions the contagion of the County Kildare creeping into West Wicklow; Ravell Walsh's letter gives us some idea of that contagion as he mentioned some incidents that had occurred in Kildare. The very fact that Ravell Walsh was in Dunlavin and felt it necessary to write to Cooke about conditions in the village verifies the fact that West Wicklow was very close to events in Kildare, and that geographical diffusion of ideas and innovations was ongoing between the two regions. O'Neale Stratford and Ravell Walsh may, of course, have met in Dunlavin during the week and decided to write separately to Cooke, in the belief that 'two heads are better than one' or, in this case, two letters might be noticed in Dublin Castle! Be that as it may, the fact remains that both men were uneasy about the arms in and around Dunlavin. Ravell Walsh's letter makes it clear that attacks on ultra-Loyalist figures had already begun in Kildare – and where Kildare led, West Wicklow usually followed. The relevant extract from Ravell Walsh's letter read:

My Lord, Being in the County of Wicklow yesterday, I received the following private information, which I think it my duty to communicate: viz. – that there is one field piece in the house of Mr. Hobson of Tubber near Dunlavin, and that there are eight Pateraroes in the house of a Mr. Armstrong Ryves of Whitestown in the same neighbourhood which, though at present in the houses of well affected men, may fall into the hands of enemies as the above mentioned places adjoin the County of Kildare.

Undoubtedly, the evidence from the letters written by both Stratford and Walsh point to a tense situation in Dunlavin and its hinterland in the summer preceding the massacre. There was obviously quite a high level of United Irish activity, and, as if to strengthen the evidence still further, a letter from John Smith, the Castle spy, was written to Cooke on 16 June 1797, only one week after the other two reports. [12]

The picture of the West Wicklow area painted by Smith was a violent one. There was ample evidence once again of the cross-county boundary nature of the disturbances. Dunlavin village was at the centre – geographically and metaphorically – of United Irish activity in the local region. The other villages mentioned by Smith ring Dunlavin on its eastern side, and recruiting into the Society of United Irishmen seemed to be continually and openly going on. Smith also made a point that was taken up by many letter-writers in their epistles to Cooke. In fact, Smith's opinions echoed those of the Hon. Benjamin O'Neale Stratford, who was very put out by the fact that many of the local magistrates seemed to him to be very lax about doing their duty. Smith also had suspicions about the liberal magistrates, and resorts to using irony, referring to them as 'our sapient magistrates' in this letter. To Smith, the effect of over liberal magistracy was very apparent, and he refers to violence and 'running battles' being fought in West Wicklow.

June 1797 was obviously a tense, violent time in and around Dunlavin, and the village and the surrounding area was regarded as a hive of United Irish activity, and was closely watched as the year 1798 began. Liberal magistrates too were targets in Castle and hard-line Loyalist eyes – and Morley Saunders of Saundersgrove was certainly seen as a liberal! Extracts from Smith's letter confirm this.

A junta, belonging to Ballymore-Eustace, Dunlavin, Donard and Hollywood are continually promoting mobs under the pretence of cock fighting etc., but their real motive is to sow the seeds of sedition, for it is notorious to all in this part but the Magistrates, that men from Dublin or the North attend to swear people in as

United Irish Men, and they are called by the country people Recruiting Sergeants!

Warming to his topic, Smith continued:

To give a still more forcible idea of the vigilance of our sapient magistrates, I shall take the liberty of informing you Sir, that from within one mile of Blessington is a place near where I live called Ballymore Cross, a space of scarce a mile, and where there are nine whiskey shops, some unlicensed, the majority of which are kept by men of atrocious character – are full most nights, some are full all night. Riots are daily committed and last Sunday was a week there was a regular battle between some mountaineers and Baltiboys men ...

O'Neale Stratford, Ravell Walsh and Smith all sent evidence of unrest in and around Dunlavin to Cooke. Their letters from June 1797 – eleven months before the Dunlavin massacre – indicated that Loyalists were well informed about events in Dunlavin; and that the village and its hinterland was regarded as a trouble spot to be watched carefully.

However, if United Irishmen were to be convicted successfully, hard evidence was needed. Hard-line Loyalist fears regarding the leniency of the magistrates did not take into account the fact that those self-same magistrates could not act harshly if they lacked such evidence. Even if suspects were arrested, they might walk free if the courts could not convict them. This led to a type of revolving door system in the prisons, which did little to ease Loyalist fears or anger. Evidence of this scenario in action in the Dunlavin hinterland is contained in a letter written by Judge Robert Day from Naas on 16 August 1797. [13] Day stated:

Sixteen prisoners have been this evening discharged, each of whom I have no doubt would be acquitted, and who now, instead of the triumph and audacity inspired by impunity, carry home with them impressions of the moderation and mercy of that Government which they are taught to abhor ... Thus Connolly has committed twelve or fourteen as implicated in the same offence, and though the information be very loosely drawn, and the committal such as they might well be bailed upon ... I have been forced to grope my way here for want of evidence, and much time has been wasted in dispatching expenses through this county for the justices.

With such a revolving door system in operation, Loyalists

obviously felt threatened, and wanted to join together to resist
the threats posed to them by Republicanism, Defenders, United
Irishmen and, on what they saw as 'their' side, Whiggishness
and weak magistrates. The Orange Order, recently formed in the
north of the country, was one way for Loyalists to express their
feelings, and the movement spread rapidly. Orangeism was widespread in West Wicklow – and crossed the county boundary into
Kildare too, of course. With Dunlavin and its hinterland seen as
something of a hotbed of sedition and potential rebellion, it was
only natural that the Orange Order should take root among the
local Loyalist population. Evidence of the activities of the
Orangemen was contained in a letter that was found in the
drawing room of John Harte on 27 March 1798. Evidently the
Orange Order, like Dublin Castle, had spies within the United
Irish movement! [14]

> We are very glad too, that you got yourself made a United Man,
> for you will know all their secrets, you are the only man in that
> county that we can depend upon to give us all intelligence ... We
> understand the barony you live in is very strong and in general
> the whole county. You had better make out a list how many
> United men in the country, as you said you could do it and send
> it to us in Naas ... and we will all know better what to do, may
> our orange cockade be strengthened, now over from our society
> at present.
> I.H., I.C., C.W., D.J. 4 friends,
> Burn this letter as soon as you read it.

United Irish documents of the County Wicklow committee
were not the only papers to escape burning obviously! In fact,
perhaps one could say that the efficiency of the Kildare
Orangeman rivalled that of the Wicklow United Irishmen, as this
letter fell into the hands of the United movement! Inefficiency
aside, the growth of the Orange Order in the vicinity of Dunlavin
and its environs gave rise to another threat – one which was very
real at the time, but which, (understandably in the light of
subsequent events), has tended to be overlooked in the popular
memory of this period – the threat of Orange violence.

We tend to think of 1798 as the year of the great Irish
Rebellion, and there is a lot of justification for this view.
However, Republican hopes fuelled Loyalist fears. The Orange
Order had been born as a result of violence. After a decade of
tension between Republicans and Loyalists, a pitched battle
between the Protestant Peep O'Day Boys [15] and Catholic

Defenders took place at the Diamond near Loughall in Co. Armagh on 21 September 1795. The Defenders, who had provoked the conflict, were completely routed, and that evening the victorious Protestants established a secret 'Orange Society' to protect their own economic and religious interests. [16] Moreover, during the mid 1790s, local 'causes cèlèbres' like the Battle of the Diamond had a definitive sectarian tinge. [17]

The spread of the Orange Order into the Dunlavin hinterland also saw the spread of sectarian tensions throughout the area. Evidence of the threat posed by Orange violence was to be found in the correspondence of the Hon. Benjamin O'Neale Stratford – of all people – to the Castle. Stratford was, as we have seen an Orangeman himself (Lodge 176) and, at first glance, is not the most obvious person to leave any record of Orange violence – actual or threatened. However, one document survives in which he played down the notion of any Orange plot, and suggested that any reports of such a plot were a wild fabrication spread by the Defenders (a term often interchanged with United Irishmen in Loyalist correspondence). [18]

The very fact that he felt it necessary to write to Cooke to make this clear to him was, though, an indication that there was more here than met the eye! Stratford's letters were written from an Orange point of view, and he seemed to be trying to engage in a damage limitation exercise with the Castle authorities. Towards the end of his epistle, Stratford claimed not to be alarmed by the weight of numbers of his opposition, as he saw it. But – who was writing to the Castle?

The very fact that Stratford was writing to Cooke at all suggested that he was running scared. His closing paragraph smacked of boyish bravado, and if there was an element of bluff found here, the previous contents of the letter may also contain some element of bluff. The threat of Orange violence could very well have been a lot more real that Stratford made out to Cooke. At the very least, it is logical to assume that the threat of Republican United Irish violence and possible rebellion did not go ignored in Loyalist circles. Orangeism could answer violence with violence (as at the Battle of the Diamond for example); and threatened violence with threatened violence. Rarely throughout all of history has the threat of impending violence gone unanswered!

The village of Stratford-on-Slaney was something of an exception anyhow, as there was a large Presbyterian (Dissenter) population there due to the presence of the Orrs and the textile mill. Orangemen here faced conditions somewhat similar to those in the north-east of the country – with Papist and Dissenter elements to contend with – and again it is reasonable to assume that the Orange reaction in Stratford could be somewhat similar to that of Ulster's Orangemen. Relevant extracts of O'Neale Stratford's letter read as follows:

> Our neighbours from the counties of Dublin and Kildare ... have sent emissaries hither who have industrious propagated a report that the Protestants under the title of Orange Boys were determined to assemble and murder the Roman Catholics and burn their houses and had fixed on Thursday night last for beginning, and that the town of Stratford-on-Slaney was on that night to be set fire ... As the most part of the inhabitants of that town are, and I fear not unjustly, suspected to be United Irish Men, it occurred to me that such a vile report was calculated for mischief of the worst sort ...

Stratford finished his letter with an assurance that he was not alarmed by the threat: 'I request the advice of the Government how to act and to know if I may continue to keep up a nightly patrol as the Protestants in this part, except myself, are really alarmed, from the numbers of the other class ...'

There is no doubt that the region was polarising along sectarian lines as people rang out the old year of 1797, and the new year of 1798 dawned. The year may have changed, but very little else had in Stratford's next letter. The language of the sectarian divide was obvious in this letter; the alienation of Protestants and Catholics (religious terms which were often interchanged with the political terms Loyalists and Republicans); the fear and loathing expressed for the Catholic priests ('villains' according to Stratford) and once again Stratford referred to the village of Dunlavin as being at the centre of events.

This letter, dated 10 April 1798, was more than sectarian in tone; it was bordering on hysteria. [19] No doubt the many outrages of that Spring of 1798 made Stratford edgy. Basically, the response of the government to continuing and increasing United Irish activity in the country was to clamp down hard on suspected Republicans – in other words the Catholic populace. The military's reign of terror spread from Ulster into Leinster. County Kildare merited special attention – the activities of Captain Swayne in Prosperous and Colonel Campbell in Ballitore were notorious. Once again, events in Kildare had a major impact on, and spread into, the West Wicklow area. Naturally enough, the actions of the military spawned resentment among the populace and even more instances of Republican, Defenders, United Irish – call it what you will – violence occurred. As things worsened in the Spring of 1798, there was no doubt that outnumbered Loyalists were living in fear of the threat posed by the Catholic masses – the 'mob' – all around them.

Stratford's letter of April 10th is typical of a man who sees danger at every turn, and his statement about 'every Catholic in this country being sworn', though probably an exaggeration, does show that the United movement was growing apace in Dunlavin ('at the head of the whole') and its hinterland. Indeed, the swearing of United Irishmen was going on quite openly in West Wicklow generally, and according to John Smith the Dunlavin Corps were deeply involved in membership of the Society! An anonymous warning was enclosed with Stratford's letter. Evidently Stratford's fears were not ephemeral, and it was easy to see why Stratford was fearful – with only such anonymous warnings to go on – and blindly accused all Catholics, as he was unable to identify the guilty. An extract from the letter provided evidence of Stratford's fears:

> I sometime since communicated to Government that Bartle Griffin one of my Corps, and brother to the person of that name now I believe in custody in Town, could give great information. He knows every Catholic in this country to be sworn and some time since declared it to Mr. King, my First Lieutenant, that all except himself were. However, in the list I enclosed Mr. Cooke last post (taken at that fellows, Michael Kearns now bailed out and a very designing villain the next so in this country to the priests of this town and Dunlavin, who I really believe to be at the head of the whole), you will perceive Griffin's name first as the officer intended, and six following non-commissioned officers.

Stratford also enclosed an anonymous warning that he had received:

> Honoured Captain these few lines is to let your honour understand the view of this kingdom as I have a little knowledge of it. The united men of this kingdom both great and low, they are all to turn out in the space of one hour through the kingdom. They expect to go on with this unlawful tyranny in less than a fortnight ... Entrust no Roman in your corps ... they expect the most part of the army of this kingdom to join them as there is thousands would ...

The Michael Kearns of this letter, was probably the Baltinglass carpenter who later joined Michael Dwyer's band of rebels and who left Dwyer during the winter of 1799-1800. He was arrested on 5 March 1800. [20]

Stratford's letter adds to the violent picture of Dunlavin and its hinterland, which is emerging in this chapter. Another reason for the vital nature of Stratford's correspondence as a source regarding the Dunlavin massacre is the fact that many of those shot on Dunlavin Green were members of the Saundersgrove Yeomanry – and hence from the Stratford-on-Slaney (Rathbran) area. Events in and around Stratford had a huge bearing on the eventual outcome on Dunlavin Green.

That Benjamin O'Neale Stratford suspected a general plot, and felt vulnerable in the midst of a largely Catholic population is obvious, but he also took action to prevent any Republican attacks – hence his nightly patrols – and, hence also his constant correspondence to Cooke in Dublin Castle. Stratford continued to suspect all around him, and another letter provides insight into his mindset. [21] Once again the priest of the parish came in for vitriolic attack as being at the bottom of the whole business. The sectarian overtones were still to be seen in this undated letter, describing how a false message revealed another plot, which he foiled:

> His [the messenger's] plan thus was a concocted plan in order to get the foot away, that an attack might be made on the town on which account I had the cavalry under my command (except such as went in search of the fellow under arms) all night with the remainder of the corps and I am certain thereby prevented further mischief intended hereabouts. I hear Mr. Saunders' arms were destined to be taken; mine and Lord Aldborough's attempted. From two letters without names and strong circumstance, I have every reason to believe the priest of this parish to be at the bottom of all this business and that he is aided by persons of property ... There is no doubt but whose names though hinted to me I don't as yet choose to mention not through fear, I know it not, but delicacy ... I should have taken the fellow who imposed on us, had he not been well acquainted with the country and crossed a bog, the party was so near him that he threw off his cap, coat, sword and hilt which we have.

Once again, Stratford's bravado was a bit unconvincing. Given the circumstances of the times, it is hardly likely that any Loyalist in the local area, (let alone one who constantly wrote about the local situation to Cooke), did 'not know fear'. Indeed,

as with his other letters, this epistle only highlighted the volatile situation that had developed in West Wicklow in late 1797 and early 1798. In fact, Stratford knew this as well as anyone at the time, and when one compares the boyish bluster of his letter with the tone that he had used in an earlier letter (from November 1797), it verifies the fact that his 'knowing no fear' is unlikely.

In the earlier letter, Stratford acted as spokesman for the local gentry, and asked that County Wicklow be proclaimed, so bad was the situation within its borders. [22] The response to this request was interesting. Only two baronies were proclaimed – Talbotstown Upper and Talbotstown Lower. The village of Dunlavin and its environs straddled both baronies, so here was further evidence that the Dunlavin area was regarded as a United Irish heartland.

Of course, the strength of Wicklow's Whig politicians may have had a part to play in the fact that other baronies were not proclaimed, but whatever the reason, the fact remains that Dunlavin and its immediate hinterland were excluded from Co. Wicklow's 'general amnesty' regarding its proclamation!

In O'Neale Stratford's November 1797 letter he stated:

> Mr. Richard Nickson of Killinure in the county of Wicklow was on the night before last wantonly and inhumanly murdered by the Defenders, and that several cattle have been haughed and stolen and arms taken by persons of that description who are become more desperate from the idea that the Government will not proclaim, that they are well armed and increasing to an alarming degree ...

O'Neale Stratford had good reason to be worried about the situation in November 1797. The United Irishmen may have been complaining about being poorly armed but another source from November 1797 confirmed that there were arms 'floating around' the local district.

The following list compiled by Major Joseph Hardy must have been alarming, to say the least, for the Loyalist population of the area. Another point to remember here is that, if these arms were found ['taken'] or given up voluntarily ['surrendered'], what must the overall number of subversive arms have been? As far as Loyalists were concerned, this list was probably only the tip of the iceberg – barely scratching the surface of a possible huge underground rebel arsenal! Hardy's list must have made grim reading for Loyalists: [23]

	IRON FOUR-POUNDERS	BRASS PATERAROES	MUSKETS	FOWLING PIECES	BLUNDER-BUSSES	PISTOLS	BAYONETS	PIKES AND SHAFTS	SCYTHES ON SHAFTS	SWORDS AND CUTLASSES	BEARDED SPEARS
Captain Ryves' Cavalry	1	8	34	53	6	15	11	–	–	15	7
Earl of Aldborough's Cavalry & Infantry	–	–	7	11	–	1	7	4	–	–	4
Captain Eustace's Cavalry	–	–	62	32	2	16	8	–	–	3	–
Captain Saunders' Infantry	–	–	15	8	9	6	5	7	–	9	10
Captain Harrington's Infantry	–	–	6	7	1	1	–	–	–	2	–
Captain Wainwright's Cavalry & Infantry	–	–	44	76	3	17	12	–	–	17	–
Captain Hume's Cavalry	–	–	37	58	7	11	8	5	3	14	–
Hon. Captain Stratford's Cavalry	–	–	11	24	2	7	9	3	4	17	9
Captain Hornridge's Cavalry	–	–	7	9	4	8	2	–	–	8	–
TOTALS	1	8	223	278	34	82	62	19	7	85	30

Hardy's list was accompanied by a note that stated:

> This return falls short of the number in the different depots of
> Baltinglass, Hacketstown, Tullow, Dunlavin and Coolatin as
> several stand of arms have been brought in by other parties of
> which there is no general return but a more correct one shall be
> made from the different depots.

If the situation in Wicklow was worsening in late 1797 and
early 1798, what of the other side of Dunlavin's hinterland?
Across the Kildare border the situation was also deteriorating.
Ballitore was a village almost equidistant from both Stratford-
on-Slaney and Dunlavin. Local men here often joined the
Narraghmore Yeomanry Corps, some of whom were also shot in
the Dunlavin Green massacre. As in Stratford-on-Slaney, events
in Ballitore were also crucial in the period before the Dunlavin
massacre. Ballitore, like Stratford was something of a religious
'melting pot', as both villages had sizeable non-Catholic and
non-Anglican populations, (Presbyterians in the case of
Stratford; Quakers in the case of Ballitore) and the atmosphere
in both places (as in Dunlavin itself) was tense, as 1797 gave
way to 1798. A unique record of events in Ballitore has survived.
The diary kept by Mary Leadbeater constitutes a vital primary
source. Towards the end of 1797, Mary Leadbeater wrote: [24]

> Soldiers now constituted part of the inhabitants of Ballitore; the
> Cork militia were stationed here. William Cooke, of Ballylea,
> about three miles hence, was attacked by a number of men, who
> set fire to his house, and demanded his arms. The house was
> burned, the family went to Baltinglass, and we all saw with dread
> the approaching flames of discord.

The premonition of 'the approaching flames of discord' was to
prove, unfortunately, all too true. The Leadbeater diary
contained more instances of violence in and around Ballitore as
the spring of 1798 wore on. Early in 1798, Leadbeater wrote: [25]

> Amongst other precautions, the names of the inhabitants were
> posted on the doors of each house, and the authorities had
> liberty to enter at any hour, night or day, to see whether they
> were within or not. This appeared a necessary precaution, yet it
> exposed the quiet of families to be sadly broken in upon. Houses
> were now searched for fire-arms, proving the wisdom of our
> friends in banishing all such weapons from theirs. Notices were
> put up demanding the arms taken by the 'United men' to be

restored, on pain of allowing the military to live at free quarters;
for many nightly incursions had been made by these robbers to
plunder houses of whatever arms they contained. A detachment
of the King's County militia was at this time sent here from Athy,
where Sandford Palmer, an old Ballitore Boy, was stationed as
their captain. The men were very well liked; perhaps it was for
that reason they were so soon removed ... They were replaced by
the Tyrone militia, mostly composed of professed Orangemen,
wearing the ribbon of their party.

Obviously, the 'reign of terror', which had been so effective in
Ulster, was now spreading to the Ballitore region (well within
the Dunlavin hinterland). The enforced billeting of soldiers in
people's houses (Free Quarters) never applied to Wicklow, but
County Kildare was different as Leadbeater testified. [26]

Hitherto the soldiers were quartered in our houses but found
themselves in provisions; the threat respecting free quarters was
now put into execution; foraging parties went into the country,
shops and private houses were searched for whisky, which was
ordered to be spilled; and seditious papers were sought for ...
Robert Bayley was pursued because he attempted to take away
one of his own horses; his horse was captured, and himself made
a prisoner. Ephraim Boake's house was plundered, and he very
narrowly escaped personal injury.

The diary also recorded the continuing (and increasing)
violence – probably only fuelled by the Free Quarters tactic and
it continued:

These attacks on the most loyal people amongst us were not to
be borne. Some of the inhabitants went to Colonel Colin
Campbell, who commanded the district, and got protections ...
Great waste was committed, and unchecked robbery. One
hundred cars loaded with hay, potatoes, oats etc. led by the poor
owners, and guarded by soldiers, were in one day marched into
Ballitore. Colonel Keatinge urged his yeomen to take with a
sparing hand; to remember that this was the 'scarce season,'
when the new food was not yet come in and the old was nearly
exhausted, and not to bring famine upon the country. But he
spoke to deaf ears, for pity seemed banished from the martial
bosom... Public Notice was given that the nightly patrol should
be withdrawn, to give opportunity for returning the arms of
which the 'United men' had possessed themselves, and that if
not returned within a stated time, the whole neighbourhood
should be burnt.

These were tense times in both Ballitore and Stratford-on-Slaney. The ultra-loyal clergyman of Stratford-on-Slaney, Rev. Christopher Robinson, confirmed this fact in a letter (written anonymously from Baltinglass, but definitely in Robinson's hand). [27] Robinson supported O'Neale Stratford's efforts to seek out and confiscate hidden armaments. He was well aware of the tense situation that prevailed in the neighbouring villages of Stratford and Ballitore (both of which also neighboured Dunlavin). Robinson also voiced concerns about liberal, 'democratic' gentry, and indeed this was hardly surprising. Robinson's own politics were obviously of the ultra-Orange variety. Robinson even voiced doubts about the loyalty of the Honourable Benjamin O'Neale Stratford, who (as his letters indicated) was of the ultra-loyal school of thought. This letter of 14 May 1798 confirmed the story which was unfolding in Mary Leadbeater's diary at the same time. The letter is dated almost a fortnight before the massacre on Dunlavin Green, and the abundance of weapons in the region is once again evident as these extracts show:

> The detection of Rebels and recovery of concealed arms, have been pretty successful this week past throughout the neighbourhood of Castledermot, Timolin, Ballitore, and Baltinglass ... The terror excited throughout the lands of Timolin, Rathtoole, Ballinure and Baronstown all in the parish of Baltinglass and county of Wicklow by the active measures adopted in the above mentioned neighbouring towns ... that night being the 11th, eight cavalry pistols, two of them belonging to Moone and Talbotstown cavalry, and one to Baltinglass do, were left at Mr. Robinson's back door ... on Sunday night about two hundred of pikes, swords, guns, pistols etc., etc., were brought to Mr. Harrington's house to be delivered up to the Magistrates, and to get protections, so the knot is effectually now broken in the parish of Baltinglass and about 800 stand of different kind of weapons are already come in, and if the leaders and instigators of this accursed, murderous conspiracy are not now fully made known, it must be the fault of the Magistracy.

The area of Dunlavin and its hinterland was a volatile place in May 1798. Places on the Kildare side of the village (such as Ballitore), and on the Wicklow side (such as Stratford-on-Slaney) were in a state of flux and uncertainty. Dunlavin was in the eye of the storm, and it could not hope to escape. Inevitably, that storm broke in its full fury in Dunlavin later that month, and men from both Stratford and Ballitore as well as Dunlavin itself were hanged from the market house pillars or lay dead on the village green.

NOTES

1: Cullen, L. M., Politics and Rebellion – Wicklow in the 1790s, in Hannigan, Ken, and Nolan, William (editors), County Wicklow: History and Society, Dublin, 1994, p460.

2: Cullen, in Hannigan and Nolan, 1994, p.456.

3: N.A.I. 620/35/55.

4: N.A.I. 620/30/89.

5: MacSuibhne, Peadar, Kildare in '98, Leinster Leader Ltd. 1978, p.185.

6: Leadbeater, Mary, (editor John MacKenna), The Annals of Ballitore, Stephen Scroop Press, 1986, p.58. (There is a full version of Leadbeater's diary in the library of N.U.I. Maynooth).

7: The village of Stratford was actually built as a model industrial town by the Second Earl of Aldborough (1780's). Chavasse, p.45.

8: Cullen, in Hannigan and Nolan, 1994, p472.

9: O'Donnell, Ruán, The Rebellion of 1798 in County Wicklow, in Hannigan and Nolan, 1994, p.369.

10. N.A.I. 620/31/65.

11. N.A.I. 620/31/45. Pateraroes were small cannons, often used on ships.

12. N.A.I. S.O.C. 3086.

13. N.A.I. 620/34/14.

14. N.A.I. 620/36/1.

15: Whelan, Kevin, Fellowship of Freedom: The United Irishmen and 1798, Cork, 1998, p. 44.

16: Beckett, J. C., The Making of Modern Ireland 1603-1923, Faber and Faber Ltd., 1966 (reprinted 1973), p.257.

17: Foster, R. F., Modern Ireland 1600-1972, Penguin Books, 1988, p.272.

18: N.A.I. S.O.C. 3099.

19: N.A.I. 620/36/186.

20: Dickson, p.103.

21: N.A.I. S.O.C. 3119/1.

22: N.A.I. 620/33/32.

23: N.A.I. 620/33/102.

24: Leadbeater, p.59.

25: Leadbeater, p.60.

26: Leadbeater, p.61.

27: N.A.I. 620/3/32/5.

Tober House, the Powell family seat burned out during the 1798 period, was never rebuilt

TERROR

The first few months of 1798, were punctuated by violent incidents in and around Dunlavin. Loyalists perceived the town and the other urban settlements around it as an oasis of government control amidst a surrounding desert (the countryside) where the United Irish movement was openly thriving. To Loyalists, acts of nocturnal Republican violence must have increased tensions within their communities. The fact that the enemy did not wear a uniform and lurked within the larger rural Catholic population only served to fuel Loyalist fears – understandably, as the Republicans were like spectres to them, and almost equally hard to capture! As early as the autumn of 1797 a reign of terror was unleashed and in 1797 that terror reached Dunlavin. The objects of the terror were the

village blacksmiths of Dunlavin. Blacksmiths came in for
particular persecution as suspected pike-makers – Owen Finn of
Narraghmore, for example, was executed in 1798 and the
Thomas Egan referred to below again narrowly escaped the
hangman's noose on the day of the Dunlavin massacre (24 May
1798). A vivid account of the persecution of the blacksmiths
read thus:

> In the morning of the 20 October last [1797] between the hours
> of one and two, Lieutenant H___ of the Antrim Militia, Richard
> Fowler of Dunlavin and Thomas Butler of the County of Kildare
> went to the house of Michael Egan, and having broken open the
> door, desired him and his son Thomas Egan to come down out of
> their beds – they were not even allowed to dress themselves –
> and on the very instant that they appeared, they were knocked
> down and received many desperate stabs: naked and bleeding as
> they were, they were then conveyed to the guardhouse of
> Dunlavin, and on daring to complain of such treatment were
> again knocked down and beaten in a most unmerciful manner.
>
> On their arrival at the guardhouse, they were offered reward and
> to swear against thirteen [United] Irishmen, but on the solemn
> declaration of the father and the son that they had no connection
> with persons of that description, they were again stabbed with
> bayonets. After having nearly killed the father, they dragged the
> son to a private part of the guardhouse and by every kind of
> cruelty and torture they could invent endeavoured to extract
> information from him; when not receiving any (as the poor man
> had none to give) the barbarians a third time inflicted several
> wounds upon him ...
>
> They then left the son and went to the father, whom they used
> exactly in the same manner, and again returning to the son they
> said that since he would not give them any information they
> would hang him. To this they proceeded and, putting the rope
> around his neck, led him to the winding staircase where (again
> not being able to obtain information from a person who had none
> to give) Lieut. H___ ordered Mr. Causker, a corporal, to tie him up,
> which was instantly done – he was then turned off.
>
> They then threatened the father that they would kill him also if
> he would not inform; but at this time, a gentleman of profession,
> hearing the shrieks of the relatives of these miserable men, came
> to the window and prevailed on the barbarians to let Thomas
> Egan be cut down.
>
> He was then cut down, but not before he was entirely deprived of
> his senses. One would have imagined that an hospital or an

infirmary would be the place to where the wretch would then have been conducted. No such thing. He was hurried to the gaol of Wicklow, where he was confined thirteen weeks and laden with the most heavy irons; but we understand he has sworn examinations against the persons concerned in the above horrid transactions.

Michael Egan the father, a man upwards of seventy years of age is lying in his bed in a most helpless situation; his breast and shoulder bone broke; and even if he survives, will never be capable of benefiting either himself or his family ... the son was hanged three times in the presence of his aged father, with every aggravating circumstance of barbarity – and this without any colour of legal authority whatsoever, but avowedly by the inhuman and illegal process of torture to extort accusations from the agony of the sufferers.

Upon the son refusing a bribe, the father was violently beaten before his face. The young man was cut down senseless and life-less, his tongue hanging out of his mouth, but was nevertheless kept several days in the guardhouse. In six days he was taken with his hands tied behind his back to Wicklow gaol, where he remained in most monstrous contempt and violation of the law in a dismal cell loaded with very heavy irons. [1]

In the days immediately preceding the Dunlavin massacre, however, the situation deteriorated rapidly. The already tense village of Dunlavin grew even tenser, as it became evident that the United Irish movement was indeed planning a rising – a rising that seemed imminent in the month of May 1798. Of course, the military response (which caused even further resentment) was to clamp down even harder on the troubled countryside. In April 1798, the house of John Dwyer (a relative of Michael Dwyer), who lived in Seskin in the Glen of Imaal, was looted and burned. The reign of terror had reached into the remote glen itself. Dwyer was a suspected United Irish Baronial Delegate. Indeed he probably was a baronial delegate, because, 'Imale district and that bordering on the Co. Kildare was represented by one of the O'Dwyer's and a young man named Hayden, both of whom were shot afterwards in the massacre of Dunlavin on the 24th May 1798'. [2] John Dwyer was brought to Dunlavin market house, which served as a temporary prison during these troubled times. He remained in captivity for about a month, and was in the market house on the morning of the massacre. Thus, he was in custody for about a month before he was shot, and was definitely among the first – if not actually the first – of the executed men to be taken prisoner.

Across the Kildare border, too, the military clampdown was enforced with rigour. In Ballitore the clampdown was quite effective and the once tiny number of captured United Irish arms was increasing in volume in May 1798.

Once again, Mary Leadbeater's diary provided an invaluable resource regarding events in and around Ballitore. The 'foremost gentleman' of Ballitore was Squire Keatinge (sometimes spelled without the final 'e'). We are told in the diary that Squire Keatinge, having raised a regiment, now became a colonel. [3] However, Keatinge was noted for his liberal views, and such a Whig was not the best man to lead a corps of yeomen in the eyes of more hard-line Unionists. Keatinge's corps was constantly under suspicion for United Irish activities. Indeed, in this respect Keatinge's corps were very similar to the Saundersgrove corps of Morley Saunders. As the harsh tactics of the military – particularly the full-time military – continued, it was quite natural for action to be taken against the suspected members of Colonel Keatinge's corps. In May 1798, Keatinge bowed to Loyalist pressures and decided to leave the area. Leadbeater recorded this episode:

> He and his lady left the country. They left their dear Narraghmore – left it never to return, and their loss has never ceased to be felt and deplored. A large quantity of arms was left as directed, but broken into pieces, and thus rendered useless. The clouds gathered darker and darker in our political horizon. [4]

With Keatinge gone, whatever protection he had given to his men had also disappeared. The way lay open for a full scale Loyalist backlash in the area, and the military presence was stepped up to enforce such measures as were deemed necessary to root the United Irishmen out of the local yeomanry. Once again, the observant Mary Leadbeater noted the increasing number of soldiers – and the different uniforms – in her diary. [5]

> To the Tyrone militia were now added the Suffolk fencibles; and the Ancient Britons, dressed in blue with much silver lace – a very pretty dress – came from Athy, seized the smiths' tools to prevent them from making pikes, and made prisoners of the smiths themselves. I could not see without emotion poor Owen Finn and his brother, hand-cuffed and weeping, as they walked after the car containing those implements of industry which had enabled them to provide comfortably for the family. Several of

these were whipped publicly to extort confessions about the pikes. The torture was excessive, and the victims were long in recovering; and in almost every case it was applied fruitlessly. Guards were placed at every entrance into the village, to prevent people from entering or leaving it. The village once so peaceful exhibited a scene of tumult and dismay, and the air rang with the shrieks of the sufferers and the lamentations of those who beheld them suffer. These violent measures caused a great many pikes to be brought in: the street was lined with those who came to deliver up the instruments of death.

Obviously, the terror tactics were now in full swing, and this deterioration in the situation led directly to the arrest and imprisonment of some members of the Narraghmore corps of yeomen who were later shot on Dunlavin green. Thanks to Mary Leadbeater and her habit of writing down information about events around her in the diary, we have a vivid, eyewitness primary source relating to the day that these men were taken prisoner. [6] Her diary regarding that May day over two hundred years ago recorded:

A party of military from Naas entered Ballitore and took prisoners, twelve of our neighbours, whom they removed to Naas gaol. Most of the villagers stood outside their doors to see them depart. They looked composed for the most part, though followed by their weeping wives and children. One child, with his cries of 'O father, father!' excited great compassion. Six yeomen were taken prisoners to Dunlavin. I was walking in our garden when they passed on a car, with their coats turned inside out, and one of their guards, a mere boy, cried out to me in a tone of insulting jocularity. We, who did not understand this case, were only qualified to see one side, and, though we forbore audibly expressing our disapprobation, our looks betrayed the depression of our minds. This excited jealousy of us: how ill-founded! For who could expect us to rejoice at the misery and degradation of our fellow-creatures and neighbours, or even to behold them unmoved. These unfortunate yeomen were shot! There was too much exultation in the military; they were not aware, perhaps, how deeply an insult is felt and resented, and that an injury is sometimes more easily pardoned.

The arrest of the six yeomen was part of a wider tapestry of events that was unfolding in the local area. The prisoners were openly humiliated and paraded before the populace as turn-coats. The young guard obviously thought that the military were stamping out subversive activity and he appeared to be 'on a high'. Leadbeater recorded sympathy for the prisoners, although she seemed to think that the government must have its reasons for such actions. Nevertheless, she failed to understand these reasons. We must remember that Mary Leadbeater was a woman of her times and women were not usually seen to hold opinions on political matters. In addition to her female status, Leadbeater was also a Quaker. Like Catholics, Quakers were not members of the established church, and had to be careful in relation to what they both said and did. Leadbeater's religious principles did, however, lead her to observe that there was 'too much exultation in the military'. Once again, this observant woman hit the nail on the head. The populace could only be pushed so far. If the reign of terror continued unabated, something had to snap. This is exactly what happened in late May, and it was no accident that Kildare (and, of course, West Wicklow) was the first area in Leinster to experience rebellion at that time.

Although the situation in Kildare had worsened in May 1798, the rebellion itself was unexpected. The authorities seemed to think that the reign of terror was working – indeed, had worked – and General Ralph Dundas wrote a reassuring letter to Dublin Castle on 16 May. [7] Whether he believed that the region was actually pacified, or whether he was trying to reassure the authorities that the real situation was not as bad as they might have heard elsewhere, one thing is very evident – Dundas was confident that the situation in Kildare was now under control as he wrote:

> Be assured that the head of the Hydra is off, and the County of Kildare will, for a long while, enjoy profound peace and quiet.

One week after this letter was written, the revolt broke out in Kildare! Where Kildare led, West Wicklow usually followed. Despite the fact that one source of information – John Smith – was lost to the government, the scene in West Wicklow was very much akin to that in neighbouring parts of Kildare.

Incidentally, as early as the autumn of 1797, John Smith was in danger of having his cover blown, as the following extract from a letter dated 15 September 1797 indicated: [8]

> But an event that happened yesterday has fully confirmed the danger I am in. Charles Reilly, the son of the person I lodge with in the course of conversation with his mother who was scolding him for having used me very ill, spoke these words to her, 'Wist

woman – don't I know he is nothing but an informer and I'll have him fixed when ever I please' – which words he spoke in the hearing of my wife whose honour may easier be conceived then discredited.

Even with Smith off the scene, however, the military clampdown in West Wicklow was achieving results. There were other informers. Captain Benjamin O'Neale Stratford prided himself on the quality of his information and the information of both James Dunne and Joseph Hawkins contributed to the Dunlavin massacre. Events in West Wicklow in May 1798 were influenced by an influx of people – some Republicans, some perhaps not – escaping from Kildare's reign of terror. Like General Dundas in Kildare, Wicklow's Major Joseph Hardy was confident that the county was under control as the following extracts from a letter dated 22 May 1798 (only a couple of days before the Dunlavin massacre, and the general rebellion in West Wicklow) amply testified: [9]

> My Lord, I have the pleasure to acquaint you that the spirit of insurrection is fairly broke in this county, and though I have been eight months in it, both in civil and military capacity, had no idea the evil had so generally spread, and pervaded the whole mass (military excepted and even they not totally untainted) except some few staunch Protestants, but hardly a Papist who was not corrupted ... Sergeants of twelve bring in their pikes together, black smiths set down the names of them they made for, full information about their secretaries and treasurers, some of whom are in custody ... Several parts, or spots, still resist but as there is a general surrender, all must yield by steady perseverance.

In the light of the subsequent Dunlavin massacre, Hardy's opening paragraph was both interesting and revealing. He spoke of how the military were 'not totally untainted' in relation to United Irish activities. The local military – the yeomen – especially were under suspicion in many areas. Many yeomen were Catholic, and the increase in sectarian tensions during the Spring of 1798 meant that these Catholic yeoman became the targets of Loyalist suspicions. These included some members of Colonel Keatinge's corps in Kildare. Six of them had been arrested together and carted off to prison in Dunlavin market house, there to join local republican figures such as John Dwyer of Seskin who had been imprisoned during the military clampdown.

The West Wicklow equivalent of Colonel Keatinge's Narraghmore yeomanry was undoubtedly the Saundersgrove corps. Time and again, Loyalist suspicion in West Wicklow hinged on this group of yeomen. The result of these Loyalist suspicions regarding the Saundersgrove corps was that a yeomanry test – essentially an oath – was introduced. Some liberal yeomanry commanders, however, held out against administering this oath. Such a course of action naturally deepened the suspicions of the Loyalists, not only of the largely Catholic yeomanry, but also of their Whig commanders, some of whom were magistrates. Morley Saunders of Saundersgrove was one such liberal figure. Even though, the regional situation was deteriorating rapidly in May 1798, Saunders did not see any need (or at least stubbornly did not want) to implement the yeomanry test on his corps. It was only when Saunders received new information and evidence about his corps that he called them out on parade and twenty or so of the corps were taken into custody. They were escorted to Dunlavin market house, where they were imprisoned with the members of the Narraghmore yeomen and some local United Irish sympathisers who were already in the building. This arrest and imprisonment of the Saundersgrove contingent took place on 22 May 1798. That was a Tuesday. On Wednesday night and Thursday morning the whole area became awash with violence as the rebellion broke out.

The Dunlavin massacre occurred on Thursday 24 May 1798. One aspect of the massacre and the injustice of it all which has been passed down orally through the generations concerns the yeomanry test – the oath. The Saundersgrove men were paraded, arrested and imprisoned (as one might expect United Irish sympathisers to be) – but they were also shot before they were given a chance to actually take the yeomanry oath. This fact has survived vividly in the folk-memory of the massacre. Why were they shot before they could take the oath? Why was the fatal decision taken? In order to understand the decision more fully, an examination of the character of the men involved in the taking of that decision is necessary. The Dunlavin garrison on the day of the massacre comprised three units – Captain Richardson's Wicklow militia, Captain Ryves' yeoman cavalry and Captain Saunders' yeoman infantry.

There is no doubt that Morley Saunders is popularly perceived as the central figure in the Dunlavin massacre, and he is held responsible for the decision to execute the men in the local popular memory. But was Saunders responsible, either solely, or even to the greater degree, for what happened?

Morley Saunders lived in Saundersgrove, a big house near the village of Stratford-on-Slaney (on the Dunlavin side of Lord Aldborough's model village). Stratford was also the home of Aldborough's ultra-Loyalist younger brother, the Honourable Benjamin O'Neale Stratford. In fact, one of the biggest ironies regarding the local gentry of that time was that the liberal Morley Saunders was actually a nephew of Lord Aldborough, and hence also of Benjamin O'Neale Stratford. It must have been very galling for the staunchly Orange O'Neale Stratford to have a nephew who was widely seen as a noted Whig (and a very liberal magistrate to boot, as Saunders was a member of the local judiciary). Such a liberal figure was probably quite popular among the mass of the populace, and we can imagine local sarcasm and wit regarding his family connections with O'Neale Stratford and the Aldborough clan. Saunders was by no means the only liberal figure among the gentry and aristocracy who inhabited the Wicklow-Kildare borderlands around the Dunlavin region. Colonel Keatinge of Narraghmore, was Whiggish, as were the Harrington Walls of Grangecon. In West Wicklow, apart from Morley Saunders, the greatest champion of liberal values was William Hume of Humewood. However, one vital distinction must be made between Hume and Saunders. Hume was a member of parliament for Wicklow and as such was a major figure with considerable political influence.

The fact that the two Talbotstown baronies were the only ones to be proclaimed in Wicklow, for example, shows the strength of the liberals' clout in political terms. Saunders, on the other hand, was more what might be termed 'Minor Gentry' and did not have the same political influence. He lived very close to Aldborough's territory in Stratford-on-Slaney, and was thus an easier target for dissatisfied and worried Loyalists.

Liberal he might have been, but Saunders was no less patriotic than his fellow members of the gentry. Thus in the troubled times of an imminent French invasion (and the December 1796 debacle in Bantry Bay ensured that the French threat remained uppermost in the minds of everyone), Saunders was one of the many gentry figures who found himself in command of a corps of part-time soldiers (yeomen), a force which was formed to assist the regular military and to show suitable defiance in the face of any French invasion – rumoured or real! There are many indications that Captain Morley

Saunders entered into his military role with gusto, and he seems to have been quite proud of his yeomanry corps. Indeed, Saunders' uncle, Benjamin O'Neale Stratford commented on his nephew's pride and the 'uncommon pains' that he had taken with his corps. [10]

Morley Saunders, perhaps like many of the minor gentry nationwide, was probably attracted by the uniform, the military planning and the prestige that went with the position of captain of the yeomen. Really, as long as the French did not invade, the phenomenon of the 'Yeos' was probably a bit like playing soldiers – and who wouldn't like such a game as long as he was the captain?

Captain Morley Saunders also had another leadership role in the local community. This was as a magistrate. Liberal magistrates came to be looked on as a threat by the more hard-line Loyalist population, especially as the overall situation became more tense from late 1797 onward. The thought of local yeomen gaining military knowledge, experience and expertise under the command of such a Whiggish figure was a frightening one for Loyalists. To make matters worse, in this time of worsening sectarianism, the Saundersgrove corps of yeomen were mainly Catholics. The spectre of armed, trained Catholics within the local region, waiting for a suitable opportunity to stage a United Irish rising was, no doubt, very frightening for local hard-line Loyalists, who were becoming more isolated as 1797 wore into 1798. These Loyalists continued to write to the Castle, and Cooke received many venomous attacks on Saunders in his correspondence.

One such letter (anonymous but again written by Christopher Robinson) dated 16 May 1798, just over a week before the Dunlavin massacre. [11] Robinson was one of the ultra-Loyalist school and the language that he used was quite revealing. He refers directly to 'Republican Assassins' and 'fiery Jacobins', both of which terms suggest a direct link to events in France.

On 21 January 1793 King Louis XVI of France was executed despite last minute Girondin (rivals of the Jacobin faction) efforts to save him. The use of such terms in Robinson's epistle indicated what a politically aware time the late 1790s was in Ireland generally, and in the Dunlavin hinterland as well.

The letter named quite a few liberal local figures, but the most heartfelt attack is reserved for Morley Saunders and his corps of yeomen (or 'Republican Assassins'). Colonel Keatinge of Narraghmore was also mentioned as a French Revolutionary sympathiser in this letter, parts of which read:

> It is shameful to see how Mr. Saunders of Saunders' Grove still labours to nurture and screen that hellish group of Republican assassins, the heads and leaders of Stratford-on-Slaney. It is also unpardonable how he connived at and cherished them and those of his own Corps and every other description of rebel since the first outset of this abominable system, and how he and Mr. Travers, the parish priest of Baltinglass, with these fiery Jacobins of Stratford-on-Slaney, humbugged, browbeat, and cajoled by arms, the inhabitants of their whole neighbourhood and one another into a motley but inveterate union of arms, bloodshed and anarchy ... I fear our high Sheriff, Mr. Carroll is too much infected with the Whiggism of his uncle Bagnell, and the liberty and equality of his cousin Keatinge ... Mr. Harrington of Grangecon, is a very great detriment in the way of getting in the arms, as he and Saunders are labouring to lump the arms for each land and grant a general protection without any further discriminating between the guilty and innocent ... I wish Mr. William Hume of Humewood was properly cautioned from screening the disaffected of his own neighbourhood.

This letter implied that quite a sizeable proportion of the Saundersgrove yeomanry corps were subversives. Saunders was accused of harbouring 'every description of rebel since the outset of this abominable (yeomanry) system'. Robinson also accused Saunders of being in league with the Catholic priest, Fr. Travers, and here Robinson echoed Benjamin O'Neale Stratford's sentiments. O'Neale Stratford believed that the local Catholic priests were 'at the head of the whole'. John Smith also thought that the local Catholic clergy merited special mention. Despite these views regarding priests in the area, Robinson, thought that Saunders was in league with Fr. Travers. No wonder Loyalists were anxious. One can only wonder what Edward Cooke in Dublin Castle must have conjectured!

Three days later, on 19 May 1798, not quite a week before the Dunlavin massacre Robinson wrote another letter to Cooke. [12] The very fact that the hard-line Robinson saw fit to write two letters within three days indicated that the situation in Dunlavin and its hinterland was becoming a lot more unstable in the week or so before the massacre on the fairgreen. Once again, Robinson was concerned with some of the liberal local gentry, and Morley Saunders figured prominently. Specific reference was made to the Saundersgrove yeomanry, and it is alleged that a half-dozen or so of the corps were involved in a plot to kill Saunders himself. Robinson's letter also mentioned that only three or four of the whole Saundersgrove corps were non-Catholics. Given the rising sectarian tensions, it was no surprise that Robinson, who implied that all Catholics were dishonest and thus subversive, perceived the presence of a trained and armed Saundersgrove Catholic corps so close to him as a threat. Saunders was once again mentioned in the same breath as the Catholic priest, and Robinson even went so far as to suggest that Morley Saunders himself was a United Irishman. This was, of course, unsubstantiated, and it is extremely unlikely that Saunders ever had any connection at all with the Society of United Irishmen.

West Wicklow, however, was adjacent to Co. Kildare, where some aristocracy and gentry figures (Lord Edward Fitzgerald and Wogan Brown for example) were involved with the United Irishmen, and Robinson evidently thought that the Kildare phenomenon had spread into West Wicklow in the person of Morley Saunders!

Extracts from Robinson's letter included the following:

> It is melancholy to think how slowly the inhabitants of this town and Southern farms of the parish of Baltinglass are delivering in their concealed arms. If it were possible to get an honest or loyal parish priest to put in place of William Travers, the arms would soon come in, but that I verily believe is impossible, as it is inconsistent with the very object and principles of their Religion. I hear this morning that six men of Mr. Saunders' yeomen are discovered to have conspired some time back to assassinate him. He need have expected no better fate from the villains that he enroled. It is terrible to think how he temporises and cringes to those rebels ... Cornet Joseph Cardiff of Lord Aldborough's Cavalry was sworn a United Irish Man by John Whittle his brother in law of the Ballimore Cavalry and his nephew Anthony Metcalf of Donard, Shopkeeper, and he even heard that Mr. Saunders was sworn a United Irish Man by Mr. Maxwell of Stratford-on-Slaney, near twelve months ago ... Mr. Joseph Fox now in Dunlavin Guard House can if he pleases corroborate his testimony, as he was, I understand, an under Secretary and attestor to Mr. Headon. Those two men know more material information of the quantities of arms in each parish and in the whose hands they are, than all the men within five miles of them, and if such men be whipped and then liberated farewell to the recovery of arms!

This letter corroborated the fact that prisoners such as Joseph Fox had been taken to Dunlavin. The Market House in the town, built by the Tynte family c.1737-1740, [13] had been pressed into service as a prison during the worsening local situation.

Robinson's correspondence regarding Morley Saunders provided a hard-line Loyalist view of this West Wicklow Whig. Saunders' liberal tendencies, his almost wholly Catholic corps of yeomen, his stance against the test oath for yeomen and his lenient magistracy were no doubt noticed by the other side as well. United Irishmen, Catholic tenant farmers – in fact the mass of the local population – would have seen Saunders as a passable, popular figure among the local gentry. In comparison to his uncle Benjamin O'Neale Stratford, for example, Saunders would have been much more acceptable to non-Loyalists generally.

However, as the situation deteriorated that May, Saunders was under mounting pressure to adopt a more hard-line attitude. Saunders and his corps were in the eye of the storm, both because his corps was largely Catholic in its composition and because Saunders was a less formidable target than the powerful figure of Hume. [14] Things really came to a head when a spy named Joseph Hawkins provided more information about the Saundersgrove corps. The sequence of events after this information had come to light was more or less as follows. The recipient of the information told Saunders about it.

As pressure mounted on him, Saunders found it harder to withstand the increasing anger of his fellow Loyalists, and a corporal was arrested. As a result of his interrogation, new facts emerged and arrests were made; and when the news of the rising in the towns and villages around Dunlavin reached Saunders and his fellow officers, the prisoners were taken out and shot.

The outrage caused in the village of Dunlavin (and beyond) by the massacre was mostly vented at Morley Saunders. In the Ballad of Dunlavin Green, Saunders is vilified no less than three times.

> Bad luck to you Saunders,
> for you did their lives betray;
> Bad luck to you Saunders,
> bad luck may you never shun;
> Michael Dwyer in the mountains,
> to Saunders he owes a spleen.

Certainly the ballad writer, who reflected the views of the larger populace, had it in for Saunders. The fact that none of the other officers is mentioned in the ballad is very significant. After all, the massacre was more or less what was to be expected from the other officers. However Saunders – liberal Morley Saunders – who was seen as different by the local Catholic population, surely he would protect the men of his corps? Saunders, it was felt locally, would not let any harm come to his men. These men were his pride and joy. The fact that he did not protect them heightened the shock for the local people, and their revulsion is plainly seen in the Ballad of Dunlavin Green. Even the Honourable Benjamin O'Neale Stratford referred to Saunders as 'both their commandant and friend' [15] in one of his letters.

To make matters even worse, a night (or two) before the massacre, when the men were imprisoned in Dunlavin market house they were actually visited by Saunders. Seemingly, the gist of Saunders' message to the prisoners was something to the effect of, 'You are my tenants, my corps, my people. You will be alright, I'll look after you.' [16] While the exact words have not survived in the folk memory for two centuries, the story of Saunders' visit to the prisoners certainly has, and with it a loathing for Captain Morley Saunders, who is still seen in the light of a Judas.

However, if we are to liken Morley Saunders to anyone in the gospel story of Christian Holy Week, perhaps Pontius Pilate would be a more appropriate comparison. Like Jerusalem of old, Dunlavin was a turbulent town, especially on the day of the massacre itself. Rumours and an influx of excited, tense, frightened and uninformed people (many of them Loyalists) would have added to the mounting pressure on Morley Saunders. [17] Like Pilate, Saunders was not in sole command. Just as the Jews had their own leaders in Jerusalem, so there were other captains in command of detachments of troops in Dunlavin that day. If the fatal decision to execute the prisoners was made on that very turbulent day, perhaps Captain Saunders was simply outnumbered by the combined opinions of Captain Ryves and Captain Richardson, who had possibly panicked on that fatal morning. To investigate this as a possible scenario, the characters of the other two captains, Ryves and Richardson, must be examined.

William Ryves (also spelled Reeves) was the captain of the Dunlavin Yeoman Calvary corps. Despite John Smith's letters, this corps of yeomen was never under the same type of suspicion as the Saundersgrove corps regarding membership of the society of United Irishmen. One reason for this is possibly the fact that this was a cavalry corps, and as one had to be reasonably affluent to own a horse in the 1790s, the corps did not include too many rank and file members of the local community. In other words, the members of Ryves' cavalry corps probably saw themselves as being (and in class terms probably were) a step above the members of Saunders' infantry corps. Like Saunders, Ryves was also a local magistrate. However, unlike Saunders, Ryves did not have the name of being a liberal magistrate. One can imagine local miscreants hoping to make a court appearance before Morley Saunders rather than before William Ryves, as Saunders was a rather lenient member of the gentry.

There were actually two branches of the Ryves family in residence near the village of Dunlavin at this time. The first branch was in Whitestown and it was headed by Armstrong Ryves (who was later involved in some escapades involving Michael Dwyer). This man is not to be confused with William Ryves. This second Ryves family lived in Rathsallagh House. [18] William Ryves was seen by his peers as a loyal man and a sound officer. One contemporary letter [19] stated that 'Captain Ryves is sensible, cool, loyal and persevering'. This view, coming as it did from the ultra-Orange Christopher Robinson, is quite revealing. After all, this is the writer who, in the same letter, refers to Captain Benjamin O'Neale Stratford as being only 'pretty loyal, but he is vain and wavering in such a good and great cause'. However, Stratford's correspondence to Cooke in Dublin Castle showed that he [Stratford] was actually a hard-line Loyalist. Yet, according to Robinson, Ryves was actually a more loyal (and better) officer than Stratford! High praise, indeed, from Robinson for Captain William Ryves. There seems to be no doubt that William Ryves took his yeomanry duties very seriously, as a letter, dated 9 May 1798, about a fortnight before the Dunlavin massacre, showed. [20] Some extracts read thus:

It is vexatious to see how the guilty are flying from the punishment they have so richly earned, for want of proper measures being timely adopted by the Magistrates for securing them ... It was a very wrong mode at first adopted in enroling yeomanry, for Noblemen and Gentlemen, who wished to make themselves appear of consequence in the eyes of Government, to muster up a set of poisoned papists into their Corps, and in that case the wretched tenant, though his heart burned to overthrow the present constitution, yet dare not refuse to comply with his vain Lord, and then made it up with his priest, that he might enrol under a heretic, to save his cattle from being drove, and on conditions that he should be ready to aid the cause of Erin go Bra, when called upon, and use his diligence in the mean time, as an intermediate link to corrupt the militia and soldiers, and by his own appearance and proficiency in arms instruct the common people, and excite in their minds a desire to imitate them ... If you think proper to have the persons named in the within list apprehended, it should be done speedily least they may abscond.

The list of nine men was enclosed with the letter and was entitled – A list of persons who can give effectual information respecting the present Rebellion, the number of arms concealed.

The names on the list were:

Thomas Walsh of Mullamast near Ballitore
Doctor Johnston of Ballitore
John Moore of Blackwrath
Joseph Fox of Stratford-on-Slaney
Roger McGuire, smith of said Stratford
James Dunn, Yeoman in Mr. Saunders' Corps
James Doyle of Rathbran
Pierce Headon of Ballyhooke, and
One Colgan of Ballyhooke.

The letter concluded: 'Captain Ryves, and a few chosen men of his Corps, with a party of Regulars or Militia would be the best men to take these last mentioned.' It was significant that Captain Ryves, rather than the more geographically adjacent Captain Saunders, was seen as the best man to take the suspects into custody.

Indeed, the presence of James Dunn on the list once again brought to light the fact that Saunders' corps was seen as harbouring suspected rebels. James Dunn was not among those executed on Dunlavin Green, but there was a John Dunne from the neighbourhood of Narraghmore shot. [21] Whether these men were related or not is impossible to say. The James Doyle mentioned in the list was not shot on Dunlavin green either, but two Doyles from Rathbarn – Morgan and Thomas – were, and it is quite probable that the James Doyle mentioned here was a member of the same family. Both Joseph Fox and Pierce Headon had been taken into custody ten days later. [22]

William Ryves was no liberal. He did not believe in using kid gloves, and during the deteriorating situation in May 1798, he did not offer any general protection as an inducement to United Irishmen to bring in hidden arms. His protection was only offered on an individual basis – after the hidden arms had been produced. Ryves, therefore, was a lot more hard-line in his political views than Morley Saunders. Another point that emerges about William Ryves is that he does not seem to be a man susceptible to attacks of panic. He was, by all accounts, quite a cool customer. More evidence of Ryves calmness and clarity is to be found in the court-martial papers dating from the period immediately after the 1798 rebellion.

Ryves was sole witness against seven prisoners – Ned Fitzharris, John Perkyns, Patrick Connor, Edward Doyle, Ned Quinn, Thomas Coyle and John Condra – in Baltinglass on 2 April 1799. [23] He was obviously a reliable, lucid witness and the court martial reached a verdict on his evidence alone – a successful prosecution by a clear, hard-headed witness performance. The evidence, then, shows us that Captain William Ryves was an efficient officer.

There was, of course, another captain in the village of Dunlavin on the day of the massacre. That was Captain Richardson of the Wicklow Militia, who had been sent from the Ballitore area to bolster the military presence in Dunlavin in mid May 1798. Richardson was not a local man and so was somewhat more detached from the local populace than either Ryves or Saunders. Being an outsider, he probably had a clarity of view regarding the whole situation in the Dunlavin area that was not afforded the local captains. However, the fact that he was in a strange place could have made him more susceptible to panic on the fatal day. Against this suggestion, though, documentary evidence seems to indicate that Richardson was a good man to have on your side in times of crisis.

On 23 May 1798, hard-line Loyalist Benjamin O'Neale Stratford provided the following revealing insight in a letter: 'I wish we had Richardson with our county militia here. He is near us in Dunlavin, and very well, I saw him yesterday.' [24] Stratford, a hard-line Loyalist, saw Richardson as a reliable officer. Incidentally, there is no evidence in this letter to suggest that Richardson was cracking under the strain of the tense Dunlavin situation either, as he was 'very well'. Richardson had come from the Ballitore area, where the military had been clamping down hard on the local populace. Indeed, there was quite a lot of carnage in the neighbourhood of Ballitore and Narraghmore during the rising itself, but that lies outside the terms of reference of the present study. One point to note, however, is that Richardson had been part of the Ballitore clampdown prior to his reaching Dunlavin. Another document stated that 'the light company of the Wicklow militia under Captain Richardson ... by that day's [24 May 1798] exertions cut down and dispersed the rebels'. [25]

Another contemporary document confirmed that the efficient Richardson remained on in Dunlavin until early June. [26] It stated: 'Captain Richardson still at Dunlavin. I have consented to the Ancient Britons, ten in number, joining their regiment from Dunlavin.'

Richardson, like Ryves, was no liberal. They both came across in documentary evidence as cool, efficient officers. Ryves, according to one document, 'sticks too much to the quibbles of the court of law and forgets the now necessary roughness of the soldier'. [27] Yet the morning of the massacre in Dunlavin saw no court of law assemble. The prisoners were shot without a trial, and before they had a chance to take the Yeomanry Test Oath. If a snap decision to shoot the prisoners in Dunlavin Market House was taken on the morning of the massacre, events must have taken a real turn for the worse and the outlook in Dunlavin that morning must have been very bleak to make cool, rational officers like Captain Richardson and Captain Ryves, along with the liberal Captain Saunders decide to execute large numbers of non-tried suspects at the market house and on the fairgreen in Dunlavin.

One possibility was that Ryves was given information by a Loyalist prisoner who had been released from jail when the rebels attacked Ballymore-Eustace that Dunlavin was to be attacked. Thus he was prepared to repel the attack. [28] However, repelling an attack was one thing, executing unarmed prisoners was another. A loyalist history of the rebellion maintained that, 'after a skirmish in Dunlavin, twenty-eight imprisoned and disarmed yeomen were summarily shot after consultation among Reeves's officers'. [29]

However, the only small-scale skirmish near Dunlavin occurred after the massacre and the village was never threatened!

The situation in Dunlavin on the day of the massacre must now be examined. Was the fighting in and around the village very bad? If the liberal Captain Saunders was outnumbered by the two other captains (though the above passage places Captain Ryves in overall command), what exactly were the circumstances that led the three captains in Dunlavin to come to the fatal decision to execute their prisoners on that day over two hundred years ago?

NOTES

1: Press report quoted in Chris Lawlor: Loose Ends from the Dunlavin Area 1797-1803, in Dunlavin Festival of Arts Brochure, XVIII, Naas, 2000, p.20-22.

2: Luke Cullen MSS. Quoted in Dickson, p.26.

3: Leadbeater, p.56.

4: Leadbeater, p.62.

5: Leadbeater, p.62.

6: Leadbeater, p.63.

7: N.A.I 620/37/90.

8: N.A.I (S.O.C.) 3111.

9: N.A.I 620/37/128.

10: N.A.I.620/37/133.

11: N.A.I 620/3/32/5. This letter was enclosed (by Cooke?) with another letter, also from Robinson. Although these letters are anonymous, they may be compared with document 620/38/51, which does contain Robinson's signature, and the handwriting is obviously the same.

12: N.A.I. 620/37/109

13: Samuel Lewis in Topographical Dictionary, 1837 attributes the building of the market house to the Right Honourable R. Tynte (vol. 1, p. 583). The Tynte family tree drawn out by Lord Walter Fitzgerald in the Journal of the Kildare Archeological Society, Vol VII No. 4, July 1913, p.222 mentions Robert Tynte of Old Bawn and Dunlavin who died in June 1760; however, his father, James Worth Tynte only died in 1758, and so would have been head of the family c.1740 (though, of course, his son Robert could have undertaken the Market House project).

14: Cullen, in Hannigan and Nolan, 1994, p.467.

15: N.A.I. 620/37/133.

16: I am indebted to local historian Fr. Joe Whittle SDB for this piece of information.

17: N.A.I. 620/37/211A tells us 'every Protestant family escaped assassination by flying that day to the garrison towns'.

18: Rathsallagh house (the original building) was burned out during this period, but the old stables were converted into a fine country house, which now contains a luxurious hotel and golf course.

19: N.A.I. 620/3/32/5

20: N.A.I. 620/37/43.

21: Mary Leadbeater's Diary for 24 May 1798 contains the following information: 'About three o'clock in the afternoon, John Dunne and many others came as far as the bridge with pikes, and Dr. Johnson turned them back.' However, as the John Dunne executed on the green in Dunlavin would have already been in custody by this date, Mary Leadbeater's 'John Dunne' must be a different man; though it is possible he was a relation of the man executed. James Dunn, though, was the yeomanry corporal whose information regarding the others led to their arrest.

22: N.A.I. 620/37/109

23: N.A.I. 620/17/30/9.

24: N.A.I. 620/37/133.

25: N.A.I. 620/37/211A.

26: N.A.I. 620/38/23.

27: N.A.I. 620/3/32/5.

28: Power, Patrick C, The Courts Martial of 1798-99, Irish Historical Press 1997, p.84.

29: Musgrave, Sir Richard, Memories of the Irish Rebellion – 3rd Edition, 1803, Round Tower Books Reprint, 1995, p.222. Musgrave was retrospectively trying to justify the massacre.

 erected
to the memory of the
36 patriots
who were executed here
on the 24ᵗʰ of May
1798.

1798

Monument at
Dunlavin Green
to commemorate
the 1798 massacre

YEOMEN - SAUNDERSGROVE CORPS		LOCAL MEN FROM DUNLAVIN	YEOMAN - NARRAGHMORE CORPS	
AMES MARA	RICHARD KELLY	JOHN DWYER	JAMES KEATING	MARTIN WALSH
OHN WILLIAMS	MORGAN DOYLE	PETER HAYDEN	THOMAS KEATING	ANDREW CART
NDREW RYAN	THOMAS DOYLE	PETER KEARNEY	DANIEL KIRWAN	DARBY BYRNE
ATRICK DUFFY	MAT FARREL	LAURENCE DOYLE	THOMAS KIRWAN	JOHN DUNNE
AMES DUFFY	JAMES MORAN	JOHN BRIEN	MARTIN GRIFFIN	THOMAS MEILE
OHN WEBB	CHARLES EVERS	- HAWKINS	LAURENCE DOYLE	
ATRICK CURRAN	WILLIAM DWYER		EDWARD SHAUGHNESSY	
AVID LEE	THOMAS BRIEN			
AT KAVANAGH	DAVID PRENDERGAST			

MASSACRE

On 23 May 1798, the situation in Dunlavin and its hinterland was tense, but fears of an impending rising seemed to be on the wane.

The military crack-down, the reign of terror (especially in Kildare and West Wicklow), the capture of rebel arms, the arrests of United Irish leaders – all of these factors lulled the area (and indeed most of the country) into a false sense of security. Then, quite suddenly, extraordinary news burst on

Kildare. An express galloped into Dundas' headquarters in Kilcullen: a rising was expected at any moment in Dublin and the adjacent district. [1] The pre-arranged signal for such a rising was very simple – the mail-coaches from Dublin to the provinces were to be stopped. However, the plan went wrong and four of the five mail-coaches got through. The one that was stopped was going north, and had little effect, as north Dublin, Meath and Louth were relatively quiet and housed large Loyalist populations. (There was a rebellion in Ulster, but it did not begin until well into June, by which time the Leinster rebels had failed.) However, on that night of May 23rd, the Munster mail-coach was approaching Naas. A party of rebels attacked it and the passengers were brutally murdered. The coach was set alight, and this was the torch that started the rising in Kildare – and of course West Wicklow followed.

The burning of the Munster mail coach meant that much of Kildare was in full revolt from May 24th onwards. Some idea of the confusion and turmoil that must have reigned in the area is evident from the following table: [2]

Battles and Engagements in Co. Kildare

Prosperous	24 May
Clane	24 May
Old Kilcullen	24 May
Naas	24 May
Monasterevan	24 May
Narraghmore and Red Gap Hill	25 May
Rathangan	25 May

Many of the places mentioned here are well within the Dunlavin hinterland. In particular, the links between Dunlavin and Naas have been already outlined. The battle for Naas on May 25th was a particularly vicious affair, and the rebels, led by Michael Reynolds of Johnstown, took very heavy casualties. Basically the rebels attacked the town of Naas from the Dublin Road. They advanced up the main street, but were caught in a deadly bottleneck, as the military had installed artillery at the top of the town. The use of grapeshot made the rebels disperse, and cavalry pursued the fleeing rebels. About three hundred rebels were killed, and more than eight hundred pikes and about twenty five guns were recovered from the town and surrounding fields the next day. On that day too, three rebel sympathisers were hanged on the main street of Naas. The rebel leader, Michael Reynolds. escaped and was later prominent in

the second battle of Hacketstown. Although the battle in Naas
and the rebels' attempts to capture the jail had ended in failure,
rumours abounded. Mary Leadbeater's diary gave a vivid
description of the situation in Ballitore on 24 May 1798: [3]

> The morning of the 24th of the Fifth-month [May] orders came for
> the soldiers quartered here to march to Naas. A report was
> circulated that Naas gaol had been broken open – that Dublin
> was in arms, and so forth. All was uncertainty, except that some-
> thing serious had happened, as the mail-coach had been
> stopped. The insurrection was to begin in Dublin, and the mail-
> coach not being suffered to leave the city was the signal for
> general revolt. This purpose being defeated by the vigilance of
> government; the mail-coach had got to Naas before it was
> stopped, yet its detention there persuaded the people that the
> day was their own. They threw off the appearance of loyalty, and
> rose in avowed rebellion. In the morning the Suffolk fencibles
> first marched out, nine men remaining to guard their baggage at
> the mill, which was their barrack. The Tyrone militia followed
> taking their baggage with them. All was hurry and confusion in
> the village. Several who had kept out of sight now appeared
> dressed in green, that colour so dear to United Irishmen, and
> proportionally abhorred by the loyal. The Suffolks went by the
> high road, the Tyrones through Narraghmore. As they marched
> out, a young woman privately and with tears told their lieutenant
> her apprehensions that their enemies lay in ambush in
> Narraghmore wood. He was therefore prepared to meet them, and
> sad havoc ensued; many on both sides fell, particularly among
> the undisciplined multitude. The court-house at Narraghmore
> was attacked, and many met their death there. We heard the
> report of firearms, and every hour the alarm increased.

The violent engagement in Naas, and the evident turmoil and
confusion in Ballitore and Narraghmore as recorded by Mary
Leadbeater had huge implications for Dunlavin. The village of
Dunlavin awoke on the morning of 24 May 1798 to find that the
whole area surrounding it was up in arms. It was to be a Fair day
in Dunlavin. As more people arrived in the town during the
morning, many rumours were flying around. No doubt the false
news that reached Ballitore – heavy fighting in Dublin, the jail in
Naas successfully captured by the rebels etc. – also reached the
neighbouring village of Dunlavin. The local Loyalist population
were quite alarmed, and more and more Loyalists arrived into
the town as the morning wore on. It was a Summer's day, and
the area was experiencing a period of fine weather, so many
people were obviously up with the lark and from early morning

onwards there was an influx of people, including many Loyalists fleeing to the garrison town of Dunlavin for protection as they found the surrounding rural hinterland up in arms on that May morning. Extracts taken from a letter dated 29 May 1798 sent by Christopher Robinson to Cooke provided a good overview of events in the area: [4]

> About 9 o'clock a.m. on Thursday the 24th May 1798 the Rebellion broke out through the entire neighbourhood of Dunlavin, Ballitore, Baltinglass, Stratford-on-Slaney, Castledermot etc., and the men, women and children joined in procuring arms of all description. They sung horrible songs and never before heard by any loyalist, to excite the Rebellion. They openly declared extripation to the Protestants; not one Papist out of 100 but assembled that day, first in a tumultuous manner in small parties and then joined in bodies of about 200, 300, 400, or 500. The milita, particularly the yeomanry corps of Dunlavin, Baltinglass, and Hacketstown, as also the light company of the Wicklow Milita under Captain Richardson, behaved most gallantly and by that day's exertions cut down and dispersed the rebels so effectually as to prevent a plan they had formed of forcing the garrison of Dunlavin and Baltinglass that night, instead of which many of them fled to the mountains and joined their camps on the hills ... It is therefore much to be wished for in that quarter that Morley Saunders Esq. would entirely desist from interfering so incessantly with the other magistrates in favour of rebels, or from enroling such men in place of those of his Corps of Yeoman that were shot for treason; or from embodying a multitude of the men of Stratford-on-Slaney whom he must know were United Irishmen ... and it is equally to be desired that Captain Stratford and Captain Richardson of the Wicklow Light Company would be firmly supported in finding out and bringing such rebels to condign punishment, as they in general seem inclined to do their duty in support of the present establishments but by the interference, and influence, and duplicity of other gentlemen and officers of doubtful character, they are baffled in their endeavours to punish the traitors and protect and cherish the man of honour and loyalty.

This letter mentions a rebel plan to take Dunlavin, which was a garrison town. The local United Irishmen did indeed have a plan to take the garrison towns in the area. In hindsight, the rebellion was really too disorganised for such a plan to succeed, but the inhabitants of Dunlavin on that morning did not have the benefit of hindsight. They found themselves plunged in at the deep end, right in the thick of an insurrection in the area. Rumours, and the ever-swelling numbers of frightened Loyalists arriving in the town seeking refuge, each with his or her own story to tell (and we may be sure that many of them lost nothing in the telling) added to the very tense situation. Dunlavin was situated between the villages of Stratford-on-Slaney and Ballymore-Eustace. Both of these villages were the scenes of skirmishes on 24 May 1798. The Battle of Stratford began with a surprise attack on the town, which fell into rebel hands. However, success was short lived as this account testified. [5]

> The same day [24 May 1798] other attacks were made by rebels in different parts of the counties of Kildare and Wicklow – about one o'clock they appeared in the neighbourhood of Baltinglass to the amount of at least four or five hundred. Thirty of the Antrim Militia under the command of Lieutenant Macauley and Cornet Love, with twenty of the Ninth Dragoons, were sent to attack them; but the instant that they were advancing upon them in the town of Stratford upon Slaney [sic], Captain Stratford appeared at the other end of the town, with part of his corps. The rebels were attacked on both sides, and completely routed, leaving near two hundred men killed, besides many wounded amongst those who had made their escape.

The violence in Stratford-on-Slaney was mirrored by violence in Ballymore-Eustace, which was also the scene of a skirmish on the morning of May 24th. Indeed, the element of surprise meant that the rebel attack on Ballymore was almost successful, and Lieutenant Beavor's Ninth Dragoons suffered seven fatalities, along with a lieutenant of the Tyrone militia, before the attack was repulsed. Members of the Ancient Briton regiment [6] then executed twelve rebels, captured during the engagement, in reprisal for the rebel attack.

News of the attack on Ballymore-Eustace reached Dunlavin from a local youth, Charles Doyle of Merginstown. The town was already on edge, and the danger now seemed to be getting closer and closer. John Williams, the son of one of those executed, provided an account of Doyle's arrival in Dunlavin. [7]

> A young man named Charles Doyle, the son of a wealthy widow farmer from Merginstown, came into the town apparently in a great fright. He had been with the insurgents on the previous night in the attack on Ballymore Eustace. He returned home ... he went to Dunlavin. This report filled the ruling party with the greatest alarm.

When this report reached the three captains in charge of Dunlavin's garrison, it was followed by the arrival of a party of Ancient Britons from Ballymore-Eustace. These soldiers reported not only the attack on Ballymore-Eustace, but also the subsequent executions there. This may have set a precedent for Saunders, Ryves and Richardson to follow during their hurried consultation. [8] John Williams, whose father was shot on the green continued his account: [9]

> Morley Saunders, Ryves and Captain Richardson of the Wicklow militia were by, or made acquainted with Doyle's report and being apprehensive of the insurrection becoming formidable they were filled with rage and confusion and the prisoners were ordered out to the fair green, each two men being tightly tied together.

Whether the liberal Morley Saunders advised against the executions and was overruled by his fellow captains, or whether (as seems less likely) either of the other two – Ryves perhaps in an effort to keep the town calm and cool or Richardson as a detached outside influence – advised against executing the prisoners but was overruled by his two peers, is immaterial. Perhaps all three captains concurred on the same course of action. Dunlavin was in the eye of the hurricane – the neighbouring villages of Stratford and Ballymore had been attacked; rumours about Ballitore, Naas and even Dublin abounded; the large temporary Loyalist population of refugees from the rural hinterland was terrified and an attack on the village itself seemed imminent. All of these factors meant that the suspected United Irishmen inside the market house constituted a potential threat. If the village was attacked and the prisoners were liberated, what mercy could the Loyalists expect from them? If an attack was in progress, the men in the market house comprised a dangerous fifth column within the village itself. Were they to escape (or be liberated by sympathisers in the confusion of such an attack), they had the potential to turn the tide of battle. These unpalatable facts, in the words of John Williams, filled the three captains 'with rage and confusion' and so the fatal decision was taken.

There has been some confusion about the date of the massacre. This was caused by the account written by a Dunlavin curate, Father John Francis Shearman, who was writing in the 1860s. [10] Despite the time lapse, Shearman assured readers of the veracity of his account. 'The memory of these events is still green in Dunlavin,' he wrote, 'but few unless one in my position could elicit much information on a subject always dangerous to touch in that locality. I append other episodes, for the truth and correctness of which I can give every guarantee.'

There is one error in his account though. He dated the massacre as 26 May 1798. However the massacre actually occurred on May 24th. There are at least three reasons to confirm this.

Firstly, if the massacre occurred after Charles Doyle had arrived with news of the skirmish in Ballymore-Eustace, then it was the morning of May 24th.

Secondly, the incident with Fr. John Murphy at Boolavogue in Wexford definitely occurred on May 26th and he had already received news of the Dunlavin massacre. This would be impossible if the massacre had also occurred on May 26th.

Thirdly, the rebellion in this area had failed by May 26th and the danger to the Dunlavin garrison had abated, so there was less likelihood of prisoners being executed.

In fact, later dating of the Dunlavin massacre on May 26th probably relied on Father Shearman's account for its authenticity. Once he had dated the event, later commentators probably relied on his account, accepting the date given without question. Thus the date probably became ingrained in local tradition as well and hence the myth of the massacre happening on May 26th grew up in the region.

The correct sequence of events was as follows. The arrest of James Dunn, a corporal in the Saundersgrove unit, on 21 May 1798 resulted in information against other members and their detention on May 22nd in Dunlavin. They were there when the rebellion broke out on the night of May 23rd, and they were massacred in cold blood the following morning. [11]

There has also been some confusion about the actual number of men executed in Dunlavin on that day. This arose because some prisoners were hanged from the market house while others were shot on the fairgreen. Sources do not agree regarding the names of the victims. [12] There is no doubt about what happened next as all sources are in agreement.

Some prisoners in the market house were taken out – the men of the Saundersgrove corps and the Narraghmore corps being joined by some local United Irish suspects – and paraded through the town, from Market Square, through Main Street and along Stephen Street to the fairgreen. It seems quite probable that the men did not realise that they were to be executed literally until the last minute. Possibly they thought they were being moved to another location. They made no resistance to parading through the village and there was even a band playing to accompany the marching men. When they had reached the fair green, they were tied together and shot in cold blood. The actual executions were carried out by the Ancient Britons who had arrived in Dunlavin that morning from Ballymore-Eustace. [13]

These men were alleged United Irishmen, but they had never been tried. Similarly, the Saundersgrove yeomen had never been given a chance to actually take the test oath. Once they had been taken prisoner at the parade in Saunders Grove House itself, they had been imprisoned in Dunlavin market house, from where they were taken for execution. Other prisoners were hanged at the market house. [14]

A most vivid account of the massacre has survived. [15] It is reproduced here:

> Some days before this savage execution, Captain Saunders of Saunder's Grove near Stratford-on-Slaney reviewed his yeomen corps and announced that he knew by private information all who were 'United Men' and told all those who were sworn as such to step forward. Many, believing he had certain information as to their movements, came forward.
>
> One man, Paddy Doyle, got a hint from Captain Saunders' butler that his master had no certain knowledge as to their sentiments, except a suspicion of their loyalty. When his name was called he said: 'It was only United Irishmen [now] to come forward, [and he] was not one.'
>
> The remainder took the hint and the Captain was foiled. Those who so unintentionally betrayed themselves were pinioned and marched as prisoners to the market house of Dunlavin for confinement till their fate would be decided.
>
> Next day as Captain William Ryves of the Rathsallagh corps of Yeomen was on the lookout for insurgents on the hill of Uske his horse was killed by a ball aimed at its rider. Captain Ryves got himself to safety, rode to Dunlavin and then it was determined to shoot the prisoners of the Saundersgrove corps and others of the Narraghmore yeomanry, in all 36 men.
>
> Next day, May 26th about 8.06, these unfortunate men were marched to the green which is situated on the rising land of the village of Dunlavin, at an elevation of more than 400 feet above sea level, commanding a most magnificent prospect. The men were placed in a hollow on the north side of the green midway

between the last house of the street opposite Sparrowhouse road and the chapel.

A platoon of the Ancient Britons stood on the higher ground on the south side of the Boherboy road and fired on the unfortunate men with dread effect. All fell together dead and dying. Of the 36 men a few were only wounded. After the first fusillade the Ancient Britons returned to the market house to complete their savagery by flogging and hanging other unfortunate prisoners to strike terror into those who were going to the market for rations [etc].

On the green, when all was quiet and the men left for dead; their friends and sympathisers [beholding] the remains watching from behind the neighbouring fences, the soldiers wives came to rifle the bodies of the murdered men. One poor fellow was only wounded; when he felt his watch being taken away made an effort to retain it, but in vain for the savage woman got up her husband who dispatched the unfortunate man by firing a pistol into his ear.

Another man, Peter Prendergast, who was wounded in the belly so that his bowels protruded, lay as dead and offered no resistance to the [plundering] and escaped. Towards evening the bodies, which were not [already] carried away by their friends, were carried to Tournant cemetery and there buried in a large pit. Prendergast being found alive, a woman replaced the entrails and bound him up in her shawl and had him carried in security to [his] home where he recovered and lived to an advanced age.

Some few persons still living have a vivid recollection of these cruel and savage times. One old man remembers going to the market with his father and saw men writhing in the agonies of death hanging between pillars of the market house. He tells of one event which he witnessed and which relieves the savagery of the scene.

A man, John Martin, snatched a sword from one of the soldiers. He was dragged to the M(arket) H(ouse), the sword taken and hanged up on a peg. The delinquent was let away at the intercession of a magistrate present. While this was pending a soldier's wife took the sword from the peg to cut the rope by which one Tomas Eagan, a blacksmith, was hanging and blowing in death's agony. He came to and found means to escape to Dublin.

In this account, the author laid the blame, to put it simplistically, on William Ryves rather than Morley Saunders. This was not the case in the most popular version of the ballad

Dunlavin Green, where Saunders, rather than Ryves, was repeatedly vilified. This ballad was definitely written by a sympathiser with the executed men, and it shows a knowledge of the people involved and their families.

Local oral tradition maintained that the Catholic priest of Dunlavin was the author of the ballad. If this was indeed the case, the man who wrote the ballad could well have been Fr. Paul Byrne, who died on 15 December 1799, aged thirty four, and who had a brother living in Rathsallagh (from where William Ryves hailed). Fr. Byrne is buried in Tornant graveyard, where the executed men were also interred. [16]

The ballad itself is an example of a broadside ballad. With cheaper printing, many ballads of this kind were written and issued as broadsides (i.e. on sheets of paper) because they were good propaganda. Elite writers usually looked on broadside ballads as low and vulgar, something that belonged to the people as an expression of free speech and democratic protest. Broadside ballads had become less popular in England by the 1790s, but in Ireland the 1798 Rebellion kept the genre alive, and indeed it has survived into modern Irish balladry. [17] The ballad, which appears in full in the appendices of this book, certainly captured the sense of injustice felt among the populace regarding the Dunlavin massacre.

Although the ballad can be viewed as Republican propaganda, there is no doubt that, in essence, much of it is historically correct. Reading the ballad raises some interesting points.

Stanza one tells us that 'false information' led to the executions. This is unlikely though. Local Loyalists had good reason to suspect that the Saundersgrove corps of yeomanry harboured members of the Society of United Irishmen. The documentary evidence provided in this book so far confirms this though many more documents have certainly been lost or destroyed over the years. No doubt much verbal information was also collected by Loyalists. One letter [18] mentioned that 'the clearest proof' was received about Republican activists in the Saundersgrove corps.

Stanza two could refer to the parade at Saunder's Grove House, when the men were arrested. However, locally the stanza is taken to refer to the parade from the market house to the fairgreen in Dunlavin on the fateful morning.

In stanza three we are told, 'quite easy they led us as prisoners through the town'. The lack of resistance or protest offered indicated that the men probably thought they were going to be moved to another location.

Stanza four showed that the writer had personal knowledge and acquaintance with the victims and their families (or at least with some of them). Among others, Father Byrne was the possible author and the ballad was certainly penned by someone from the locality.

A venomous attack on Saunders is launched in stanza five. The fact that Saunders is mentioned three times in the ballad indicates the local level of amazement that the liberal Morley Saunders could allow such a thing to happen and has certainly built up Saunder's culpability in the local folk memory.

Stanza six referred to the aftermath of the executions, and the prolonged guerilla campaign waged by Michael Dywer and his band in the Wicklow mountains long after the main rebellion had ended.

The ballad also names some of the men shot on the fairgreen. There has been some confusion as to whether 35 or 36 men were executed. (Of course the fact that one man escaped death may have caused this). A list of the known victims appears in the appendices of this book.

Some sources say the men were tied together before being shot and this has raised an anomaly about numbers. If the men were tied and executed in groups of five, as one source suggested, [19] this would imply that only 35 men (as opposed to 36) were shot. However, John Williams (son of one of the executed men) stated: 'It was the lot of my father, the only Protestant that was shot, to be tied to Mat Farrel, a brave and resolute man.' [20] This primary source indicates that the men were tied together in groups of twos and threes. Perhaps some of the twos and threes were shot together, thus causing the later confusion regarding groups of five. However, if 36 men were shot that day, only 35 died. The escape of David Prendergast from death that day was nothing short of miraculous. Considering that the Ancient Britons were shooting at point-blank range and at stationary targets, and 'the aim was so sure and deadly that the first volley done the business', [21] the fact that David Prendergast was not killed is absolutely incredible. Prendergast was tied up with the others and was shot in the stomach. Prendergast fell and lay quite still among the dead bodies until the soldiers left the scene of the execution. He then managed to creep from the pile of bodies into an adjacent ditch or drain (one of the 'dykes of Dunlavin Green' mentioned in the ballad). The shootings took place on the lower end of the green, beside the present Catholic church. There was quite a deep drain beside this end of the green until it was filled in during mid-1970s. David Prendergast was discovered, having lost a lot of blood from his abdominal wound. He was rescued and smuggled out of the village to the house of Mr. Lee in Griffinstown (an outlying townland). Amazingly David Prendergast recovered fully from his wound, and lived on until 1842 in his native Ballinacrow. [22]

His mentor, Lee, was not so lucky. Lee was arrested as a rebel and sent to prison for his republican sympathies. He spent time on a prison ship (or ships) in Dublin Bay – possibly the Hieram and definitely the Peggy. Lee's attitude did not change in prison. Lee was not released until late in 1803, five years after he had been Prendergast's saviour. He was unrepentant to the last. [23] Prison obviously failed to reform Lee's views!

The Dunlavin massacre was a watershed in the early days of the rebellion. It entrenched the views of both sides. It represented a 'crossing of the Rubicon' by the authorities and many rebels regarded it as the event that pushed them beyond the point of no return. The decision to execute these men was taken under extraordinary conditions. Dunlavin was a beleaguered town, there was an influx of terrified Loyalists and skirmishes had occurred on both sides of Dunlavin along the road (Stratford-on-Slaney and Ballymore-Eustace). There was also the possibility of an imminent United Irish attack and rumours were flying around everywhere.

In addition, events were fuelled by ongoing Loyalist suspicions about the liberal Morley Saunders and his treacherous yeomanry corps, some now interned in the market house and a threat if the attack did come. This Loyalist view of Saunders continued even after the worst threat in West Wicklow was over and the back of the rebellion broken. The ongoing rift in the Loyalist community and the enmity against Saunders before the massacre meant that 'the local circumstances of the preceding weeks made the Dunlavin event particularly chilling'. [24] There was undoubtedly, as we have seen, a hard-line Loyalist element out to get Morley Saunders and his corps, and Saunders had to bow to increasing pressure on him in Dunlavin as that confused morning of May 24th wore on.

That morning saw a volatile village – a town in turmoil – in Dunlavin. One commentator has noted: 'At Dunlavin, it is true, the victims were yeomen, and there was good reason to suspect their fidelity. All over that region, the yeomen and especially the Catholic yeomen had gone over to the rebels. The garrison expected an attack at any moment. It is at times like this that one expects atrocities to occur.' [25] This logic – i.e. that the decision to shoot the prisoners was taken out of mounting panic among the garrison and its commanders on that Thursday morning – is excellent. There is no doubt that the garrison thought itself to be in a tight situation, and wild rumours probably caused panic in some quarters.

One point cannot be over-emphasised at this juncture. It is simply this – though an attack seemed imminent to the garrison, no such attack on the village of Dunlavin took place before the massacre. Dunlavin does not come into the category of Stratford-on-Slaney, where rebel deaths were caused by actual fighting, or the category of the Ballymore Eustace, where the executions by the Ancient Britons were carried out as a direct measure of revenge and reprisal for Loyalist casualties received during the fighting.

There was a minor engagement involving Captain Richardson's Wicklow Militia near Dunlavin later on, in the afternoon of May 24th. [26] However, this incident was small scale, and no evidence of it is found in local folklore. Given the rebel defeats elsewhere and the Dunlavin massacre earlier in the day, the rebels' courage deserted them when they met armed resistance, and they dispersed quite quickly into the surrounding fields and on to the nearby mountains. What is clear is that this event occurred after the massacre on the fairgreen, and so could not have had any bearing on the decision to shoot the prisoners.

Any panic that was felt that morning was because of the threat of an impending, rather than an actual, attack on the village. Another commentator has written: 'It is probable that the proximate cause of the massacre was fear that if the garrison was attacked the prisoners would escape.' [27] Certainly this scenario is plausible, even probable. But given the nature of the captains in charge that day, it is not possible that the fatal decision was not taken on the spur of the moment?

The authorities had been implementing a policy of state terrorism in West Wicklow for months and the methodical way in which the condemned men were bound together and shot on Dunlavin fair green disabuses any contention that the garrison acted out of panic. It is more likely that the executions were a reprisal intended to intimidate wavering rebels in Talbotstown and to punish those whose comrades had inflicted heavy casualties in Ballymore-Eustace. [28] These men were shot as an example to the whole area. The executions cannot be taken as a direct reprisal for an attack on the village of Dunlavin, because no such attack occurred. However, as an indirect reprisal for other rebel attacks in the area, (especially at Ballymore-Eustace, as Ancient Britons who had arrived from that village performed the executions), the massacre made perfect (if grim) sense. However, the apparent speed of the fatal decision that morning – a snap decision – raises another question. Was the fate of the prisoners – or of the Saundersgrove men at any rate – actually sealed before the day of the massacre? One contemporary source suggested that this was indeed the case.

If the motive behind the decision to execute the prisoners was fear of imminent attack, and if the massacre was not a reprisal (as no attack had been mounted on the village), it certainly was done to set an example to all Republicans and United Irish sympathisers in the area. In this, the massacre succeeded, as not all sworn United Irishmen followed the rebels into arms, and of those that did, many returned home after the first unsuccessful day. News of the massacre influenced many luke-warm rebels' decisions to quit their efforts and return home. The rebels had successfully taken no West Wicklow village, and many neighbouring Kildare towns, including the strategically important centre of Naas, had withstood the rebels' attacks. A significant rebel victory in the local area might have changed the situation, but defeats and news of events like the massacre in Dunlavin dampened many rebels' ardour.

Christopher Robinson expressed indignation that many rebels who had returned home were receiving pardons from military commanders. [29]

> Vast numbers returned in the night to their houses and are claiming protection on pretence that they had not joined in the rising. Others of them say they were forced to join, by this means and the connivance of some country gentlemen, aided by protections they obtained in groups from General Dundas, and some from Col. Campbell; they are (and some of them the most daring and culpable traitors the country ever produced) now evading the punishment so justly due to Rebels of so horrible a description.

However, Robinson's political views were very hard-line, and what the ultra-Orange clergyman failed to realise was that the whole area was very tense and volatile in the wake of the skirmishes and the Dunlavin massacre. The protections handed out by Dundas and Campbell, among others, showed that they felt a need to pour oil on troubled waters and reduce the tension locally by taking a merciful and lenient stance, at least with rank and file rebels. However, Robinson did not have such insight and tact!

The Dunlavin massacre certainly acted as a deterrent to rebel forces in the village and its hinterland. However, the event may not have hinged on a snap decision. A letter, dated 23 May 1798, from O'Neale Stratford in Stratford Lodge to Cooke in Dublin Castle suggested that the decision may well have been taken before the day of the massacre and the fate of the Saundersgrove men at least may have been sealed before the morning of May 24th. [30] The contents of the opening piece of this letter shed new light on the fatal decision, and if one reads between the lines, the executions of May 24th were a fait accompli before that date.

In consequence of some serious and interesting information, though far from well, I rode to Dunlavin and there made out to Mr. Saunders' full conviction that most of his corps and servants were United Irish Men. I really pity my dear nephew; he had indeed taken uncommon pains with his Corps and was both their Commandant and friend and had the day but one before, on my mentioning my suspicions more strongly than I had done for some months before, called on each on parade and informed them he had heard it and desired that if any were so they would voluntarily confess it. He offered to swear they knew nothing about any such thing, yet on the clearest proof he yesterday called them out, twenty beside the one I had before in custody, among whom were five of his servants, Moran and the other young lad, Prendergast and Farrel two of his masons, the Duffys, Williams, Sub-Constable Doyle, his smith, his slater etc. etc. The most horrid and infernal plan was formed against his life and all his family, which I trust in God I have prevented, indeed my dear fellow expressed his thanks in the prettiest manner, yet none did I deserve. I only would have done what common humanity demanded of me by any man and was my duty – a ten fold obligation for affinity friendship, esteem, long acquaintance etc. etc. He has not as yet satisfied me; the worst are still in his house, and the Corps must be better thinned. Sorry am I to say that we have now the clearest proof of the intentions of the Catholics' intention, but as Government are appraised of it, I trust proper means will be used to put a total stop to the business in which the priests (that is the majority of them) will be found deeply concerned.

This letter was written on the day before the massacre. Stratford had met Saunders in Dunlavin on the previous day – Tuesday, May 22nd. The reason for O'Neale Stratford visiting Dunlavin was some information which he had received on the previous day – i.e. Monday the 21st. Doubtless this was 'the false information' referred to in stanza one of the Ballad of Dunlavin Green. This letter (and much other documentary evidence as we have seen) suggested that the information reached O'Neale Stratford via the spy Joseph Hawkins.

Hawkins was probably also in contact with Morley Saunders on the Monday. Perhaps more than one name was mentioned in this information, but it certainly led to one arrest (whether as the sole person informed against or as a ringleader is unclear, and really unimportant as events unfolded). That was the arrest of Corporal James Dunn, and he was the man referred to in the letter in the phrase 'beside the one I had before in custody'. The arrest and interrogation of Corporal Dunn led to his giving information against other members of the corps. Whether Dunn gave this information voluntarily, or whether torture was used to extract it, is unclear, but one thing is fairly certain – by giving this information Corporal Dunn probably saved his own life as he was not among those executed on the fairgreen. (The John Dunne who was shot was a member of Colonel Keatinge's Narraghmore corps.)

According to the letter, '[Saunders] the day but one before (i.e. Monday) called on each one on parade and informed them he had heard it (i.e. accusations of United Irish membership) and desired that if any were so they would voluntarily confess it'. The yeomen, however, were not asked to take the test oath, not dismissed from the corps by Saunders and not given a chance to resign from the corps. Corporal Dunn's information, given, or extracted, on the Monday night changed the situation.

The corps was assembled again the next day (the day after the parade at Saunders Grove House) and this time arrests were made. The letter referred to 20 men who were taken into custody. Of these, 18 were executed, including all of those named in this letter, so Stratford's figure may be a rough one, rounding up from 18 to 20. The members of Saunders' yeomanry corps who were arrested on Tuesday, May 22nd were marched to Dunlavin and imprisoned in the market house, which was probably looked upon as the most suitable local building to hold such a large number of inmates. It was there that Morley Saunders visited them and tried to ease their fears.

This visit was made on the same day as Stratford's letter was written.

One fact that leaps out from this letter is that Benjamin O'Neale Stratford was sure that he has finally convinced Morley Saunders about the guilt of the arrested members of his corps. There are several indications of this in the letter. O'Neale Stratford 'made out to Mr. Saunders' full conviction that most of his corps and servants were United Irishmen'. The phrase 'to Mr. Saunders' full conviction' indicates that Saunders was at last convinced. O'Neale Stratford says that 'on the clearest proof he [Saunders] yesterday called them out'. Saunders, who had procrastinated so long about taking any action against his corps and for whom he 'had indeed taken uncommon pains ... and was both their commandant and friend', was left with no excuse and had no alternative but to act.

Evidently Hawkins' information was quite explosive and very convincing. The Ballad of Dunlavin Green refers to 'false information', but this was certainly not the view of Morley Saunders. The information received evidently referred to a plot to kill Saunders, referred to in the phrase, 'the most horrid and infernal plan was formed against his life and all his family'. So Saunders believed Hawkins' story. The 'clearest proof' referred to in the letter finally awakened Saunders to the danger that he was in. O'Neale Stratford noted Saunders' reaction when he wrote: 'My dear fellow expressed his thanks in the prettiest manner.' Was this the Morley Saunders who for weeks before had defended his corps, his pride and joy, in the face of mounting hard-line Loyalist wrath? Saunders' reaction was suggestive of a man in a daze, a man who did not know what to think, a man who had learned an awful truth and is now 'going with the flow' of O'Neale Stratford's suggestions. At this point the liberal Morley Saunders had a change of heart. His defences were down – O'Neale Stratford obviously noticed this. 'I really pity my dear nephew,' he wrote. The avuncular reference is also significant. Though O'Neale Stratford often mentioned Saunders in his correspondence, he usually gave him his proper title. The reference to 'my dear nephew' indicated that O'Neale Stratford now felt that he had a degree of control over Saunders which was hitherto not the case. Indeed, the whole tone of Stratford's narrative and his use of the past perfect tense in relation to the corps ('He had indeed taken uncommon pains.') might be taken to indicate that Stratford thinks that the problem is now solved and that the liberal Morlely Saunders has now been converted to a more hard-line Loyalist stance. The past tense is actually used throughout this passage, indicating that O'Neale Stratford thought that the execution of the men was all but done!

The dazed Saunders was now as putty in the hands of his uncle, O'Neale Stratford, whose hard-line tendencies meant that he favoured harsh measures. O'Neale Stratford wrote: 'He [Saunders] has not as yet satisfied me; the worst are still in his house and the corps must be better thinned.' For O'Neale Stratford, the arrests were not enough. He stated in this letter, dated one day before the massacre, that the Saundersgrove corps 'must be better thinned'. With the suspects already in jail, he now wanted the men executed. The use of the chilling phrase, 'I trust proper means will be used to put a total stop to this business', indicated a finality of purpose. O'Neale Stratford was not satisfied with the measures already taken. Had he already advocated a 'final solution' to Saunders? Admittedly, this would involve a trial, but with the 'clearest proof' and the testimonies of Hawkins and Dunn (and of O'Neale Stratford and Saunders himself) the outcome of such a trial would surely have been a foregone conclusion. The fact that rebellion broke out in the local area on the Wednesday night and the Thursday morning meant that there was no time to try the prisoners, but their death warrants had been sealed at the suggestion of O'Neale Stratford before the morning of May 24th even dawned.

Morley Saunders' visit to the prisoners in the market house on the previous night can be reinterpreted in the light of this scenario. This visit was the action of a man who, knowing that he finally had to bow to the pressure of his peers and realising that his peers were right about the United Irish element within his corps, was trying to salve his conscience? Did Saunders visit the men to further convince himself of their guilt and were his soothing promises simply a front to diffuse the already tense situation?

Certainly the visit of Morley Saunders to the market house partly explained the sense of amazement felt by the writer of the Ballad of Dunlavin Green regarding the liberal captain's failure to step in and save the condemned men on the morning of the massacre. The line 'Bad luck to you Saunders, for you did their lives betray' was perhaps truer than even the writer realised, as there is documentary evidence of a preconceived plan between Saunders and his uncle, O'Neale Stratford, to execute the prisoners.

Whatever the truth about the fatal decision to execute the

prisoners in the market house, there is no doubt about the outcome. On the day after Benjamin O'Neale Stratford penned his letter, there were over forty men executed in the village of Dunlavin.

NOTES

1: Pakenham, p.129.

2: Mac Suibhne, p.3.

3: Leadbeater, p.63-64.

4: N.A.I. 620/37/211 A.

5: Dickson. Letter from Lt. Macauley of the Antrim Militia to Major Hardy, quoted on p.30.

6: This Welsh regiment, the Ancient British Light Fencible Cavalry, had acquired a reputation for notoriety in many places, particularly Newtownmountkennedy. For an account of their activities see Myles V. Ronan, (Editor) Insurgent Wicklow 1798, chapter 2, Clonmore and Reynolds Ltd., Dublin, 1948.

7: Dickson, p.34.

8: Musgrave. 'A consultation among Reeves' officers' is mentioned on p.222.

9: Dickson, p.34.

10: N.U.I. Maynooth, Shearman Papers XVII, quoted in Chris Lawlor, Dunlavin Green Revisited, in Dunlavin-Donard-Davidstown Parish Link, Vol. IV, No. 3, November 1998, p.6-7.

11: Cullen, in Hannigan and Nolan, 1994, p.468-469.

12: Thirty victims are named in Shearman Papers XVII. Thirty four are named in Dickson. One is named in Leinster Leader, 25/9/1948 and one more is named in Mac Suibhne. The total number of named victims now rises to fifty-two allowing for different Christian names, but some (e.g. Shearman's Peter Prendergast and Dickson's David Prendergast) are obviously the same man. However it seems safe to assume that the death toll in the village that day must be revised to a figure somewhere in the mid-40s at least.

13: Mac Suibhne, p.2.

14: O'Donnell, in Hannigan and Nolan, 1994, p.349. More evidence of hangings is given in Mac Suibhne, p.188-189, in the following passage: Dunne who was hanged in Dunlavin was a forefather of Mick Dunne, Ballyshannon. Another brother was hanged in Carlow. The judge asked him did he know anyone in Carlow who would get him off. He said, yes, pointing to a neighbour from Narraghmore. But the neighbour denied all knowledge of him. There was a good deal of this. This Dunne lived in Blackhall. They moved to Ballyshannon and Dillons moved in. There were different hangings in Dunlavin. Evidence of A. Hendy and Paddy Lynch. Also, during his address at the opening of the refurbished market house on 25 May 1979, Mr. Frank Goodwin stated: 'During the rebellion of 1798 [the market house] was fortified and garrisoned for the protection of many families who fled to this town from the battles in the surrounding countryside. It is said also that people were hanged in those days from the colonades above our heads.' Frank Goodwin, The Market House, Dunlavin – Restoration and History, Dunlavin Community Council, 1979, p.11.

15: N.U.I. Maynooth, Shearman Papers XVII, quoted in Chris Lawlor, Dunlavin Green Revisited, in Dunlavin-Donard-Davidstown Parish Link, Vol. IV, No. 3, November 1998, p.6-7.

16: Fr. Patrick Finn, The View from the Mountains, in Dunlavin, Donard, Davidstown Parish Link, vol. 3, October 1997, p.1.

17: Hodgart, Matthew, (Editor) The Faber Book of Ballads, Faber & Faber Ltd., 1965, p.18-21. The use of the present tense in the ballad means that it is probably a primary source.

18: N.A.I. 620/37/133

19: Tattoo at Baltinglass: '98 Commemoration Ceremony, in Leinster Leader 25/9/1948, p.3

20: Dickson, p.34. Dickson also mentions that Coogan says Prendergast, Evers and

Farrel [were] tied together.

21: John Williams quoted in Dickson,p.34.

22: Lawlor, Chris, Dunlavin in 1798, in the Tenth Annual Dunlavin Festival of Arts Brochure, 1992, p.56. Local oral tradition maintained that Prendergast was dragged out of sight and hidden in a pig sty until he could be spirited away after dark. The pig dung congealed and acted as a kind of poultice, helping to stem the bleeding from his wounds and possibly saving his life. I am indebted to Mr. Michael Deering of Lemonstown for this piece of information.

23: Dickson, p.245. The following account relates to Lee's unrepentant attitude: [The prisoners] were marched straight to the Provost. We remained there for three days and nights. Our female companions were then sent to Kilmainham and we, the male prisoners, were sent to the Hieram tender lying nearly opposite to the Pigeon House. Capt. Bogie and Lieut. Draper were the officers. Our usage with regard to food and drink was tolerable. We had occasional visitors, but they never put any improper questions to us. This was too good for us and after a few weeks we were sent from the Hieram (to) the Peggy then lying in the same water. The changes were very much for the worse ... In the Hieram we met with people who told us our neighbour Lee in whose house Davy Prendergast took shelter on his escape from the massacre of Dunlavin where he had been shot . . . remained so long in that tender that it is quite evident he was actually forgotten there. An inspecting officer said to him one day; 'Lee, if you ever get ashore I hope you will have quite forgot your generosity and be more loyal.' 'If I ever get ashore, Sir, and have the means I will be even generous than ever'. The retort was sent to the Castle and Lee thinks it got nearly a year's confinement.

24: Cullen, in Hannigan and Nolan, 1994, p.469.

25: Pakenham, p.156.

26: N.A.I. 620/37/211A. Also O'Donnell, in Hannigan and Nolan, 1994, p.349 contains the following passage: Later in the day two to three hundred rebels in the vicinity of Dunlavin, a separate group from those repulsed from Stratford, may well have been about to attack before they were confronted by Richardson's militia and the mounted yeomen (probably Ryves's cavalry corps) and driven off into the mountains.

27: Dickson, p.34.

28: O'Donnell, in Hannigan and Nolan, 1994, p.349.

29: N.A.I. 620/37/211 A.

30: N.A.I. 620/37/133.

The Market House in Dunlavin

AFTERMATH

The Dunlavin massacre had a huge effect on many people, one of whom was the future rebel leader Michael Dwyer of the Glen of Imaal. Dwyer was born and raised a Glensman. His father, John Dwyer had married Mary Byrne of Cullentragh. [1] Michael was their eldest son. The family moved from the townland of Camara to the townland of Eadstown in 1784, when Michael was about twelve years old. Eadstown was not quite as remote as Camara, but it was still situated well within the Glen of Imaal. In the early 19th century Camara was 'two thirds rocky and green pasture intermixed with heathy pasture with coarse grass through the heath; high and exposed with heath pasture on the mountain top'. [2] The move to Eadstown improved the Dwyer family's circumstances. John Dwyer was a farmer and the young Michael showed all the signs of following in his father's footsteps. Indeed, as Ireland was largely unaffected by the Industrial Revolution which had swept through parts of Britain in the late 18th century, there was little else for a young Glensman to aspire to as a means of livelihood. Land was life and working the land was vital to the tenant families in remote rural areas such as the Glen of Imaal.

Despite the long and laborious hours spent on the land, the

young Michael Dwyer did receive some schooling. He could certainly read and write; letters written by him at the time of his captivity in Kilmainham jail reveal a clearly legible and highly embellished script, with an accomplished knowledge of spelling and punctuation. The anti-Catholic penal laws meant that formal education was an undreamt-of luxury for Catholic children during the late 18th century, but Dwyer attended a hedge school run by Peter Burr. Burr was a protestant graduate of Trinity College and he was a liberal and progressive thinker. [3] A schoolmaster named Birr (probably the same man) was a member of the United Irishmen and he later ran for election as a captain in the Imaal area. [4] Burr instilled a sense of patriotism, a love of Ireland and things Irish, into his students. Coupled with this, he instilled a sense of injustice regarding British rule in Ireland and hinted that the land of Ireland might be fought over again in future times. [5] The land tenure system also did much to nurture a sense of injustice in the small tenant farmers, who laboured long and hard on farms that could never be theirs, as the landlord system did not allow them to buy out their holdings.

There was also a sectarian element in the area. [6] In the 19th century Catholic farmers in the Glen of Imaal were targeted for eviction as the Earl of Wicklow pursued a policy of populating the glen with protestant families. [7] The Howard family held the title of Earl of Wicklow. They had extensive lands, not only in Wicklow, but also in Donegal. The Howards first came to Ireland in 1636. In 1667 Ralph Howard M.D. acquired estates in north Arklow and the Glen of Imaal. With them came Shelton Abbey, which would become the family residence. Although the Howards lived at Shelton Abbey near Arklow in East Wicklow; they retained a land agent in the Glen of Imaal. Later, in 1776, when Michael Dwyer was four years of age, another Ralph Howard was elected to peerage as Baron Clonmore of Clonmore castle, County Carlow. His daughter, Alice, inherited Castle Forward and its land in Donegal. The Howard family were respected members of the Ascendancy. They were also the principal landholders in the Glen of Imaal; in the early 19th century they held 2,330 acres of land in the glen, nearly four hundred acres more than the second largest landholders, the Hutchinsons. [8] In common with many others, Michael Dwyer, the son of a tenant farmer, found himself growing up in a landlord system that stifled the dreams and aspirations of those at the bottom of the landholding ladder.

The young Dwyer was a passionate lover of nature. [9] However this does not and cannot take away from the fact Dwyer's youth was laced with hardship. The Glen of Imaal was a beautifully scenic area, but it was also a marginal one. About thirty five miles (56 kilometers) south-west of Dublin, the glen was physically separated by the Wicklow Mountains from the more populated eastern parts of the county. It also offered a great contrast to the adjacent rich lowland areas of County Kildare. This reinforced its status as a distinct regional unit – an isolated outlier of county Wicklow. [10] The quality of much of the land in the glen was poor. Much of it was taken up with heath and bog, and some was too rocky for agriculture. The soils, particularly on the higher slopes, were acidic and soil erosion had exposed great granite outcrops in many places. The area experienced much orographic rainfall and much of the winter precipitation fell as snow. Given such conditions, life for a young Glensman was anything but easy.

There is a breed of dog known as the Glen of Imaal terrier. Today, we are told that this game little terrier comes from 'a wild Irish Glen, steeped in the romance of Irish history and legend'. Bred long and low to the ground with powerful head and legs bowed, 'this game little dog guarded their stock and fought many a fight for wagers away from the watchful eyes of the Law'. These terriers 'are still well endowed with the characteristics with which they served their masters long ago in the mountains and glens of Wicklow'. [11] In a word, the Glen of Imaal terrier was hardy.

This was also true of the Glenspeople. Dwyer's upbringing was hard; life was a struggle. There were bad years when the weather made survival precarious for a family of tenant farmers in a remote and infertile Wicklow glen. The only break from the laborious existence of the tenant farmer came in the form of illicit gambling sports such as dog or cock fighting and in the consumption of alcohol in the cabins of the family or neighbours, or in the shébeen.

The young Dwyer was probably introduced to these pursuits from an early age. Such intervals were few and far between however, and everyday life centred on working the land. The long and difficult hours of physical toil 'toughened up' the young man though. On the eve of the 1798 rebellion he was about five feet ten inches in height, full-breasted and very straight in the back with a short neck and square shoulders. He had long legs and big feet, black hair and a dark complexion, large dark eyes, a short nose and a wide mouth with evenly spaced teeth. [12] According to his brother John, Michael was a 'well-behaved, good natured young man; moral in his conduct, civil and obliging to his acquaintances and very true to his friends; by no means quarrelsome but always of a bold and daring disposition'. [13] In his late twenties, Michael Dwyer too was 'hardy'. It was a trait that he would need and one that would serve him well in the long campaign ahead.

Michael Dwyer had also joined the United Irishmen. The exact date of his enrolment in the organisation is uncertain, as is the identity of the person who administered the United oath. Certainly the United Irish movement was gaining strength daily in West Wicklow during the summer of 1797. In May of that year, the organisation was openly recruiting in Hollywood. [14] Throughout the summer of that year, a United Irish recruitment drive, spearheaded by William Putnam McCabe, took place across County Wicklow. [15] Dwyer joined the United ranks around this time. [16] Thus he was a member of the outlawed organisation during the reign of terror that was visited upon Dunlavin parish and the Glen of Imaal in late 1797 and early 1798. The situation deteriorated as tensions rose to boiling point and on 24 May 1798 the terror reached its height as the rebellion broke out in West Wicklow and the Dunlavin massacre unfolded.

The Dunlavin massacre had represented the first attempt at a policy of ethnic cleansing within the yeomanry. [17] This ethnic cleansing was not based on grounds of race or religion (at least one protestant was executed), but rather it was based on political views. West Wicklow was a politically aware and active area in the 1790s, and the policy implemented on Dunlavin green boiled down to rooting out United Irishmen, rebels, Republicans, French sympathisers, armed Catholics and any other feared category of yeomanry. Given the circumstances, the executions at Dunlavin, including that of John Dwyer of Seskin, affected Michael Dwyer deeply and the killings instilled in him a thirst for revenge, which was left unsatisfied even at the time of his ultimate surrender in December 1803. [18] Whatever might have been his previous determination, the arrest and ill-treatment of his father, the destruction of his cousins and neighbours in the slaughter in Dunlavin gave a fixity of purpose to that determination, which could scarcely be relaxed. [19]

Dwyer's protracted military campaign against the authorities began on the day of the massacre on Dunlavin green – to be exact, when news of the massacre filtered through to the Glen of Imaal.

The first consequence of the Dunlavin massacre was that it confirmed Loyalist supremacy in the village during the critical week at the end of May 1798. Any United Irish plans to seize the local garrison towns and establish control of one of the main routeways to Wexford and the south-east were now in tatters. The massacre was an effective deterrent. However, a major side effect of the massacre was that a high level of tension continued in evidence in and around the village of Dunlavin. The resentment of the local populace grew, fuelled as it was by sympathy for the executed men and their families. Like many Republicans (and Loyalists) both before and after them, they had become martyrs. A letter from Colonel Campbell in Athy to General Dundas in Kilcullen revealed that the situation in Dunlavin remained tense enough for Captain Richardson and his men to be left in the village until early June. [20] However, by the date of this letter, June 2nd, Dunlavin's immediate danger had passed and the threat of rebel success in the area was diminished. Colonel Campbell wanted to recall Richardson's men and the Ancient Britons, who had stayed in Dunlavin after their arrival from Ballymore-Eustace. Apart from the half-hearted attempt made on the afternoon of May 24th, no further attack was made on the village of Dunlavin after the massacre. Undoubtedly, the massacre had the desired effect from a Loyalist viewpoint, and the town of Dunlavin remained a safe haven in a sea of skirmishes in the surrounding villages of the Dunlavin hinterland.

If the town itself remained safe, it was a different story in the rural areas surrounding it. The rebel encampment on Blackmore Hill remained a threat for a while and there were numerous violent incidents in Dunlavin's rural areas. Rathsallagh House, the seat of William Ryves, was burned out during this period. After the rebellion had ended, Mary Shackleton (a local Quaker lady) and a friend went to Rathsallagh in order to retrieve 'some of our plundered property' which Squire Ryves, as a magistrate, was safeguarding until it was reclaimed. She wrote:

> The way seemed long, lonely and dreary. The large old mansion of Rathsallagh exhibited a melancholy air. Its neglected appearance, barricaded windows, the absence of the female part of the family and the presence of a military guard made us think

our own situation preferable, as we were permitted to enjoy
domestic comfort. Some of our things were here and while the
squire restored them to us, he smiled, and warned us of our
danger of being robbed again. He foretold but too truly.

Captain Ryves died in February 1803 and was succeeded by
his son, William, a solicitor, who took over as captain of his
father's yeomanry corps. [21] Evidence of other violent incidents
in the immediate area of Dunlavin was recorded in the claims for
compensation made after the 1798 rebellion. The following list
provides a snapshot of the level of unrest. [22] Question marks
indicate tears or smudges in the original list.

Name/Area	Nature of Loss	Amount Claimed
John Barden *Crehelp*	House, potatoes, meat, tools, fuel fire	£14.08.08
Paul Barden *Crehelp*	House, cattle, meat, tools, fuel fire	£173.04.04
George Barret *Merginstown*	House	£47.06.06
John Barret *Crehelp*	House, meadow	£44.09.06
William Crampton *Merginstown*	House	£43.03.01
Mary Doyle *Merginstown*	House, clothes, cash, a stallion	£84.00.02
Edward Fisher *Merginstown*	House burned, furniture, clothes	£863.17.01
Richard Fisher *Merginstown*	A House	£28.04.03
Mary Hanbidge *Merginstown*	House, a mare, sheep, furniture, provisions	£126.19.07
Esther Miley *Merginstown*	Car, furniture, house, timber	£41.10.00
Andrew Morris *Griffinstown*	Haggard destroyed	£25.04.7
Andrew Morris *Griffinstown*	House, furniture, cattle, timber	£357.16.03
Patrick Mullally *Lemonstown*	2 mares, a bull, Hill sheep	£37.14.01
Patrick Mullally *Crehelp*	Cash, clothes, butter	£30.19.08
George Powell *Dunlavin*	Livestock	£39.18.00
Matthew Powell *Tober*	House, crop, timber	£37.16.00
William Powell *Tober*	House, pigs, timber, crops, clothes	£?
Gilbert Rawson *Tober*	House, a ladder, furniture, oats	£13.09.02
Joseph Toole *Crehelp*	A house	£27.03.07

continued on next page

Samuel Wallis		
Oldcourt	Cattle, horses, provisions, oats, hay	£?
Christopher Walsh		
Oldcourt	Corn, sheep, furniture, clothes	£ ?
Richard Whittle		
Merginstown	House, sheep, flax	£22.12.9
Thomas Wilson		
Griffinstown	House, furniture	£24.014
Mary Wornell		
Merginstown	House, furniture	£57.12.0

Local oral tradition maintains that Tober House, the seat of the Powell family, was burned out at this time. However, it was no accident that the townlands of Merginstown and Crehelp suffered the most, as these townlands are both on the eastern (mountainous) side of Dunlavin, and the rebel activity centred around Blackmore Hill stretched as far as these townlands, and was a foretaste of further prolonged rebel activity in the Wicklow mountains under Michael Dwyer. As late as June 5th it was reported that the country outside of Wexford was quiet apart from Blackmore Hill, [23] but the Blackmore Hill rebels dispersed about this date. [24]

Apart from the rural areas immediately surrounding the village, many settlements in the Dunlavin hinterland also suffered violence during 1798 rebellion as the following extracts testify: [25]

> Blessington: The Marquis of Downshire has a handsome mansion ... the interior was burned by the insurgents in 1798 and has not been restored. Ballymore-Eustace: The late Earl of Milltown took a lively interest in this spot ... but owing to the disturbances of 1798 he went abroad. Boystown or Baltiboys: there are several gentlemen's seats, among them are Tulfarris, the seat of R. Hornidge, Esq. which was partly burned by the insurgents in 1798.

Evidently, although the Dunlavin massacre was successful in preventing an attack on the village itself, the resentment and bitterness that it engendered in the local populace spilled over into acts of violence within Dunlavin's immediate and extended hinterland.

Indeed, the massacre at Dunlavin had repercussions further afield even than the extended Dunlavin hinterland. News of the massacre had far reaching implications. The Dunlavin event was unlike incidents in surrounding towns and villages. These surrounding settlements had experienced violence and death too, but they had all seen some military action. Places like Naas,

Narraghmore and Stratford-on-Slaney had been the scenes of battles or skirmishes. Even the Ballymore-Eustace executions had been carried out in direct retaliation for a rebel attack on the village. Dunlavin was different.

What happened in Dunlavin was the shooting of disarmed and defenceless prisoners, suspects who had not been tried or given a chance to resign from the yeomanry, when no attack on the village had taken place. Perhaps it was a pre-emptive measure or perhaps there was a pre-conceived plot to shoot the men. Either way, the incident in Dunlavin came under the heading of 'massacre' rather 'battle', 'skirmish' or anything else. Dunlavin was not the end of it, however. A similar massacre occurred in the ball alley in Carnew very shortly after the Dunlavin event. News of the Dunlavin massacre spread rapidly southwards, as did the unsubstantiated rumours about rebel victories in Kildare, Carlow and West Wicklow.

Local folk memory sees the Dunlavin massacre as the most important causal factor behind the Boolavogue incident, and the start of the County Wexford rebellion. In the words of one historian: [26]

> It was the afternoon of Saturday, 26 May [1798]. As the priests [Fr. John Murphy of Boolavogue and Fr. Michael Murphy of Ballycanew] hesitated, two extraordinary pieces of intelligence swept through the villages of North Wexford. The first was the news of two terrible atrocities. At Dunlavin ... the panic struck garrison had taken their prisoners ... and shot them ... a drunken mob of Loyalists at Carnew had taken ... prisoners ... and executed them in a ball alley. To Wexford men, it seemed there was now an official policy of extermination. The second piece of news was still more extraordinary, though it was what all United men had been hoping for. Wild rumours of the storming of Naas and Carlow, of the capture of Ballitore and Kilcullen and most of County Kildare had at last reached Wexford. Fr. Michael was still undecided, but it was enough for Fr. John. [He] agreed to lead a campaign of resistance.

The Wexford rebellion had begun, and news of the Dunlavin massacre influenced Fr. John Murphy's decision to rebel. Ironically, the severity of the fighting in Wexford has tended to obscure events in the Wicklow-Kildare region in subsequent studies of the 1798 rebellion. However, the ferocity of events in Wexford also meant that Michael Dwyer went there to join the rebel armies in the field. In May 1798 Michael Dwyer, though a member of the Wicklow United Irishmen, did not hold a position of seniority within the County Wicklow organisation of the society. Dwyer was not implicated by informers operating in and around Stratford on Slaney in April, shortly before the outbreak of hostilities in West Wicklow. [27]

Stratford-on-Slaney was the scene of a battle on 24 May 1798, the same day as the Dunlavin massacre. The insurgent leaders at Stratford were Thomas Kavanagh and Martin Burke. Rebel losses were high and Thomas Kavanagh was executed. [28]

Local folklore sometimes has it that Michael Dwyer fought in this battle, but this was not so. In fact, Dwyer was in hiding on the slopes of Lugnaquilla at the head of the Glen of Imaal during those crucial early days when the conflict started in the surrounding region. [29] Though not an elected officer within the United Irish network, the arrest of many senior figures such as Peter Hayden, John Dwyer of Seskin and the schoolmaster Peter Burr had thrust the more junior but up-and-coming figure of Michael Dwyer more into the limelight. Dwyer came to be viewed as an important organiser at local level and the attentions of the authorities forced him into hiding during the week preceding the outbreak of rebellion. Thus Dwyer was cut off from the earliest hostilities in West Wicklow and, although he undoubtedly received some accounts of events such as the Dunlavin massacre and the battle of Stratford, he may have been unaware of the existence of insurgent camps in the border areas of Counties Wicklow, Dublin and Kildare. [30] However, definite news of the defeat inflicted on Crown forces at Oulart Hill in County Wexford reached Dwyer on Tuesday 29 May. [31] On that day, Michael Dwyer decided to throw in his lot with the Wexford men and he set out for that county.

Dwyer's movements during the first week of June are something of a mystery. This in itself indicates that the Glensman was not a leading figure within the United Irishmen at this time. Had he been better known, or had he been a leading officer within the movement, his movements would have been noted and consequently would have been accurately traced. There is, however, no record of Dwyer having any command of significance in early June. Oral tradition that he fought at Newtownbarry (Bunclody) on 1 June 1798 is probably inaccurate. He joined up with the united Wexford and Wicklow forces just north of Gorey at the end of May. Following a sojourn at Mountpleasant, he marched northwards with the army of North Wexford. He definitely fought in the battle of Arklow on Saturday, June 9th, where he held a minor position, under such

major leaders as Anthony Perry, Esmond Kyan and the Wicklow
man, Billy Byrne of Ballymanus. [32] The Wicklow contingent in
which Dwyer now fought was known as the Ballymanus
division. During the battle of Arklow Dwyer's bravery was noted
by the Wexford men. [33] Despite their bravery, the insurgents
were halted at Arklow and fell back towards Gorey. The battle of
Arklow effectively stopped the spread of hostilities north of the
County Wexford region. Following an action at Kilcavan Hill,
Dwyer and the Ballymanus division reached Vinegar Hill on
June 20th. This was the eve of what was to prove to be the
decisive government victory of the campaign in the south-east.
The following day, the rebel forces broke and fled at Vinegar Hill.
The main body retreated towards Wexford town. Dwyer did not
go with them. Instead, he retreated northwards, rejoining some
of his comrades on the way. They spent that night at Peppard's
Castle and reached the sacked settlement of Aughrim on June
24th. [34] The survivors of Vinegar Hill began to regroup. Byrne
was no longer in command, but his older brother Garret now
decided on an attack on Hacketstown, just over the Carlow
border.

The Battle of Hacketstown took place on 25 June 1798.
Actually, this was the second Battle of Hacketstown. [35] The
settlement had previously been attacked on May 25th. On the
morning of June 25th the combined Wicklow and Wexford
forces attacked the town, hoping to capture arms and
ammunition, which were in short supply. It was at this battle
that Michael Dwyer was given his first significant command, as
he led one of the flanking parties on that day. [36] The
effectiveness of Dwyer's command over some of the men under
him on the eve and the day of the battle of Hacketstown
(especially those who had been drinking) has been questioned.
It is possible that this point was made to distance Dwyer from
atrocities such as murder and arson committed by drunken
rebels. [37] Whatever the real situation regarding Dwyer's
leadership qualities at the time of his first command, a
determined Loyalist resistance meant that the attackers' losses
were high as the defenders picked them off from within stone
buildings. Solid resistance from well armed forces within well-
fortified positions amply demonstrated that, without cannon,
the rebels could not hope to take such positions. Once again,
Dwyer's courage was noted at Hacketstown. With two brothers
named Laffan [Laphen] from Kilmuckridge, he managed to climb
the barracks wall using scaling ladders. [38] Despite this gallant

effort, the barracks proved too tough a nut to crack and the rebels eventually had to withdraw. Following a protracted engagement and the burning of nearly eighty houses, the deaths of Captain Hardy and eight Loyalists were far outnumbered by rebel losses. [39] One major loss to the rebel leadership was Michael Reynolds of Johnstown, near Naas, who had been very prominent in the battle that day. [40]

By late June, the great Irish revolution of 1798 was drawing inexorably toward its conclusion in the south-eastern part of the country. However there was a brief respite and a resounding rebel victory at Ballyellis on 30 June 1798. During this engagement, the same Ancient Briton regiment responsible for atrocities in Newtownmountkennedy and the executions at Dunlavin, sustained losses of about thirty dead. [41] Michael Dwyer took an active and prominent part in this action [42] where he fought with Edward Roche, before chasing and killing a 'huge Briton' when he 'clove his head nearly in two with a captured sword'. [43] Although a resounding success, Ballyellis was not a major victory. Moreover, the rebel forces failed to pursue their advantage and nearby Carnew was not taken.

One ballad about Michael Dwyer, rather unusually, concentrated on the earlier part of his career as a United Irishman and his involvement in the 1798 rising. It mentioned a number of incidents, including the second Battle of Hacketstown, in which Dwyer was involved. It was published (with footnotes) in the late 19th century. [44] The ballad contains stanzas such as:

> But soon the boys,
> they did him join,
> And Hacketstown surrounded,
>
> With pike and gun,
> they made them run,
> Their schemes were soon confounded.

Despite the heroic imagery of this ballad, by July the tide of war had firmly turned in favour of the government forces. Retreat into the fastnesses of the Wicklow Mountains was now the only sensible option for the beleaguered rebel forces, but Michael Dwyer could scarcely have imagined just how long his resistance would last in these fastnesses as he and his comrades trekked towards Glenmalure in the first week of July 1798.

The Wexford rebellion had failed and, although other parts of the island of Ireland saw further bloodshed later in that fateful year, the last chance of success for the United Irishmen died with their defeat in the south-eastern theatre of war. Brief but false hopes flickered as rebel armies took to the field in Antrim, Down, Mayo and elsewhere. These hopes were crushed along with the armies that engendered them.

Meanwhile, the remnants of the army of North Wexford, including Michael Dwyer and the surviving members of the Ballymanus division, had reached the relative safety of Glenmalure. There was now a council of war among the battered army's leaders. Debate raged about whether to stay in the shelter afforded by the remote glen or to move out of it and try to link up with other rebel forces elsewhere. One section of the army embarked on an expedition through Kildare and into Meath. The mastermind of the successful ambush at Ballyellis, Joseph Holt, accompanied this force, though it was against his better judgement. Dwyer and Miles Byrne of Monaseed remained in Glenmalure with a skeleton force, guarding the wounded members of the division. [45] Dwyer was responsible for the defence of the secluded valley at this time, and he was referred to as 'the Governor of Glenmalure'. [46]

The Meath expedition was a fiasco. Following rebel defeats at Clonard and Rynville Hill, the majority of the force disbanded and only something between four hundred and a thousand rebels were left in the field in Wicklow. [47] Joseph Holt had been wounded twice and even had to feign death to escape with his life during the Meath debacle. [48] Following Holt's return to the Wicklow Mountains on 16 July 1798, Dwyer rejoined the main army. At this stage the 'general in chief' of the reduced force that remained in the mountains was Joseph Holt.

Holt was a protestant from Redcross and his role in the Wicklow rebellion was rewritten and watered down by 19th century Catholic historians. One account tells us that there were men far superior to Holt in the qualifications of a warrior. [49] However, the truth was that Holt was the only surviving rebel leader of note willing to take command of the few hundred survivors in the Wicklow Mountains. [50]

The rebels' only hope of success lay in a successful French invasion, but Holt received news of the French General Humbert's surrender on 9 September 1798. [51] Despite this, Holt continued to hold out, but the failure of the French and the onset of winter persuaded him to seek terms with the authorities. Joseph Holt surrendered, on his own terms, on November 10th – the day of Wolfe Tone's trial [52] – and the main body of the battered rebel army in the Wicklow Mountains disbanded.

Michael Dwyer had evacuated Glenmalure with the remainder of the insurgents on 6 August 1798 and on the next day they arrived in the Glen of Imaal. [53] Dwyer was home! The glen of Imaal was geographically remote and the community within it was a close-knit one, which meant that Dwyer had many friends ready to shelter him locally. Even some elements of the yeomanry in this area were prepared to harbour Dwyer. [54] Here, in Imaal he also had an extended web of kinship could rely on the popular support which was one factor behind the longevity of his mountain campaign. [55] Knowledge of such support and shelter influenced Dwyer's decision not to avail of a protection, which was offered to him in August. He may have even received such a protection, but not availed of it. He also feared becoming the target of a Loyalist reprisal attack. [56] A protection might be all very well, but with the memory of the Dunlavin massacre and other incidents fresh in Dwyer's mind, no doubt he may have felt that such a protection might not be worth the paper that it was written on. Dwyer considered the option of taking a protection, but ignored it and September saw him involved in the Battle of Keadeen [Kaigeen]. [57] Dwyer and his men had decided to continue the fight.

As the last stanza of the ballad Dunlavin Green implies, the Dunlavin massacre certainly meant that Michael Dwyer and his rebel band had many sympathisers in and around Dunlavin, Donard and the Glen of Imaal. [58] The executions on Dunlavin green and other acts of terror had set a chilling example and engendered much resentment among the local United Irishmen, and many inhabitants of the Imaal area were only too willing to give their support to Dwyer and his followers. This support was vital and all the more necessary following Holt's surrender in November, leaving the intrepid Dwyer as the only leader of note still at large in the Wicklow Mountains.

From this time onward, much of the information about Michael Dwyer becomes anecdotal. The great rebellion was over and the last remnants of Holt's fighting force had disappeared. Dwyer stood alone and his band of followers, though faithful, was very small. No more than fifteen men usually accompanied Dwyer. [59] Sometimes the number of followers was as low as three. Given these conditions and the overwhelming odds, many of the episodes relating to Dwyer concern his narrow escapes form the authorities.

Early in December 1798, for example, Dwyer and some of his men attended a christening at Killalish, and their presence in the area became known to the authorities. They were sheltering in the house of the family of Peter Hayden (who had been shot in the Dunlavin Massacre), before they escaped over the mountain from the pursuing Highland regiment. [60]

Dwyer and his men did still pose a threat to the forces of the crown however. On December 8th, or thereabouts, there was an episode in the townland of Sruhaun. One account mentions that two yeomen named Magennis were shot because they were going to report Dwyer's whereabouts, [61] but it is more probable that they were shot because they refused to surrender their arms. Later that day, Dwyer's men also shot two other soldiers and a farmer named Young. [62] The latter shooting happened at Tuckmill.

Whatever the truth of the Sruhaun exchange, it proved that Dwyer still posed a threat to crown forces and their supporters in and around the Glen of Imaal. As the year 1798 drew to a close, many areas had been pacified by the authorities in the orgy of violence that followed in the wake of the attempted revolution. This bloody aftermath, coupled with the loss of life during the actual fighting meant that over thirty thousand fatalities resulted from the civil war that was the rebellion of 1798. Resistance had been crushed nearly everywhere, but the Wicklow Mountains was a notable exception.

Violent incidents continued to punctuate the area around Dunlavin parish as the following extract shows.

In August 1798, some yeomen, returning from Vinegar Hill, went to Kilbelet to the house of John Metcalf, a respectable farmer descended from a Yorkshire family who settled about Donard after the Battle of the Boyne. Metcalf fled and was chased up the side of Church Mountain and murdered beside the mearings of the townland of Woodenboley. His assassins, two brothers, had been in his employment previously and owing to some disagreement left their master. They were soon after convicted of sheep stealing and got the alternative of joining the army or suffering death for the crime. For their last escapade they were allowed to go unpunished. [63]

Incidents such as this influenced Dwyer's decision to fight on. As 1799 dawned, despite very determined efforts to surround and capture him in the month of December 1798, [64] Michael Dwyer from the Glen of Imaal, a captain of the United Irishmen, who had 'risen through the ranks' and gained in prominence during the rebellion itself, held out in that glen against all the might of the forces arrayed against him.

NOTES

1: Dickson, p.22.

2: Heaney, Deirdre, Land and Life in the Glen of Imaal 1830-1901, Unpublished B.A. Thesis, N.U.I. Maynooth, p.8.

3: O'Donnell, Ruán, The Rebellion in Wicklow 1798, Irish Academic Press, Dublin, 1998, p.69. See also John Thomas Campion: Michael Dwyer or The Insurgent Captain of the Wicklow Mountains: A Tale of the Rising in 1798, Cameron, Ferguson, 1869, (also Gill, 1910) p.5.

4: Dickson, p.23.

5: Campion, 1869, p.6.

6: N.U.I. Maynooth Library, Shearman Papers, XVII, p.169. Regarding the systematic evictions of Catholic farmers, Shearman wrote: Should there be a man so daring as to raise his voice above the common herd he is set down as a turbulent spirit and entails on himself a persecution of the lowest and meanest character unworthy of the noble proprietors whose only excuse is that they act thus led only by the invidious whisperings of avaricious agents and their cowardly myrmidons.

7: I realise that 'Protestant' is a complex term, including many shades of opinion and belief. I use the term here to refer to members of the Church of Ireland and apologise to all who might take issue with the simplistic terminology but religious argument is not central to this book, so I hope that the content and context in which it is used is clear.

8: Heaney, p.10.

9: Campion, 1869, p.4.

10: Heaney p.2. Heaney wrote: The isolation from the more populous eastern parts of the county, where the county administration is based, naturally leads to a feeling that the area is somewhat of a backwater.

11: http://members.tripod.com/granitefields/new_page_3.htm (visited 4/4/02).

12: Dickson, p.24.

13: Hoxey, Elaine and de Lion, Caoimhin, Michael Dwyer: Battle of Doire na Muc, Donard, 1988, p.4.

14: N.A.I. 620/30/89.

15: Cullen, in Hannigan and Nolan, 1994, p.449 et seq.

16: Dickson, p.25.

17: Lawlor, 1998, p.123.

18: O'Donnell, 1998, p.178.

19: Ronan, p.49.

20: N.A.I. 620/38/23.

21: http://www.turtlebunbury.com/history/history_houses/hist_hse_rathsallagh.htm (visited on 2/2/07).

22: Lynott, John, 1798 Claims, in the Ninth Annual Dunlavin Festival of Arts Brochure, 1991, p.15.

23: Dublin News 5 June, in Glasgow Courier, 9 June 1798.

24: O'Donnell, in Hannigan and Nolan, 1994, p.357.

25: Lewis, Samuel, A Topographical Dictionary of Ireland (1837), quoted in: Dermot James, and Séamas Ó Maitíu, (editors), The Wicklow World of Elizabeth Smith 1840-1850, The Woodfield Press, 1996, p.151-154.

26: Pakenham, op. cit. pp.169-170.

27: O'Donnell, 1998, p.69.

28: Wicklow County Council, Wicklow commemorating 1798-1998: Calendar of Events, p.8.

29: O'Donnell, 1998, p.165. See also Dickson, p.36.

30: O'Donnell, 1998, p.165.

31: Dickson, p.36.

32: Power, Pat, The Battle of Arklow, in Wicklow Historical Society Journal, Vol. 2, No. 4, May 1998, p.24.

33: Dickson, p.38.

34: Dickson, p.38.

35: Carlow County Council/Carlow Urban District Council: Carlow '98 Bicentenary Commemoration 1798-1998: Schedule of Events, p.12

36: Wicklow, 1998, p.18.

37: Duffy, Robert, One Hundred Years Too Soon: Hacketstown and 1798, Hacketstown Community Council, 1998, pp.32-37

38: Duffy, pp.42-43. See also O'Donnell, p.251.

39: Wicklow, 1998, p.18.

40: Lawlor, 1998, p.90.

41: I am indebted to Mr. Paul Haycock of Wigton, Cumbria, for this piece of information and for his information regarding the Ancient Briton regiment, which appears in appendix eight.

42: Dickson, p.44.

43: Dickson, p.45 and O'Donnell, 1998, p.259.

44: On Captain Dwyer, in R. R. Madden: Literary Remains of the United Irishmen of 1798 and selections from other popular lyrics of their times, Dublin, 1887, p.110-112. The full ballad appears in appendix three of this book.

45: O'Donnell, 1998, p.277.

46: Dickson, p.47. Also Wicklow, 1998, p.19.

47: Ronan p.49. Also Wicklow, 1998, p.20.

48: O'Donnell, 1998, p.280. Also Wicklow, 1998, p.20.

49: Ronan, p.49.

50: O'Donnell, in Hannigan and Nolan, 1994, p.365.

51: O'Donnell, in Hannigan and Nolan, 1994, p.368.

52: Kenny, Michael, The 1798 Rebellion – Photographs and Memorabilia from the National Museum of Ireland, Dublin, 1996, p.47.

53: Dickson, p.47.

54: Bartlett, Thomas, Masters of the mountains: the insurgent careers of Joseph Holt and Michael Dwyer, County Wicklow, 1798-1803, in Hannigan and Nolan, 1994, p.387.

55: Bartlett, in Hannigan and Nolan, 1994, p.386.

56: Lawlor, 1998, p.126. Also O'Donnell, p.296.

57: Dickson, p.78.

58: The standard form of the ballad ends thus: 'Micky Dwyer in the mountains to Saunders he owes a spleen, For his loyal brothers, who were shot on Dunlavin Green.' See Lawlor, 1998, pp.96-97.

59: O'Donnell, 1998, p.340.

60: Lawlor, 1998, p.127.

61: Campion, 1869, p.73-76. Interestingly, Campion entitled this chapter, Justifiable Homicide.

62: Dickson, p.96-97. See also O'Donnell, Ruán : Aftermath: Post-Rebellion Insurgency in Wicklow 1799-1803, Dublin, 1999, p.24.

63: N.U.I. Maynooth, Shearman Papers XVII, quoted in Chris Lawlor, Dunlavin Green Revisited, in Dunlavin-Donard-Davidstown Parish Link, Vol. IV, No. 3, November 1998, p.6-7.

64: Dickson, p.99.

This 1898 Wicklow '98 Centenary membership card depicts Michael Dwyer's escape from Derrynamuck.

RESISTANCE

West Wicklow remained disturbed long after the rest of the country had been subdued in 1798. Joseph Holt held out until November of that year and Dwyer amazingly did not surrender until December 1803. In 1800 a survey of County Wicklow was undertaken and it recorded that the complete baronies of Upper Talbotstown and Ballinacor (almost 100,00 acres in extent) had been 'wholly laid waste' and the survey noted that it was not safe to explore it. [1] There were 'huge unimproved wastes' all across a vast extent on the tract of country around Dunlavin and extending to the Tallaght hills amounting to between eight and ten thousand acres. [2] The survey also stated: 'From the destruction which took place in this part of the country, many have not yet rebuilt their houses or returned to the country ... almost every house in this neighbourhood has been destroyed except Russborough, which is formed into a garrison.' [3] This state of affairs was due to the activities of Michael Dwyer and his followers.

Dwyer held out for a period of more than five years, and as he was a West Wicklow man, his activities affected Dunlavin and its hinterland, just as the Dunlavin massacre affected the activities of Michael Dwyer.

The executions on Dunlavin green had set a chilling example and engendered much resentment among the local United Irishmen. As the last stanza of the Ballad of Dunlavin Green implied, the Dunlavin massacre certainly meant that Michael Dwyer and his rebel band had many sympathisers in and around the village of Dunlavin and its hinterland. Dunlavin parish extended to cover Donard, Davidstown and the Glen of Imaal. Dwyer himself came from this geographically remote and glen and some of the executed men also hailed from this area. The community within the Glen of Imaal was a close-knit one, which meant that Dywer had many friends ready to shelter him locally. Early in December 1798, for example, Dwyer and some of his men attended a christening at Killalish, and their presence in the area became known to the authorities. They were sheltering in the house of the family of Peter Hayden, who had been shot in the Dunlavin Massacre, before they escaped over the mountain from the pursuing Highland regiment. [4]

Dwyer knew that many families in the region would shield him and afford him shelter, and this influenced his decision to withdraw into the Wicklow Mountains August 1798 and embark on the next phase of his rebel activities.

This phase of Michael Dwyer's life was the one that established his renown. This renown has spread far and wide and has lasted over two centuries. The story of Dwyer's life up to and during 1798 is one of a young United Irishman who was drawn to the fighting in the Wexford theatre of operations, who had taken refuge in the Wicklow Mountains when the crown forces gained the upper hand. Admittedly, Dwyer had shown conspicuous bravery during engagements with these crown forces such as those at Arklow, Hacketstown and Ballyellis. He had been given his own command and had stayed in the field even after the demise of Holt's contingent. Holt had laid down his arms in November 1798, but Dwyer continued his resistance until he gave himself up – on terms of his own choosing – in December 1803.

In total, Dwyer continued his fight against the authorities for over five and a half years. The longevity of his campaign was staggering and his feat becomes all the more amazing when one considers the huge weight of odds stacked against him. His guerrilla war made him a legend both in his own lifetime and afterwards.

At the outset, it is important to clarify that Dwyer was not a mere criminal or bandit. From late 1798 onwards banditry and minor raids could continue as long as there were small numbers of unreconciled or outlawed rebels, but this in itself could not be considered as insurrectionary warfare. [5] However, Michael Dwyer had been a captain of a United Irish force. His family background was also entwined within the United Irish organisation. Many of his kinfolk had been deeply involved in the movement; for example John Dwyer of Seskin had been a baronial delegate. [6] Michael Dwyer's leadership qualities were noticed during the Wexford campaign and he had his own command from the time of the second battle of Hacketstown onwards. Hence Dwyer had a mandate for his actions from within the organisation to which he belonged.

One school of thought puts forward the argument that the United Irish forces formed the true Irish army of the time. The events of 1798 are thus viewed not as a rebellion, but as a war. This school of thought seems to need a legitimacy bestowed on what it would term 'the martyrs of 1798'. Therefore, the argument continues, the term 'rebels' should not be applied to the soldiers of this properly constituted army who were fighting on the soil of their own land against forces loyal to an outside monarch. However, the application or non-application of the words 'rebel' or 'rebellion' is hardly relevant to the legitimacy or otherwise of the cause espoused by these men. The American Revolution, which is also referred to as the American War of Independence, also originated as a rebellion. Unlike the scenario in Ireland some twenty years later, however, the American 'rebels' won their 'war' and were referred to as 'the continental army'. [7] The French 'Revolution' was another example of a successful 'rebellion'. In Ireland the United Irishmen were truly 'revolutionary' in their aims and aspirations, but their 'rebellion' (a much bloodier affair than the French 'Revolution' and the French reign of terror) ended in defeat. Language is strange, and perhaps it is important. Certainly it is important to modern political schools of thought, but the language of the events of 1798-1803 has come down to us through networks of both the victors and the vanquished. And, in the final analysis, language alone cannot bestow or withhold legitimacy on the organisations, events or people of the past. Informed opinion is aware of this fact.

Whatever view one takes about the legitimacy of the struggle, Michael Dwyer's status as a rebel leader was real enough. While small-scale operations were his principal modus operandi during the protracted guerrilla campaign, there was always the element of hitting out against the crown forces. Dwyer's operations were of necessity small-scale due to the dearth of numbers within his following. Moreover, any larger scale operations would have attracted the attention of the authorities and the very nature of guerrilla warfare involves small bands that hit both hard and fast before moving on rapidly. Such a campaign suited Dwyer, who was on home territory and whose fieldcraft and survival skills were of the highest order. [8] As the campaign progressed Dwyer (and, for a shorter time, Holt) became household names. They were actually far better known than many of the now more famous United Irishmen whose roles were re-appraised during the post-famine era. [9] Dwyer's exploits were well known during his own lifetime and news of his daring escapades only served to fuel the growth of his legend. He became a Romantic figure, regarded as a criminal by the state, but considered hero, champion, avenger and fighter for justice by the people among whom he sheltered. A 'social bandit' in the mould of Robin Hood, Michael Dwyer was idealised and turned into a myth who never killed but in self-defence or just revenge. [10]

The romanticism associated with Michael Dwyer was both a cause and a consequence of the composition of a number of ballads about his life. Perhaps the most romantic (in every sense of the word) of these concerned the marriage of Dwyer to Mary Doyle, which took place on 16 October 1798, while Dwyer was 'on the run' and avoiding the authorities. [11] Though certainly inaccurate, this ballad was later published [12] and it helped to establish and perpetuate the Dwyer myth. Ballads such as this presented him in a romantic and attractive light. They were passed on from one generation to the next, forming part of an oral tradition regarding the leader and his exploits. There is no doubt that many of Dwyer's exploits were hair-raising – the real stuff of which ballads were made. Narrow escapes such as the evasion of detection by assuming the disguise of a beggar man and boldly passing by the soldiers who were seeking him or lying across the rafters of Mangan's house while the yeomen searched the building at ground level [13] rank right up there with the legendary Robin Hood's entry into a hostile Nottingham in the garb of a butcher or his hiding in the branches of a tree as the sheriff's men passed beneath! Dwyer's most famous exploit during his guerrilla campaign was probably also his narrowest escape.

This occurred at the cottage of Miley Connell in Derrynamuck (also referred to as Dernamuck and Doire na Muc) on the night of 15 February 1799. For once, Dwyer's lookout system had failed to alert him of approaching danger. Information received from a spy had led the military to the very door of Dwyer's refuge. Connell's cottage was the third in a clachan of three, situated at the end of an isolated boreen. The rebel occupants of the other two cottages had already been taken. Ned Lennon and Thomas Clerk surrendered at Hoxey's house and Wat McDonnell (McDaniel), Patrick Toole, John Ashe, John Mickle, Hugh Byrne and Darby Dunn were captured at the home of the Toole family. The military, a detachment of Scottish Highlanders led by Captain Roderick McDonald, surrounded Connell's cottage and called on the men inside – Michael Dwyer, Sam McAllister, Patrick Costello and John Savage – to surrender. [14] They refused. Costello and Savage were killed in the ensuing battle of Derrynamuck. Sam McAllister also lost his life, which he sacrificed in order to give Dwyer himself a chance to escape. Dwyer emerged from the cottage and fled near naked and barefoot, before he burst through the Scottish line and ran to freedom. [15] The whole sense of the dramatic was enhanced because this event happened in the middle of a very cold winter with deep snow covering the ground. During his flight he was lucky to slip on an icy patch as the bullets from a second volley whizzed past overhead. [16] Dwyer was the only member of the rebel band to escape that night. The others were all either killed or captured.

This incident inspired the best-known literary work about Dwyer, T.D. Sullivan's poem, The Ballad of Michael Dwyer. [17] Thanks to Sullivan's ballad, Dwyer's escape from Derrynamuck is the first episode that springs to many people's minds when they hear his name. [18] Though Sullivan's ballad is the best-known example, it was not the only one to be written about the escape. Another ballad, published in 1887, referred to the same incident. [19]

After his eventful escape from Derrynamuck, Dwyer made for the house of Thaddeus Dwyer, who was a brother of the John

Dwyer shot on Dunlavin green, and thence on to either Sleivecorragh or Corragh. [20] The prisoners taken at Derrynamuck were taken to Baltinglass, court-martialled and executed (except for Hugh Byrne who turned Kings Evidence and thus saved his life). Indeed Dwyer's continuing activities in the region meant that Baltinglass became something of a 'court-martial capital' for the West Wicklow region. [21]

Some examples illustrate this fact well. On 19 February 1799 Michael Doyle was tried under Captain Bellock of the Dumfries Light Dragoons and found guilty of 'rebellion, robbery and murder'. [22] He was sentenced to transportation for life. Doyle was perhaps lucky to be transported. On 9 March 1799 James Comyns was sentenced to death when he was found guilty of 'rebellion and robbing Michael Fenton, a yeoman, of his arms and accoutrements and making for the hills with said articles'. [23] A week or so later, on March 13th, John Byrns received the death penalty for 'rebellion and carrying arms against His Majesty's forces'. [24] On Christmas Eve 1800, a death warrant was drawn up for William Genoud following his capture, escape, re-capture and subsequent court martial on 22 December 1800. [25] It is both interesting and revealing to note that the charges against these men all mention rebellion rather than brigand-like outlaw activities.

These primary sources reveal that at the time in question, many people, including the authorities, perceived that men such as Dwyer and his ilk were continuing the rebellion rather than engaging in mere banditry. Dwyer, like Holt before him, was conducting his campaign of orchestrated resistance precisely because he did have a political agenda and moreover, a specifically 'United Irish' agenda, however ill defined it may have been. [26] Dwyer was engaged in violence, but as a politically aware rebel guerrilla fighter rather than as a mere cut-throat.

Dwyer's mountain campaign of guerrilla warfare would continue long after his escape from Derrynamuck in February 1799. Indeed, when Lord Cornwallis stated in a letter of 13 July 1798, 'our war is reduced to a predatory system in the mountains of Wicklow and the bogs of Kildare' [27] he surely could not have foreseen just how long Dwyer and his followers would continue to hold out in the Wicklow Mountains.

Dwyer was involved in many dangerous escapades, near misses and scary moments. News of such exploits endeared him to the public at large both during his lifetime and after his death. The ballad-writers were not idle and ballads concerning his wider activities rather than relating to a single incident were also composed. One such song, simply entitled Michael Dwyer is the work of Paddy Heany and Peadar Kearney (famous for the Irish national anthem Amhrain na bhFiain). This ballad is short on factual material but the heroic tone and rousing chorus mark it out as yet another work that added to the already famous legend of the rebel leader of the Wicklow Mountains. [28] Ballads such as these were vital because they ingrained Dwyer and his memory into popular culture.

As noted already, Dwyer is synonymous with Wicklow in the minds of many people. He is also synonymous with the United Irish leadership. The fact that he was not one of the principal leaders during the main action of the rebellion in Wexford has been obscured by a 19th century revision of his role. The inclusion of Michael Dwyer in pictures of the United Irish leadership grouped around a table or in individual medallions on a plain background, the romantic account of his resistance written by John Thomas Campion and, above all, the numerous ballads about his time in the Wicklow mountains have helped to etch the figure of Michael Dwyer into folk-memory far and wide. Dwyer's legend had been growing throughout his guerrilla campaign [29] and posthumous literary works would later elevate Dwyer to hero status. His prolonged resistance in the Wicklow mountains had touched a communal nerve. Dwyer was more than an outlaw, more than a rebel, more than a guerrilla leader to many people. He was a symbol of hope at a time and in a place of oppression. [30] As he continued to elude capture, that symbol became brighter and the hope, instead of being dashed, grew in the breasts of an admiring public. Dwyer was a cause célebre in his day. To Republicans and Nationalists who had tasted defeat in the main rebellion, Dwyer's continued defiance burned like a beacon. Dwyer and his followers gave pride and a sense of self-respect to those whose own hopes had been cruelly denied. [31] As long as there was any hope, however slight, of another revolution or another French invasion, Dwyer would remain in his mountain lair and await developments.

As the years passed, hope of such developments faded. By 1803, the Treaty of Amiens of the previous year, though short-lived, had shattered any remaining hope of French intervention in Ireland. In July of that year, Robert Emmet's attempted revolution had petered out amid a mixture of incompetence and bad luck. [32] Meanwhile the net was tightening on Dwyer and his followers. The completion of the Military Road through the mountains was a major boost to the crown forces. This was possibly the first purpose-built road in Ireland – the purpose being to capture Dwyer and his band. Military barracks were occupied at strategic points along this road. There were garrisons stationed at Leitrim, Glencree, Seven Churches, Glenmalure and Aughavanna. [33] This new reality considerably hindered Dwyer's capacity for movement within the heart of the mountains.

Coupled with this was the fact that the military had unleashed a campaign of arrests against known or suspected friends and relations of Dwyer. This strained Dwyer's kinship network almost to breaking point. The situation was very bleak for the remnants of Dwyer's pitifully small force as the winter of 1803 drew in. Without the kinship contacts, there was a lack of safe houses. Caves and other outdoor places of refuge such as abandoned mine workings were not suitable during a winter when snow lay several feet deep on the mountains. In this era of mini ice-age, [34] cold, damp and dreary conditions awaited the Dwyer faction as they faced into their sixth winter 'on the run'. With the changed political situation in France, the debacle that was Emmet's 'flash-in-the-pan rising', [35] the large garrisons stationed along the new Military Road, a renewed military campaign against him which began on December 10th [36] and the absence of many of the arrested kin, Michael Dwyer's thoughts turned to the drawing up of terms of surrender.

Like Joseph Holt before him, Michael Dwyer did not wish to surrender unconditionally. He made overtures via his wife to William Hume of Humewood. The commander of the military, General Beresford, wanted Dwyer to surrender 'upon the mercy of government' (i.e. unconditionally) but Hume, while informing Dwyer that the actual surrender would have to be unconditional, certainly gave some assurances to Mary Dwyer. [37] The exact nature of these assurances, or at least of Hume's ability to honour them, is unclear. Certainly Dwyer's life was to be spared [38] and safe passage to America for four of his leading followers and himself was possibly agreed upon. [39] Dwyer may have been led to believe that he would obtain a full pardon on surrendering himself. [40]

Whatever the truth of the situation, there is no doubt that the United Irish Captain Michael Dwyer laid down his arms on what he believed were his own terms when he surrendered himself into the custody of William Hoare Hume, the Yeoman Captain and M.P. for County Wicklow, on 14 December 1803, [41] thus bringing to an end the brilliant guerrilla campaign which had elevated him to the status of myth.

From December 1803 to August 1805 Michael Dwyer remained a prisoner in Dublin's Kilmainham jail, as did some of his men. [42] Unlike Holt, (whose surrender had been supposedly unconditional, but, thanks to the intervention of the influential La Touche family among others, whose real terms of surrender were that he be allowed to go to Australia a free man) [43] Dwyer wanted to be shipped to the fledgling United States of America. Despite all previous assurances to the contrary however Dwyer was kept incarcerated at Kilmainham. Dwyer and his followers were committed to Kilmainham on a charge of high treason. [44] As state prisoners, they were not always satisfied with their treatment there. Michael Dwyer [45] and by Arthur Devlin [46] both wrote to William Hume from Kilmainham, complaining about their conditions and asking him to intercede with the Castle authorities on their behalf.

William Hoare Hume, son of the liberal Wicklow M.P. who was killed by rebels in a skirmish near Humewood on 8 October 1798, [47] either following in the Whiggish tradition of his father, or because he was tired of being pestered (or both), did write to Dublin Castle regarding the imprisoned rebels. [48] His letter made it clear that terms had been sought from him and that he gave assurances to the surrendering men. However, the letter merely stated that they would be sent 'out of the kingdom', so it is uncertain whether he actually agreed to grant them passage to the United States of America.

Hume's powers to grant such terms to Dwyer and his group were always suspect anyway. However, Hume argued, shipping the men out of Ireland would calm the situation in Wicklow and Dwyer's sympathisers would be deprived of their figurehead. While providing an idea of conditions in the prison and giving a flavour of Dwyer's well-documented [49] and long-running battle with Dr. Trevor of Kilmainham gaol, these letters also prove that Hume did agree to terms with Dwyer and his men.

However, unlike Holt, Dwyer did not end up in the place that he had expected. This was yet another factor in the growth of Dwyer's legend. The authorities were portrayed as 'base knaves' who had failed to keep their promises. For 19th century nationalist historians this was yet another example in a litany of deceit on the part of the crown forces.

The mythic qualities of Michael Dwyer were heightened by a sense of injustice at the treatment meted out to him. Hume's letter above hinted at a sense of disquiet among the people during Dwyer's lengthy time in prison. This disquiet developed into an outbreak of righteous indignation among Dwyer's adoring public following his departure for Australia. This phenomenon of support for the wronged leader continued posthumously and in its turn helped to sustain the cult of Dwyer in both Ireland and Australia.

Before he sailed, Dwyer had gotten wind of his destination, and he protested vigorously. Once again he desperately tried to contact Hume. [50] Despite this last minute appeal, Dwyer's captivity in Ireland finished in August 1805, when, in company with his wife Mary, his cousin Hugh 'Vesty' Byrne, Byrne's wife Rachael and their children, Arthur Devlin, Martin Burke and John Mernagh, the leader from the Glen of Imaal boarded the Tellicherry at Cobh, bound for Botany Bay. [51] So the process of ridding West Wicklow of active United Irishmen, which had started on 24 May 1798 with the executions on the fairgreen of Dunlavin, finally ended on the 28 August 1805 when the Tellicherry sailed for Port Jackson in New South Wales, Australia.

Michael Dwyer spent twenty of his fifty-three years in Australia. Though they were eventful, it was not for these years that Dwyer is best remembered. His place in history stems from his actions during the period 1798-1803 and consequently this account of the latter part of Dwyer's life story is short. The voyage on the Tellicherry took Dwyer and his comrades across vast, undreamt of expanses of ocean but it finally ended when the ship arrived at the entrance to Port Jackson on St. Valentine's Day 1806. [52] Despite initial confusion regarding the Wicklow rebels, they were each given a hundred acres of land at Cabramatta. [53] The Dwyer group may have travelled to Australia on a convict ship, but they went as free men and it seemed that a new and peaceful life awaited them in the southern hemisphere.

However, when William Bligh (famous, or rather infamous, for his role during the affair of the 'Mutiny on the Bounty') succeeded Gidley King as governor of New South Wales later in 1806, the peaceable new lives of Dwyer and his comrades were threatened. [54] Bligh was paranoid about the possibility of an uprising in the colony and, considering their background, he perceived the Wicklow settlers as a huge threat. This was one instance where Dwyer's fame worked against him. Dwyer was arrested as a possible ringleader of a rebellion that had not taken place and kept in solitary confinement on board the H.M.S. Porpoise. [55] Following an elaborate show trial, Dwyer was found guilty of 'conspiracy in order to raise a rebellion' and in May 1807 he was sent to the convict depot on Norfolk Island. [56]

Dwyer was once again a prisoner, just as he had been in Kilmainham. He was moved from Norfolk Island to Van Dieman's Land in January 1808. [57] However, moves to oust Governor Bligh were afoot in Sydney and following the so-called 'Rum Rebellion' he was removed from office. [58] With the departure of Bligh, Dwyer and his companions were pardoned and released from captivity. Under the enlightened Governor Lachlan Macquarie, on 25 August 1810, Dwyer was appointed as a constable at George's River. [59] The irony of the ex-guerrilla fighter taking up such a post was not a hindrance to the growth of the Michael Dwyer legend however. Advocates of Dwyer point out that this appointment demonstrated that Dwyer had extraordinary leadership skills and that these were recognised in the raw, new, vigorous, exciting but perhaps dangerous climate of New South Wales. This was a place where 'real men' were given a chance and were not stifled by the social immobility and Ancien Regime mentality, which existed within the 'old countries', now the 'United Kingdom of Great Britain and Ireland' – a political entity established by the Act of Union, which came into force on 1 January 1801. By 1819 Dwyer' owned six hundred and twenty acres [60] and his solid expansion of his land holding was seen as further proof of his acumen and ability. In May 1820 Dwyer was appointed Chief Constable of Liverpool and it was argued by his supporters that his rise through the system meant that he was in a better position to help other Irish emigrants-cum-convicts.

Moreover, in the heady atmosphere of the raw and fledgling colony, led by the enlightened figure of Macquarie, surely men such as Dwyer had an integral part to play in the shaping of a better life for all? Dwyer the chief constable fitted very nicely into the myth as Dwyer the just, the guardian of the peace and the champion of the oppressed. Had not he fought with the United Irishmen to achieve a better quality of life for his people? Now, in a young land, albeit in a new capacity, why should he do any differently? Indeed, could he do less now than during his idealistic days of resistance back in far off Wicklow? Dwyer now served the King that he had rebelled against, but in a place where, by doing so, he could make a difference and see many of his revolutionary principles put into action.

However, the myth and the man diverge here. Dwyer had invested in a tavern called the Harrow Inn. This was perhaps not a good move on the part of a man who was known to have a fondness for alcohol. [61] The public house brought financial problems and Dwyer was removed from his position as chief constable due to misconduct. [62] To boost his finances, Dwyer had illegally set land belonging to a woman named Ann Stroud. On Christmas Eve 1822 he was found guilty of 'having broken the colonial regulations' and was fined £20. More serious however, he lost his spirit licence and was unable to pay his creditors. Many of his possessions and some of his lands were sold, and in 1824 he was incarcerated in the debtors' prison in Sydney.

He was released in May 1825, but was in poor health when he returned to one of his few possessions that had not been sold – his house at Cabramatta. Weak and suffering from dysentery, he lived only another three months and died on 23 August 1825. [63]

Michael Dwyer was buried in Devonshire Street Cemetery, but in 1898 his remains were re-interred in Waverly Cemetery. A crowd of about 200,000 attended the re-interment and oral tradition states that the memorial stone is the highest of all the monuments over any Irish patriot and still the highest head-stone in Sydney.

The death of Michael Dwyer in Australia strengthened the legend of the wronged leader shamefully exiled by a deceitful establishment. It was now certain that this 'exile from Erin' was 'never to return'. Dwyer's acceptance of the positions of constable and later chief constable was either kept hidden or worked into the myth by portraying Dwyer as a dispenser of justice for other Irish exiles. [64] So well known during his guerrilla campaign and for his transportation against his negotiated terms of surrender, Dwyer had achieved 'celebrity status'. In those pre-mass media days, the press had made him into a 'superstar'. The longevity and romantic nature of his mountain war had captured the imagination. Posthumously also, he became a valuable symbol – an icon – for Nationalists to aspire to and for Nationalist historians to incorporate into their corpus of literature. Although his guerrilla campaign was always peripheral to the bigger picture, the never-say-die attitude that it embodied was inspirational to a Nationalist Ireland that was crying out for heroes, and who needed those heroes to sustain its growth and development.

NOTES

1: Fraser, Robert, General view of the agriculture and mineralogy present state and circumstances of the County Wicklow with observations on the means of their improvement drawn up for the consideration of the Dublin Society, Dublin 1801, p.98. [Though published in 1801, the text was written in 1800].

2: Fraser, p.81.

3: Fraser, p.91 and p.97.

4: Dickson, p.95.

5: O'Donnell, 1998, p.340.

6: Lawlor, 1998, p.59.

7: See for example: William Miller: A New History of the United States, London, 1968, p.104.

8: Bartlett, in Hannigan and Nolan, 1994, p.388.

9: O'Donnell: The Rebellion in Wicklow 1798, Dublin 1998, p.5.

10: Eric Hobsbawn quoted in Bartlett, in Hannigan and Nolan, 1994, p.391.

11: Dickson, p.85.

12: 'The outlaw's bridal' in Campion, 1869, p.16-18. The ballad appears in appendix 3.

13: Hoxey de Lion, 1988, p.13.

14: Dickson, p.106-108.

15: Bartlett, in Hannigan and Nolan, 1994, p.389.

16: The wording of this reference is taken from my sixth class history copy and was dictated to me by my teacher, Mr. Tom O'Neill in 1971. The copy is in the author's possession. The incident is verified in Bartlett, in Hannigan and Nolan, 1994, p.389 and in Ruán O Donnell: Exploring Wicklow's Rebel Past 1798-1803, Wicklow, 1998, p.30-31.

17: The ballad appears in numerous studies, including Lawlor, 1998, p.128-129. There is no doubt that this ballad posthumously helped to enhance Dwyer's reputation and added to the myth. The ballad was on the Irish primary school curriculum for many years. The name of Michael Dwyer is well known beyond his native Wicklow, and this ballad is largely responsible for this fact. To many people, Dwyer is synonymous with Wicklow. Personally on at least six occasions I have had Dwyer's name quoted to me with no prompting from myself other than to mention the fact that I hail from County Wicklow. For the record, the six instances happened in Doolin, Co. Clare; near Dunmanway in west Cork; Bayswater, London, Midtown, Manhattan, New York City; Ryde, Sydney, New South Wales and Swanston, Melbourne, Victoria, Australia. The geographical diffusion of Dwyer's name and its association with County Wicklow is impressive indeed!

18: For example see: Kieran Sheedy: Upon the mercy of government, Dublin. 1988, Foreword, p.3.

19: On an escape of Dwyer, in R.R. Madden: Literary Remains of the United Irishmen of 1798 and selections from other popular lyrics of their times, Dublin, 1887, p. 119-122. The ballad appears in appendix 3.

20: Ronan, p.90 and Dickson, 1944, p.110-111.

21: Lawlor, 1998, p.129.

22: N.A.I. 620/17/30/6. Document reproduced in appendix 4.

23: N.A.I. 620/17/30/10. Document reproduced in appendix 4.

24: N.A.I. 620/17/13/15. Document reproduced in appendix 4.

25: N.A.I. 620/17/22. Document reproduced in appendix 4.

26: Bartlett, in Hannigan and Nolan, 1994, p.393. See also Ruán O'Donnell: Aftermath: Post-Rebellion Insurgency in Wicklow 1799-1803, Dublin, 1999, p.101.

27: Letter quoted in Patrick C. Power: The Courts Martial of 1798-99, Carlow, 1997, p.80.

28: Lawlor, Chris, Loose ends from the Dunlavin area 1797-1803, in Dunlavin Festival of Arts Brochure, XVIII, Dunlavin, 2000, p.20-28. The ballad is also featured on http://www.lin-uxlots.com/~dunne/ireland/Michael_Dwyer.html [visited 8/2/2000]. The ballad appears in appendix 3.

29: O'Donnell, 1999, p.79.

30: For an excellent overview of oppression and the general situation see Cullen, in

Hannigan and Nolan, 1994, p.411-501.

31: Sheedy, 1988, p.263.

32: McMahon, Sean, Robert Emmet, Cork, 2001, p.41.

33: Freeman's Journal, 3 March 1803.

34: Sheedy, 1988, p.37. I am also indebted to Cllr Tommy Cullen of Baltinglass for information about climatic conditions at this time.

35: McMahon, 2001, p.39.

36: Sheedy, 1988, p.43.

37: Sheedy, 1988, p.47. See also O'Donnell, 1999, p.171.

38: Sheedy 1988, p.47.

39: Wicklow, 1998, p.19.

40: Wicklow, 1998, p.19.

41: Ronan, 1948, p.124.

42: Lawlor, 1998, p.139.

43: Bartlett, in Hannigan and Nolan, 1994, p.383 and O'Donnell, 1998, p.343.

44: Dickson, 1944, p.271 and Hoxey and de Lion, 1988, p.14.

45: N.A.I. 620/14/186/11. Document reproduced in appendix 5.

46: N.A.I. 620/14/186/7. Document reproduced in appendix 5.

47: O'Donnell, in Hannigan and Nolan, 1994, p.371.

48: N.A.I. 620/14/186/7. Document reproduced in appendix 5.

49: Sheedy, 1988, pp.81-123; Kieran Sheedy: The Tellicherry Five, Dublin, 1997, pp.41-63; Dickson, 1944, pp.250-271.

50: N.A.I. 620/14/186/11. Document reproduced in appendix 5.

51: Wicklow, 1998, p.19.

52: Sheedy, 1997, p.75.

53: Sheedy, 1997, p.76-80.

54: Dickson, 1944, p.276.

55: Sheedy, 1997, p.88.

56: Wicklow, 1998, p.20.

57: Sheedy, 1997, p.101.

58: Wicklow, 1998, p.20.

59: Sheedy, 1997, p.111.

60: Sheedy, 1997, p.121.

61: Dwyer's fondness for alcohol is well documented. Having grown up in circumstances where the shébeen was one of the principal diversions from hardship, his arduous guerrilla campaign – particularly during the winter months – in the Wicklow Mountains almost necessitated the use of spirits. He was intoxicated on arrival in Kilmainham [Dickson, 1944, p.250 and Sheedy, 1988 p.57]. It is probable that the authorities plied him with drink in efforts to extract information. Dwyer's letter of 21 January 1805, reproduced in the previous chapter, may also suggest a dependence on spirits. In Australia, there were numerous references to his drinking [Sheedy, 1997, p.123-137 passim]. The cause of Dwyer's death was given as dysentery and alcohol abuse is known to aggravate this condition. This note is factual, not judgemental and it must be noted that Dwyer was a product of his times.

62: Wicklow, 1998, p.20.

63: Sheedy, 1997, p.129-137.

64: Campion [1869] wrote the Australian years almost completely out of his account of Dwyer's life, giving 1805 as the year he died. On the other hand Ronan [1948] mentions that Dwyer became a chief constable: a situation of great trust. During that time he never let pass an opportunity of serving any of his countrymen who had been sent there for political offences.

The 1798 Rebellion was a decisive moment in Irish history. It shaped both Loyalist and Republican attitudes for generations afterwards. Although the enormity of the rebellion and its legacy cannot be overstated, the event itself was short-lived. The savagery of the fighting lasted through one fateful summer, by the end of which the insurrection was totally subdued. Yet resistance continued for fully five and a half years in West Wicklow, only ending when the rebels freely laid down their arms in December 1803. This resistance was centred on Dunlavin parish, through the Glen of Imaal to the summit of Leinster's highest mountain, Lugnaquilla.

The rebellion in this area opened with the horrific massacre of over forty men in Dunlavin village. Events during the months preceding the massacre meant that something had to give, and that it would more than likely involve Morley Saunders' yeomanry corps.

In the event this is exactly what happened. Whether the decision to kill these men was made on the day of the massacre or not is doubtful. Possibly the fate of the prisoners had actually been decided in advance of the day of the executions. The massacre was an appalling event. The number of men shot in the village that day constituted a significant proportion of Dunlavin's population, which was well under a thousand at that time. It is no wonder that the event has lingered strongly in local folk memory.

One thing that has kept such events alive in the local (and national) folk memory is the proliferation of ballads that were written, especially about 1798. These are usually very biased and may not be historically accurate, but once one realises this and approaches them with caution, using them in conjunction with other sources, they may be examined by historians.

Certainly many local ballads such as Dunlavin Green provide insight into events at local level. They possibly deserve more attention than many historians, both nationally and especially locally, have given them in the past. In fact, many ballads have been rejected altogether as historical sources, but local ballads and traditions, if collected and then examined thoroughly, can shed light on many long-forgotten local events, not alone during the 1798 period, but during other periods as well.

The tragic event on Dunlavin Green raises a question that re-appears at many times of crisis. This question is particularly evident at times of war, especially civil war. Basically, the question may be posed thus: How is it that people who have lived side by side in the past are capable of such savage and brutal acts? Time and again events such as this have happened in societies that are deeply divided.

In West Wicklow the roots of these divisions went back to conquest and colonisation. Wicklow was the last county to be shired in 1606 and the incoming settlers introduced new lifestyles. [1] The whole area of West Wicklow experienced bitter fighting during the 1641 Rebellion and there were many violent robberies [2] and sectarian killings such as the summary hanging of the Protestant Jane Fflood by Catholic rebels in Hollywood. [3] Following the defeat of the 1641 rebels, the land settlements of the 1660s further alienated the members of the losing side. Mostly Catholic landowners suffered; mostly Catholics were alienated and sectarianism deepened. In the Dunlavin region, the lands that had belonged to the Catholic Sarsfields [4] in the pre-1641 era passed into the hands of the Protestant Bulkeleys in the post-1641 period.

The Bulkeleys were staunch supporters of William of Orange and Sir Richard Bulkeley, the second Baronet Dunlavin, defaced Saint Doulagh's Catholic church in north County Dublin when he was returning from the Battle of the Boyne. [5] Sectarianism continued to bubble under the surface in West Wicklow throughout the 18th century.

The whole sectarian question is a troubling one in both national and local history. It removes both historians and readers from their comfort zones, but it cannot be shied away from and must be studied. It is only by studying the mistakes caused by past attitudes that present generations may hope to change such attitudes and rectify such mistakes.

The sectarian issue often arises when one group (in this case the Catholic majority) harbour constant resentment for real and perceived wrongs, while the other group (in this case the Protestant minority) live in constant fear of real or imagined reprisals and violence. This was the case, to a greater or lesser extent, in the Dunlavin region throughout the whole period of the present study. Time and again evidence of this sectarian undercurrent surfaced in the West Wicklow area, sometimes manifesting itself with frightening ferocity.

The massacre on the fair green of Dunlavin is a case in point. Dunlavin was not the only nor the largest massacre to happen in 1798. Of course, Loyalists did not carry out all massacres. The horrific events at Scullabogue [6] and Wexford bridge, [7] where rebel forces slaughtered Loyalist prisoners were every bit as, if not more, horrific than the massacre on the fair green of Dunlavin and other massacres of rebels by Loyalists. Indeed, the whole area of massacres during 1798 might prove a fruitful field of study, both from a historical and a sociological perspective.

Massacres, though, are not to be ranked in order and judged by degree. They do not form a grim numbers game. Nothing can deflect from the horror and terror in the village of Dunlavin on the day of the massacre; and nothing should. Similar massacres do not excuse the Dunlavin episode – and vice versa, of course. One commentator, who was writing about another time of crisis in Irish history (the Famine of the mid-19th century), provided a succinct observation that

could just as well be applied to the Dunlavin massacre: [8]
'Blaming people is easy and frequently erroneous; the
challenge is to understand what people do (or fail to do) and
why.'

However, at the time many rebels did blame the Loyalists
for the Dunlavin massacre and one consequence of this was
Michael Dwyer's reluctance to accept a protection and turn
himself in after the rebellion. The life of Dwyer was
remarkable by any standards. As a young man growing up in
the remote Glen of Imaal in the era of the American War of
Independence and the French Revolution, there was nothing
to suggest that his name and fame would echo through the
centuries. Yet in many people's minds, Dwyer's name springs
to mind as a defender of the 'rights of man' much more
readily than does that of Thomas Paine, the author of the
celebrated pamphlet of the same name.

This is due to the folk-memory aspect associated with
Dwyer. Dwyer held a minor enough position within the
United Irishmen before and even during the 1798 rebellion.
However, his campaign in the Wicklow Mountains changed
his status as a rebel and during the period 1799-1803 he
became to many a major figure within the United Irish
organisation. Moreover his highly publicised escapades were
an acute propaganda embarrassment for Dublin Castle. [9]

In the eyes of many, Dwyer's escapades elevated him to the
status of a hero. Although later Nationalist historians used
his guerrilla campaign as a form of propaganda, they need
not have exaggerated the facts of that campaign to do so. The
truth was as dramatic as much of the myth. Although
Dwyer's heroic status was assured at national level, nowhere
was it more keenly felt than in his own area of West Wicklow.
Older generations have passed on their knowledge of the
great man orally. Stories were told and ballads about the
Dunlavin massacre and the escape of Dwyer at Derrynamuck
were sung or recited around firesides. Growing up in West
Wicklow, one could not escape the sense that Michael Dwyer
was a hero. It was more than a sense, it was a fact!

However, examination of the historical facts revealed that
he was mortal after all. Far from the sentiments expressed in
T. D. Sullivan's ballad We're True United Irishmen, We'll Fight
Until We Die, Dwyer became a chief constable when he

settled in Australia. He had shady land dealings and spent time in a debtors' prison. He drank heavily. Yes, Dwyer was mortal. He had feet of clay. Indeed, no folk hero like Michael Dwyer could ever live up to the heroic image and the sanitised reputation that an emerging nation bestowed posthumously on him. [10]

At another level, Dwyer's feet of clay matter not a jot. He was not remembered for his shortcomings; he was remembered for his strengths. He decided to fight at Derrynamuck, and it was hardly his fault that he did not fight until he died! Whatever he may have done in later life cannot change that fact. It was Dwyer's admirable guerrilla campaign that etched him into the popular memory and many folk-ballads continued to cement Dwyer's place in folklore. Dwyer's guerrilla campaign also ensured that West Wicklow and especially Dunlavin parish remained violent places for nearly six years – seven, if one includes the reign of terror inflicted on the area from the autumn of 1797 onwards. In other parts of Ireland the 1798 rebellion lasted but a few weeks or months – truly the Dunlavin area of West Wicklow was the scene of longest rebellion.

NOTES

1: See, for example, TCD, 1641 Depositions, County Wicklow, ff 1150, 1152, 1153.

2: See, for example, TCD, 1641 Depositions, County Wicklow, ff 22, 1274, 1306.

3: See, for example, TCD, 1641 Depositions, County Wicklow, ff 1978, 1982, 1990.

4: Tallon, Geraldine (ed), Court of Claims: Submissions and Evidence 1663, Dublin, 2006, p.156,157.

5: http://www.malahide.dublin.anglican.org/blog/?page_id=32 [visited 5/7/2002].

6: Pakenham, 1972, p.226/227.

7: Pakenham, 1972, p.291/292.

8: Comerford, R. V., County Kildare and the Famine, in Lest we forget – Kildare and the Great Famine, Kildare Co. Council, Leinster Leader Ltd., 1995, p.18.

9: Kevin Whelan: Fellowship of Freedom: The United Irishmen and 1798, Cork, 1998, p.105.

10: Sheedy, 1988, p.263.

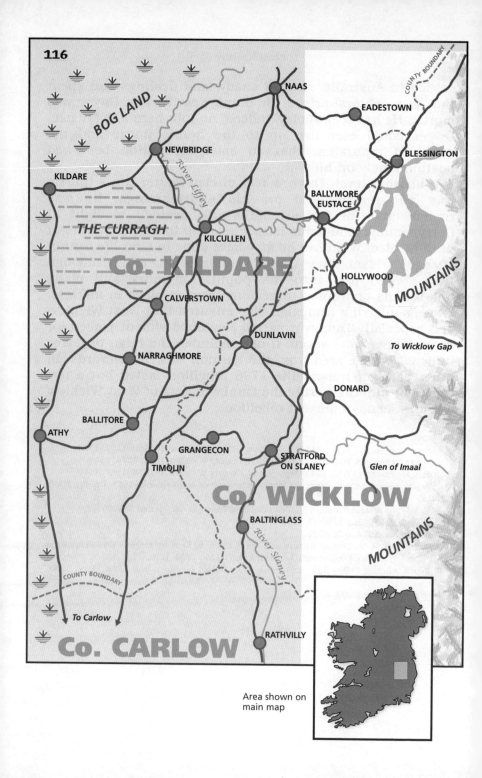

Area shown on main map

APPENDIX 1 THE DUNLAVIN MASSACRE

The Ballad Dunlavin Green

DUNLAVIN GREEN

In the year of one thousand seven hundred and ninety eight
A sorrowful tale the truth unto you I'll relate
Of thirty-six heroes to the world were left to be seen
By a false information were shot on Dunlavin Green
Bad luck to you, Saunders, for you did their lives betray
You said a parade would be held on that very day
Our drums they did rattle-our fifes they did sweetly play
Surrounded we were and privately marched away
Quite easy they led us as prisoners through the town
To be slaughtered on the plain, we then were forced to kneel down
Such grief and such sorrow were never before there seen
When the blood ran in streams down the dykes of Dunlavin Green
There is young Matty Farrell, has plenty of cause to complain
Also the two Duffys, who were shot down on the plain
And young Andy Ryan, his mother distracted will run
For her own brave boy, her beloved eldest son
Bad luck to you, Saunders, bad luck may you never shun!
That the widow's curse may melt you like snow in the sun
The cries of the orphans whose murmurs you cannot screen
For the murder of their dear fathers, on Dunlavin Green
Some of our boys to the hills they are going away
Some of them are shot, and some of them going to sea
Micky Dwyer in the mountains to Saunders he owes a spleen
For his loyal brothers, who were shot on Dunlavin Green

The standard form of this ballad [Hodgart, 1965, p.202].

A LAMENTATION ON THE HEROES WHO WERE SHOT ON DUNLAVIN GREEN

In the year of one thousand seven hundred and ninety eight
A sorrowful ditty to you I am going to relate
Concerning those heroes both clever and rare to be seen
By false information were shot upon Dunlavin green.
Woe to you Saunders, disgrace me you never shall
That the tears of the widows may melt you like snow before the sun
Those fatherless orphans! Their cries nor moans can't be screened
For the loss of their fathers, who were shot upon Dunlavin Green
Some of our heroes are 'listed and gone far away
There are some of them dead, and some of them crossing the sea
As for poor Andy Ryan, his mother distracted has been
For the loss of her son, who was shot upon Dunlavin Green
As for Andy Farrell, I'm sure he has cause to complain
And likewise the two Duffys, I'm sure they may well do the same
Dwyer on the mountain, to the orange he owes a great spleen
For the loss of his comrades, who were shot upon Dunlavin Green
They were marched from the guard house up to the end of the town
And when they came there the poor fellows were forced to kneel down
Like lambs for the slaughter that day it was plain to be seen
Their blood ran in streams on the dykes of Dunlavin Green
That we may live happy the joyful tidings to hear
When we will have satisfaction for the murders they did in that year
There were thirty-six heroes, both clever and rare to be seen
Both Loyal and United, shot one day on Dunlavin Green
Now to conclude, and finish my mournful tale
I hope all good Christians to pray for their souls will not fail
Their souls in white pigeons, a-flying to heaven were seen
On the very same day they were shot upon Dunlavin Green

The White Collection in the Library of Trinity College, Dublin.

DUNLAVIN GREEN

Of the year seventeen hundred and ninety-eight
A sorrowful ditty and I am going to relate
Of thirty-six heroes whose like were never seen
Who by false information were shot on Dunlavin Green
They were marched from the market house and up through the town
And coming to the green they were ordered to kneel down
Oh such horror and such terror, the like were never seen
When those heroes lay bleeding in the dykes of Dunlavin Green
When the sad news came to each village and each town
Some were a sowing and more were a mowing
And more were following the ploughs
While their wives were a spinning and milking the cows
They gave up the sowing and mowing and creeping stealthily along
Their briars and their ditches and leaping o'er walls so strong
They came to the green and to their grief were seen
The heroes lying in their gore in the dykes of Dunlavin Green
I am sure Nancy Ryan has reason to complain
And the two late Duffys can in sorrow do the same
And Mat Byrne whose fine son distracted had he been
At the slaughter of the heroes shot on Dunlavin Green
My curse on you Saunders, bad luck may you never shun
May the tears of widows and orphans melt you like the snow before the sun
May poverty and sorrow on you and yours be seen
For the slaughter of those heroes in the dykes of Dunlavin Green

Shearman Papers in the Russell Library, N.U.I. Maynooth

APPENDIX 2 THE DUNLAVIN MASSACRE

The Executed Men

YEOMEN – SAUNDERSGROVE CORPS

James Mara (Maher)
John Williams
Andrew Ryan
Patrick Duffy
James Duffy
John Webb
Patrick Curran
David Lee
Mat Kavanagh
Richard Kelly
Morgan Doyle
Thomas Doyle
Mat Farrell
James Moran
Charles Evers
William Dwyer
Thomas Brien
David Prendergast

Of these, the two Doyles were farmers from the Rathbarn (Stratford-on-Slaney) area. Mat Farrel was also a farmer. One of the Doyles was also a sub-constable. The Duffy brothers were masons. Five of the men were servants of Morley Saunders and there was also a smith and a slater among them.

YEOMEN – NARRAGHMORE CORPS

James Keating
Thomas Keating
Martin Walsh
Edward Shaughnessy
Andrew Carty
Darby Byrne
John Dunne
Martin Griffin
Daniel Kirwam
Thomas Kirwan
Laurence Doyle
Thomas Neile

Of these, the two Keatings were masons and were definitely related. Martin Walsh was a nailor. Edward Shaughnessy, Andrew Carty and Darby Byrne were all labourers – in those non-mechanical days many agricultural labourers were needed, of course.

NON-YEOMEN FROM THE AREA

John Dwyer, Seskin
Peter Hayden, Imaal (Keadeen)
Peter Kearney, Donard
Laurence Doyle, Dunlavin

Laurence Doyle was a local carpenter. John Dwyer, who had been in the market house for about four weeks, was a relation of rebel leader Michael Dwyer and probably a United Irish baronial delegate for Co. Wicklow. Peter Hayden's family were republican sympathisers, (if not before the massacre, certainly afterwards) and they helped Michael Dwyer later. [1]

OTHER LISTS AND NAMES

John Keeravan, {Brothers of Uppertown, Dunlavin.
Daniel Keeravan {Printed as Reeravan in The Sham Squire.
Laurence Doyle, Dunlavin.
Martin Gryffin (at 21 he came from Dublin the night before to see his father and was not connected with United men).
Duffy {Brothers of
Duffy {Baltinglass.
Mathew Farrell, Stratford on Slaney.
Michael Neil [Dunlavin].
Andrew Ryan, Shrucka.
Richard Williams, Ballinacrow.
Keatinge {of Narraghmore
Keatinge {[brothers].
Edward Slattery, Narraghmore .
Andrew Prendergast of Ballina?
Peter Kearney, Donard .
John Dwyer do, uncle to Capt. Michael Dwyer.
John Kearney, Donard.
Peter Headon, Killabeg.
Thomas Brien, Ballinacrow Hill.
John Doyle, Scrughawn.
Morgan Doyle, Tuckmill, Baltinglass.
John Doyle do.
Webb, Baltinglass.
John Wickham, Eadestown.
Wickham do.
Costelloe.
Bermingham {Brothers of Narraghmore,
Bermingham {belonging to Col. Keatinge's corps.
Patrick Moran, Tuckmill.
Peter Prendergast of Bumbo Hall, wounded in the belly and escaped. [2]

Father John Francis Shearman provides extra names for victims, and given the fact that so many sources are so definite that thirty-six men were shot, the other victims were those hanged at the market house after the shootings.

Peadar Mac Suibhne also names John Brien. [3] O'Brien was only captured on the day of the massacre. He fought under Darby Neill and Captain James O'Doherty in the Ballyshannon area. He was captured in the gravel pit at Narraghmore after the battle of Pike Bridge. He was taken to Dunlavin and was executed. He was survived by his mother. The fact that he was arrested individually and was not part of any of the groups of prisoners housed in the market house before the massacre may account for his name being omitted from both local folklore and Charles Dickson's book.

The Leinster Leader, on 25 September 1948, [4] also names Joe Hawkins. Ironically he was the spy who gave information leading to the arrests of the Saundersgrove yeomen in the first place. The fact that he was an informer would certainly have led to his name being deliberately omitted from the local folk-memory. The Leinster Leader stated: 'The order was to execute in groups of five, and finding that one group had only four men, the spy Hawkins, who had already given information leading to the arrests, was forcibly compelled to take his place in the group of four to make up five, and was executed with them.'

These lists contain some degree of overlap, but it is certain that more than thirty six prisoners were executed. The probable total is somewhere between forty five and fifty.

NOTES
1: Dickson, 1944, p.370-371 (naming 34).
2: Shearman papers in NUI Maynooth (naming 30).
3: Mac Suibhne, Peadar, Kildare in '98, Naas, 1978, p.133.
4: The Leinster Leader, 25 September 1948, p.3.

APPENDIX 3 BALLADS ABOUT MICHAEL DWYER

THE THREE FLOWERS

One day when walking down a lane as night was drawing nigh
I met a colleen with three flowers and she more young than I
'Saint Patrick bless you, dear,' said I, 'if you be quick and tell
The place where you did find those flowers
– I seem to know them well'

She took and kissed the first flower once and sweetly said to me
'This flower I found in Wicklow hills, dew wet and pure,' said she.
'Its name is Michael Dwyer – he's the bravest of them all
And I'll keep it fresh beside my breast,
though all the world should fall'

She took and kissed the next flower twice and sweetly said to me
'This flower I found in Antrim fields outside Belfast,' said she
'The name I gave it is Wolfe Tone – the bravest flower of all
And I'll keep it fresh beside my breast,
though all the world should fall'

She took and kissed the next flower trice and sweetly said to me
'This flower I found in Thomas Street, in Dublin fair,' said she
'Its name is Robert Emmet – the youngest of them all
And I'll keep it fresh beside my breast,
though all the world should fall'

'Then Emmet, Dwyer and Tone I'll keep, for I do love them all
And I'll keep them fresh beside my breast,
though all the world should fall'

ON CAPTAIN DWYER

Draw nigh, ye sons of liberty
Come listen to my story
It's truth to you I will relate
It's of Hibernia's glory

All in the chains of slavery
Since Cromwell and his damned decree
Has robbed us of our liberty
But now the time is over

Now the time is drawing nigh
When we shall be delighted
Those heroes brave on Wicklow plains
So boldly and firmly United

No Orange tyrants of the land
Nor cavalry can them withstand
They fly like chaff before the wind
With dread in heart sincerely

There is Captain Dwyer from Imail
A stout true-hearted member
That bloody twenty fourth of May [1]
He can very well remember
Then the cavalry, like birds of prey
Exulting in their tyranny
And many a bleeding victim lay
Along the streets of Stratford

This hero brave oft did declare
That he'd have full satisfaction
As soon as he could well prepare
To join in warlike action

But soon the boys, they did him join
And Hacketstown surrounded
With pike and gun they made them run
Their schemes were soon confounded

Captain Byrne was there that day [2]
As stout as Alexander,
That Hardy and his troops knew well [3]
For shortly they were conquered

To hear them bawl, to shout and run
Crying out that they were now undone
At every corner of the town
They were driven to destruction

Those heroes brave, with loud huzzas
Maintained the fight with valour
The soldiers, to protect their lives
Retired within their barrack

But soon did Dwyer, with Holt and Neal [4]
And Reynolds too, that man of fame [5]
Set the town and barrack in a flame
Which caused a deal of ruin

continued over

The next attack was in Keadun bog [6]
When they met with Captain Dwyer
One hundred cavalry and more
On him began to fire

He and six more behaved so well
The cavalry to their grief may tell
You would laugh to see how many fell
And wallowed in the mire

Out of six he lost but one
Yet they were something hasty
Of soldiers more than half a score
He gave them much vexation

To think how he had so much odds
And they were hampered in the bogs
Which made them curse and blame their Gods
That they had them forsaken

There is a curse o'er Baltinglass
And likewise o' er Dunlavin
For spilling innocent blood thereon
Which is for vengeance calling

Those vicious hearts that took delight
In deeds of blood both day and night
But our heroes brave gave them a fright
That their wits have them forsaken

Now to conclude and make an end

Let us fill up our glasses

And drink to every daring man

While time and season passes

And steady in themselves, prepare

The green cockade once more to wear

Drive tyrant villains to despair

And that's our only glory

NOTES

1: Dunlavin massacre and battle of Stratford.

2: Garret Byrne of Ballymanus.

3: Captain Thomas Hardy, Hacketstown yeomanry.

4: Joseph Holt of Mullinaveigue near Roundwood – later transported to Australia and 'Big John' Neal – later an informer.

5: Michael Reynolds of Johnstown near Naas, killed at the battle of Hacketstown.

6: The battle of Keadeen, September 1798.

THE OUTLAW'S BRIDE

As the torrent bounds down from the mountain
Of cloud-helmed stormy Kaigeen
And tosses, all tawny and foaming
Through the still glen of lone Carrageen

So dashed a bold rider of Wicklow
With forty stout men in his train
From the heart of the hills, where the spirit
Of Freedom has dared to remain!

Of grey frieze their caps and their surcoats
Their carbines were close to their knee
And their belts were well furnished with pistols
Like men who knew how to be free!

Oh! grass-green the sash on their-shoulders
Their caps crested green, with cockades
And their leader he wore a long dagger
The brightest and keenest of blades

To the right ran Imale's lovely valley
And before them was meadow and mound
And the gallop of freemen was music
The echoes sprang out to resound!

Thou leader of horsemen! why hasten
So fleetly to Brusselstown hill?
What foemen, what yeomen await thee
To question, in Wicklow, thy will?

No foemen or yeomen they're seeking
Though furiously onward they ride
But their leader, he loves a young maiden
And he's speeding to make her his bride!

'Halt!' Bridles were drawn, and they halted
There's a farmstead looming ahead
And the door of the dwelling is open
Now the leader rode forward and said

'There's somebody seeking thee, Mary
A boy who came down from Kaigeen
With forty brave bridesmen from Laragh
With cockades and crosses of green!'

Oh! Mary came out in her beauty
The loveliest maid of Imale
The loveliest flower that blossomed
In all the wild haunts of the vale

Arrayed in an emerald habit
And the green and the white in her hair
The Leader, he sprang from his courser
As light as a hawk from the air

He pressed her fair hand to his bosom
She felt the big throb of his heart
'My Mary! I'll love thee forever
'Till God on this earth will us part!'   continued over

They led out a horse on the heather
She patted his neck with her hand
Then sprang on his back like a feather
And stood in the midst of the band!

The leader was soon in his saddle
'Castle Ruddery's ruins!' he cried
'The priest's house is near to Green's river
And here is the ring for my bride'

Away dashed the cavalcade fleetly
By beauty and chivalry led
With their carbines aflash in the sunlight
And the saucy cockades on their head!

The priest he demurred and he pleaded
The maiden she blushed and she frowned
And the Leader of Forty felt nervous
And tapped with his gun on the ground!

And thus went the parley, till even
Began to fall down on the glen
And the priest thought a matron were better
To be 'mid such wild bearded men!

They were wedded 'To horse!' cried the Leader
 And the bridal pair led the hot flight
And away rode Dwyer, the Outlaw
To his mountain-cave, back in the night!

ON AN ESCAPE OF DWYER

On a wintry night as the turgid stream
Rolled down the mountainside,
From the vault of heaven no star did gleam
And nought was heard beside
But the rumbling roar of the mountain flood
As it fretted into ire
And deluged the cave where the outlaws stood
With their manly Captain Dwyer
The noble hearted Dwyer

Affection's fame ne'er warmed the blood
Of more devoted men
Drenched by snow, by storm and flood
They seek some friend to screen
But they little know that the spy is on
Nought can stay his foul desire
And he tells in gold, each ounce, each dram
Of the blood of Captain Dwyer
Of the single hearted Dwyer

Three friendly doors are opened wide
To aid the brave distressed,
Three pickets set and their arms are tried
They take themselves to rest
Through drifting snow and mountain storm
O'er glen, through bog and mire
In the dead of night the foeman comes
To seize on Captain Dwyer
On the terror striking Dwyer

continued over

The arrant Scot proposed a truce
Oh, base and treacherous man
But brave Dwyer threw back his overture
Saying 'We can die like men'
The innocent babes you will set free
Their mother and their sire
And all your vengeance heap on me
I am the captain Dwyer.
My name is Michael Dwyer

But the kilted foes around them set
And fired the house of Connel
Those hungry Scots, the hound of death
Ah, shame on you McDonnell
Spirits of the dead, the butchered of Glencoe
Look down with vengeful ire
On you, degenerate sons, the murdering crew
That sought the life of Dwyer
Of the freedom loving Dwyer

The awful blaze ascends the sky
Bullets quick are flying
Within, there is blood, but no dismay
Without the Scots are dying
And there is no surrender from the few
Not scared by balls, by wounds or fire
Nor the blazing roof cannot subdue
The noble soul of Dwyer
The lion hearted Dwyer

The noblest deed in annal found

And purest in devotion

Sam McAlister receives a wound

See that soul's emotion

But the chieftain laid the foeman low

In gasping death to expire

His winding sheet's the drifting snow

He fell by the hand of Dwyer

By the unerring hand of Dwyer

'I'll sell my life to save my friend'

Said the noblest blood of Ulster

'I'll rush out and dare the Scottish fiends,

So perish Sam McAlister

And then desperate fire they'll pour on me

Then all I do require

Is to embrace that moment and be free

My gallant Captain Dwyer

Oppression's hater Dwyer

Then the manly chief, in softening mood

Embraced his wounded friend

'Oh no, for I'll fall with the brave and good

And so struggle till the end'

But rushing forth from the leader now

The hero met their fire

And purpled o'er the virgin snow

To save his captain Dwyer

The persecuted Dwyer

continued over

The furious Dwyer with vengeance strove
Against their whole array
Disdaining death, he nobly stood
And kept the Scots at bay
Like goaded lion from his den
Or tiger from his lair
And beckoning on his last two men
The true, the faithful Dwyer
The vengeance vowing Dwyer

Brave men, they fell and nobly bled
Among the gallant slain
The name of Savage long will shed
Its memory o'er that plain
And Costeloe, that brave young man
The last to quit the fire
Was butchered by the unholy clan
As a vengeance on brave Dwyer
The high priced head of Dwyer

MICHAEL DWYER

Have you heard of Michael Dwyer and his mountain men?
Runs your blood like molten fire when you hear again
How he dashed like mountain torrent on his country's bitter foes
Like a thundering, tearing torrent on the craven yeos?

<u>Chorus</u>
Here's the chorus, chant it loudly on the still night air
As the war shout rises proudly o'er the trumpet's blare
Chant it! Peal it! Till it echoes over every hill and glen
Here's to gallant Michael Dwyer and his mountain men

When the stars of freedom vanished and our flag went down
And the nation's hope was banished from each vale and town
Borne intact through blood and fire, Ireland's banner waved again
Held aloft by Michael Dwyer and his mountain men (Chorus)

Still the nation's hopes are burning as they burned of yore
And the young and strong are yearning for the battle's roar,
But the blessed star of liberty shall never blaze again
Till we strike like Michael Dwyer and his mountain men (Chorus).

THE BALLAD OF MICHAEL DWYER

At length brave Michael Dwyer and his undaunted men
Were scented o'er the mountains and tracked into the glen
The stealthy soldiers followed, with ready blade and ball
And swore to trap that outlaw that night in wild Emall

They prowled around the valley, and towards the dawn of day
Discovered where the faithful and fearless heroes lay
Around the little cottage they formed in a ring
And called out 'Michael Dwyer! Surrender to the King!'

Thus answered Michael Dwyer 'Into this house we came
Unasked by those who own it they cannot be to blame
Then let those guiltless people, unquestioned, pass you through,
And when they've passed in safety, I'll tell you what we'll do'

'Twas done. 'And now' says Dwyer 'your work you may begin
You are a hundred outside we're only four within
We've heard your haughty summons, and this is our reply
We're true United Irishmen we'll fight until we die'

Then burst the war's red lightning, then poured the leaden rain
The hills around re-echoed the thunder-peal again
The soldiers falling round him brave Dwyer sees with pride
But, ah! one gallant comrade is wounded by his side

Yet there are three remaining, good battle still to do
Their hands are strong and steady, their aim is quick and true
But hark, that furious shouting the savage soldiers raise!
The house is fired around them! the roof is in ablaze!

And brighter every moment the lurid flame arose
And louder swelled the laughter and cheering of their foes
Then spake the brave McAllister, the weak and wounded man
You can escape, my comrades, and this shall be your plan

'Place in my hands a musket, then lie upon the floor
I'll stand before the soldiers, and open wide the door
They'll pour into my bosom the fire of their array
Then, while their guns are empty, dash through them and away!'

He stood before the foemen, revealed amidst the flame
From out their levelled pieces the wished-for volley came
Up sprang the three survivors for whom the hero died
But only Michael Dwyer burst through the ranks outside

He baffled his pursuers, who followed like the wind
He swam the river Slaney, and left them far behind
But many a scarlet soldier he promised soon would fall
For those, his gallant comrades, who died in wild Emall

APPENDIX 4 COURTS MARTIAL RECORDS

Number One

Proceedings of a General Court Martial held at Baltinglass on the 19th February 1799 by order of his Excellency the Lord Lieutenant.

President: Captain Bellock	Dumfries Lt. Dragoons
Members: Captain Blood	Clare Militia
Captain Jackson	ditto
Lieut. Eams	ditto
Lieut. De Renzy	Wicklow Militia
Lieut. Comyns	Clare Militia
Lieut. Drew	ditto
Cornet Shaw	Dumfries Lt. D
Ensign Whitedown	Clare Militia
Ensign England	Acting Judge Advocate

Michael Doyle for Rebellion, robbery and murder.

James Whelan the evidence against the prisoner having suffered death in pursuance of his Excellency's warrant, here follows the affidavit sworn by him before his death and was sworn it enclosed.

Prisoner's defence
Michael Doyle denies whole

Sentence
The court having considered the evidence contained in the affidavit sworn by James Whelan before his death are of opinion that Michael Doyle is guilty and do therefore sentence him to be transported for life.
C. Bellock, Captain, Dumfries Lt. D. and President

County of Wicklow
To Wit:
James Whelan of Fryenstown in said county being duly sworn on the Holy Evangelists and examined, said that on the evening of the 22nd of December last he went to the house of James Hughes of Stratford with John Riley of Wine Tavern and Michael Doyle of Stratford and the said Michael Doyle asked the defendant to accompany him towards Manger Bridge along the road with J. Reilly, that the said Michael Doyle after they came part of the way, pulled out from below his coat a short gun and bayonet and that Reilly had a pistol, that Michael Doyle informed the defendant that he was going to rob Farrel Doyle, that he thought it reason[able]? to rob him as after the battle of Stratford he would not give him a night's lodging or any other substance; that the said Farrel Doyle had a good quantity of bacon and money, that his wife had three rings and a pair of silver buckles, that said Michael Doyle gave this defendant the pistol and the bayonet and desired him to go into the said house and told him to

say that they came from Captain Dwyer* and that he and those with him were sent to burn the houses of James Valentine, Patrick Price and Mrs. Valentine and that if he did not behave like a stout fellow the said Michael Doyle swore he would shoot him; that the said Michael Doyle said he would not enter the house least he should be known; that the said Michael Doyle desired to give the said Farrel Doyle some stabs of the bayonet if he did not give him money. The defendant then rapped at the door of Farrel Doyle's house which he entered and told the said Farrel Doyle that there were some men at the door who wanted money and after some conversation he took a guinea and half a crown which he took out to the said John Riley and Michael Doyle. The said Michael Doyle snatched the gun from Riley and asked the defendant how much he had got. When the defendant told them Riley said he was "too soft" and the said Michael Doyle swore violently he would shoot him if he did not go in again and take the three rings and ten guineas – and desired the defendant to put all the people of the house into the room until he would go in for the bacon and also desired the defendant to get shirts etc; that the defendant went in and requested Mrs. Doyle to conceal her rings and buckles as he was not willing to take them. When the defendant went out of the house said Riley told him that he had entered the house and taken out the bacon and made the defendant assist to carry part of it up Manger Hill. The said Michael Doyle took two parts of the said bacon and Riley one which the said Riley took home with him to Randalstown to the back of his father's house and the said Michael Doyle took his part down the road towards Manger Bridge using the precaution of stripping off his coat lest it should be soiled with it. That the said Mrs. Doyle's petticoat was taken by Riley and a pair of stockings which the defendant took from Mrs. Doyle of which the said Michael Doyle and John Riley took one stocking each. That the said Michael Doyle told the defendant that he was one of the persons along with Michael Kehoe who before robbed said Farrel Doyle of [?] money and clothes of all sorts and not short of as much as would make him up forever. That said things he found concealed in a tub or chest barrel in an outhouse belonging to Farrel Doyle and that the boy who then lived with him knew how things were situated in the house. The said Kehoe had his plunder stored in his house under the ash [?], and wanted the said Whelan to go with him and take them from the said Kehoe on the night of the 6th January inst. The defendant was sick having recently too much and the said Michael Doyle went from him towards Farrel Doyle's, stayed some little time and returned with Riley and charged the defendant with having dropped some words in the town of Stratford about his former robbery of Farrel Doyle that if he was convinced of it he would instantly go to [Original torn] and asked him to now own to [Original torn] towards which in a ditch the defendant attempted to stoop down to hide a watch and pocket book. The said Michael Doyle made a violent thrust at him with a bayonet, which was fixed on a fork and short handle with two iron rings and which he drew through the thigh of the said defendant and then called out to John Riley to fire at him which he attempted to do but his pistol missed fire. Whelan ran from them and made his escape. The defendant further says that he heard the said Michael Doyle and John Riley say that they and a Curtis Doyle of Randalstown were the persons who attempted to rob the office of Messrs. Orrs of Stratford in November last and would have effectively done so had it not been for the cowardice of the men who stood frightened, who called them off before they could break open the only door which they to effect to come at the money, as they thought.

James Whelan before me this day 11th day of January 1799.

Morley Saunders

Examined bound in the sum of Fifty pounds still to appear and prosecute To be next [assizes]? being considered an evidence bound in the examination under which _____ pleaded is _____ any although it is equally believed that the_____ is a notorious defendant. *[Gaps due to tears in original document]*

[*Probably Michael Dwyer]

19th February 1799

This document raises some interesting points. Firstly, Morley Saunders was still performing his duties in February 1799. Though there is evidence to suggest that a plot to kill Saunders was afoot in 1798, there is nothing to suggest that any actual attempt was made on his life. William Ryves, on the other hand, was the object of such an attempt, when his horse was shot from under him in a sniper-like attack in the townland of Usk shortly before the Dunlavin massacre. Secondly, the townland of Freyenstown lies just outside Dunlavin village (between Dunlavin itself and Stratford-on-Slaney), so there is no doubt that the continuing violence directly affected the Dunlavin area. Thirdly, from a legal point of view, one wonders how valid the evidence of the dead man, James Whelan, was in a court of law – considering that Whelan himself obviously could not attend! Would such evidence be permissible today? However, these were violent times, and the backlash in the wake of the uprising meant that the courts martial possibly did not 'stick too much to the quibbles of court of law' to quote Rev. Robinson regarding William Ryves! Fourthly, Doyle was perhaps lucky to be transported as the other court martial records show! The next one reads as follows:

Number Two

Proceeding of General Court Martial held at Baltinglass March 9th by order of his Excellency the Lord Lieutenant.

President: Captain Bellock	Drumfries Lt. Dragoons
Members: Captain Blood	Clare Militia
Lieut. Bridgeman	ditto
Lieut Eames	ditto
Lieut. De Renzy	Wicklow Militia
Lieut. Morrice	Clare Militia
Lieut. Comyns	ditto
Cornet Shaw,	Dumfries Lt. Dragoons
Ensign Whitedown	Clare Militia
Ensign England	Acting Judge Advocate

James Comyns for Rebellion and robbing Michael Fenton a yeoman of his arms, ammunition and accoutrements and making for the hills with said articles.

Michael Fenton sworn is a Yeoman in the Dunlavin Corps of Yeomanry. The prisoner lived in his house and in October last, he one night stole witness's arms, ammunition and accoutrements, viz. a musket and a bayonet, a cartridge box with fifteen rounds, broad sword and helmet, regimental coat and waistcoat. Witness hearing three weeks ago that the prisoner had been taken by a party of the Glengary Fencibles at Radagnan near Hacketstown, went there, saw the prisoner and identified his arms and accoutrements which he still had on when taken. The arms etc. etc. were produced before the Court and Michael Fenton's name found written in the inside of the coat and waistcoat. He swore the arms etc. etc. were his own and the same the prisoner had run away with.

Prisoner in his defence said that he had drunk too much whiskey and that he had committed the robbery in a fit of insobriety.

The Court having duly and maturely considered the evidence for and against the prisoner James Comyns are unanimously of opinion that he is guilty of the crime laid to his charge and do therefore sentence him to death.

[Jotted in afterwards]

C. Bellock, Captain, Drumfries Lt. D., President
Approved Cornwallis.
Baltinglass: 9th March '99
General Court Martial
No. 10
J. Comyns
Sentence: Death Confirmed
Trial of James Comyns for Rebellion and Robbery
9th March 1799

Once again, this court martial sees a member of the Dunlavin Yeomanry in the spotlight. Michael Fenton was probably a member of William Ryves' calvary corps though, as Saunders' corps was referred to as the Saundersgrove corps. Moreover, it is doubtful that any infantryman would have a broadsword. Of course, there is no doubt that many of the local yeomen sympathised with and even sheltered Michael Dwyer and his men. Without such help, it is doubtful whether Dwyer could have held out so long. The memory of the Dunlavin massacre probably played a part in many of the yeomen's sympathies towards Dwyer. The men executed on the fair green had been mostly fellow yeomen, from a suspected corps. Thus, many local yeomen 'turned a blind eye', though the Comyns and Fenton episode is obviously not a case in point!

Number Three

Proceedings of a General Court Martial held at Baltinglass, March 13th by order of his Excellency, the Lord Lieutenant.

President: Captain Bellock	Drumfries Lt. Dragoons.
Members: Captain Blood	Clare Militia
Lieut. Bridgeman	ditto
Lieut. Morrice	ditto
Lieut Eames	ditto
Lieut. De Renzy	Wicklow Militia
Lieut. Comyns	ditto
Cornet Shaw,	Dumfries Lt. Dragoons
Ensign Whitedown	Clare Militia
Ensign England	Acting Judge Advocate

Prisoner
John Byrns for Rebellion and carrying arms against His Majesty's forces.

Joseph Hawkins sworn is a yeoman in the Honourable Captain Stratford's corps, went out with a party in October last to the Glen of Emale where many houses had been burnt by the rebels. Said Party came up with some of the rebels, prisoner was among them and witness had known him a long time before. After some shots had been exchanged the rebels ran away, the prisoner himself was pursued by witness and some other yeomen. Prisoner ran into a boggy ground and leapt over a large ditch and then fired his piece at the yeomen, who being on horseback could not follow him in the bog. Prisoner got clear off and carried his arms with him. Witness hearing that prisoner had been taken by a party of the Glengary Fencibles, went to Hacketstown and identified him. Witness swore that prisoner was the man who fired at him in the Glen of Emale.

James Fenton sworn is a yeoman in Captain Hume's corps, was out with the party that went in October last to the Glen of Emale under the command of Lieutenant Downy of the 89th Regiment. The party fell in with the rebels in the Glen and put them to fright. Witness corroborates the evidence given by Joseph Hawkins and was himself fired at by the prisoner after he had cleared the ditch.

Lawrence Doyle sworn is a servant of Lieutenant Fenton of Mr. Hume's corps, was driving a cart loaded with leather belonging to his master in November last. He was met by the prisoner who was armed with a musket and who asked him whose leather it was? Witness said it was Mr. Fenton's. Prisoner then said he did not want the leather, but that if the "rascally Orange-man" (his master) was ever in his way, he should sell leather no more. Mr. Fenton is a leather merchant.

Prisoner acknowledged the truth of the evidence and begged to be transported to any of His Majesty's Dominions.

Sentence: The Court having duly and maturely considered the evidence for and against the prisoner, John Byrns, are unanimously of opinion that he is guilty of rebelliously carrying

arms against his majesty's troops and do therefore sentence him to death.
C. Bellock, Captain, Drumfries Lt. Dragoons. President.

[Jotted in afterwards]

Approved Cornwallis
Baltinglass No. 15
Trial of John Byrns for Rebellion
13th March 1799
John Byrns
No. 15
13th March 1799

This mentions a yeoman called Fenton (probably related to the Michael Fenton of number two above). James Fenton, Joseph Hawkins and Laurence Doyle all gave evidence against John Byrns concerning an incident that occurred in the Glen of Imaal. This area, as we have already noted, forms part of Dunlavin parish and is well within the immediate hinterland of the village. Byrns, like Comyns, was not lucky enough to be transported, and the death sentence was passed and approved by Lord Cornwallis.

Number Four

Dublin 18th December 1800

Sir,

I had the honour to receive your letter communicating to me His Excellency's commands that I should point out specifically the steps necessary to be taken in the case of William Noude or Genoude in consequence of the several papers and documents transmitted to me all of which I herewith return.

You will please to inform His Excellency that in my opinion a Court Martial should be ordered to assemble, before which Noude or Genoude should be brought a prisoner. The person acting as advocate general should have the proceedings of the Court Martial which tried Noude or Genoude in his hands and lay them before the Court. He should then call on Noude or Genoude and state to him that at a Court Martial heretofore held at Baltinglass, stating the time from the proceedings, he had been tried for the crimes stated in the proceedings, setting them forth that he had been found guilty thereof; that sentence of death and execution thereon had adjudged and awarded against him which judgement could not since be carried into execution in consequence of his having broken out of prison then to demand of him if he has anything to say why judgement of death and execution thereon should not now be awarded against him agreeable to the sentence before passed. It is probable he will confess himself to be the same person who was before tried, if so the Court will record it; if not his identity must be proved by calling on Lieutenant Rawson and any other of the persons mentioned in the same information with him, which must likewise recorded if so found or a contra.

If his identity is found a warrant I think may then issue for his execution.

This I humbly beg leave to submit is the regular and proper mode of proceeding on the present occasion.

I have etc. etc.

Francis Patterson

Col Littlehales

Proceedings of a General Court Martial held at Baltinglass 22nd December 1800 by virtue an order from his Excellency the Lord Lieutenant of which Lieut. Colonel Hugh Dive of the D.Y.R. is President.

Members: Captain Alan Cobban	D.Y.R. Highland Regiment
Captain John Feeny	D.Y.R. Highland Regiment
Lieut John Gibson	D.Y.R. Highland Regiment
Lieut George MacKenzie	Caithness Legion

The President, members of the Court and Captain Robert Grant D.Y.R. Highlanders acting Judge Advocate duly sworn proceeded to identify William Genoud.

The Judge advocate having read the proceedings of a Court Martial on the prisoner

Genoud and others held at Baltinglass on the 6th November 1798. The sentence of which adjudged suffer death by being hanged and having demanded of the prisoner what he had to say in defence and why that sentence should not now be put in execution. The prisoner acknowledged himself to be William Genoud and that he was the same person tried by the foresaid court martial, but says that after he escaped from the Guard House he got a protection from the Honourable Captain Stratford and remained between three and four months at his house until he was driven from it by some yeomen.

The Honourable Captain Stratford being sworn deposes that he did write a note to Genoud saying that he would endeavour to obtain his pardon provided he would give useful information as he understood he could discover where many arms were concealed. That the Deponent wrote Government in his favour and got an answer to say that if the Prisoner made these discoveries the recommendation would be attended to ,that the deponent told the prisoner's wife of the above terms intimating to her that if the prisoner did not by a certain day came forward and made such discovery that he would consider the protection withdrawn, and says the prisoner did not come in nor make any discovery whatever.

Captain King being sworn

Question by the prisoner: Whether some time after he escaped from the Guard House if he remembered the prisoner's wife applying to him to know why her husband was pursued having Captain Stratford's protection and Captain King says he did not, but would enquire of Captain Stratford:

Answer: He did remember her asking him such a question was his answer.

Robert Grant	**H Dive**
acting as Judge Advocate	**Lieut. Colonel**
	President

Proceedings of a Court Marital held at Baltinglass on 22nd December 1800 to identify Mander or Genoud.
Warrant drawn the 24th December 1800

Additional Memorandum

I asked Genoud if he could say anything in his justification or if he could say or do anything that might incline the Government to extend mercy to him.

He replied that he could not say anything in his defence, that the crimes he was guilty of he was told deserved death, but that there were great numbers out who deserved it more than he did, that he could not now say, or do, anything that would incline Government to extend mercy to him.

I was, when leaving Baltinglass followed by Genoude's wife who told me that if he was removed from Baltinglass to one of the neighbouring prisons he would give valuable information.

Joseph Nicholson, Aide de Camp

Horse hire and expenses in Baltinglass for Edward Dowling, Richard Kirwan, Christopher Bently and John Taylor, it being unsafe for them to return last night: £0-19-6d.

Memorandum of what passed between the prisoner Genoude and Ensign Nicholson, Aide de Camp Baltinglass. 15th December 1800.

This document was dated 22 December 1800. The new century had not seen an end of violence in the West Wicklow area! William Genoud had actually been captured, escaped and been recaptured. The Hon. Benjamin O'Neale Stratford (familiar to us from some of his correspondence to Dublin Castle) appeared at this court martial. Once again, the sentence was death, and the death warrant itself was actually drawn up on Christmas Eve 1800.

APPENDIX 5 LETTERS FROM KILMAINHAM

Number One

Kilmainham Gaol
January 21st 1805

Dear Sir,

The high opinion that I always entertained of your honour and veracity induced me to surrender myself to the Government on your faith beyond that of any other gentleman of the County. The terms on which I surrendered you will be pleased to recollect. I am conscious that the violation of such terms in any manner is not with your consent or even privacy, and whereas such violation now had place, I think myself warranted in giving you an understanding through praying your enquiring into the nature of my complaints and if just your immediate remedy of them.

Agreeable to your promise I received very good treatment until the first of July 1804 (my over close confinement excepted) and which day I was ordered into the yard with the other prisoners. The allowance of tea, sugar, and spirits granted me theretofore was on said day entirely stopped from me by Dr. Trevor – after expostulating with Dr. Trevor I requested of him not to deprive me of the spirits, as my health would suffer materially by being debarred of that to which I had been, necessarily, so long accustomed. All in vain, I was deprived of the entire. I was at same time debarred the company of my wife in such sort as to prevent my breakfasting or dining with her. Dr. Trevor told me that if I did not tacitly observe his orders, he would put me into that part of the prison intended for capital offenders. I told him that asking for the spirits usually allowed me did not warrant such treatment, which was so entirely opposite to the faith of Government pledged to me by the Honourable Mr. Hume, and therefore I said I would not go unless I was forced. He called Mr. Dunn to take me over to the place appointed. I went with the jailer quietly and peaceably, fearing if I had acted otherwise I would have done wrong, and in the mean incurred your displeasure. I remained there eleven days destitute of any maintenance other than the county allowance.

Agreeable to your instructions I wrote to your uncle complaining to him of my situation; he came accordingly and caused me to be brought from my cell to the jailer's parlour, where in presence of the jailer he examined me very minutely. He could find no charge against me – I asked the jailer in his presence if he could learn from his own knowledge of one, or from the reports of any of the turnkeys or attendants, that any conduct in any degree warranted ill treatment, he declared he never knew a more quiet or peaceable man, but said Dr. Trevor is a very passionate man, upon which your uncle said that for that purpose of easily releasing myself from the present difficulty, I should beg the Doctor's pardon. I observed to him how painful it would be to beg pardon when I had not given offence of any kind but, that however painful it was, I would comply as it was his wish, observed to him at same time that I had conducted myself in such sort as to give offence to no person, considering that if my conduct was otherwise, it would be forfeiting the friendship and protection of the gentleman unto whom I surrendered and offering him the greatest insult. I returned to my cell to wait the arrival of the Doctor unto whom I told I had been sufficiently punished and would be very much obliged to him if he would suffer me to go back to my wife and children. He said he would, and asked me if I considered that it was Hume's interposition obtained my return. I said I did not know, but was satisfied his interposition would redeem me from a worse place and greater difficulties. Dr. Trevor then told me he did not punish me for any crime or offence of mine, but as an example for the rest of the prisoners!!!

I was afterwards given to understand that Dr. Trevor had been assessing my character by often times saying I was a savage or tyrant unfit for any society. Upon my being informed hereof I told Dr. Trevor 'your terms with me had been very much violated by such abuse', and he answered with an air of seeming disdain. 'Your terms, your terms, I know what your terms are better than yourself. You have no terms at all. There is no robber or highwayman could make better possible terms than saving his life, and the capital offence is where you and such persons ought to be.'

An investigation of the prisoners took place here some time after, before the Right Honourable Judges Downs and Day, unto whom I complained of the above treatment, which they seemed to disapprove very much and told Dr. Trevor it was highly improper, and said Dwyer's terms should not be by any means violated (to which lecture no attention was afterwards paid). I have never mentioned to Dr. Trevor what were my terms nor to any other person. Before the surrender of Arthur Devlin, Dr. Trevor said if he, Devlin, should surrender, Martin Burke's life should be saved and wrote a letter to that effect directed to Devlin which he received in Humewood. After his surrender such a letter was delivered to Burke's wife by the Doctor for Devlin. When Burke was afterwards sent for trial to Wicklow Dr. Trevor denied having held out any promise to him and said if Devlin had surrendered to him as he expected, and made terms for Burke as he had done with Hume, they should be treated well. Upon my mentioning to the Judges that Burke was sent for trial to Wicklow, they with astonishment asked me if Burke was hanged. I told them he was not and hoped he would never be hanged, whereas a gentleman had pledged his word for his safety. Judge Downs asked me who that gentleman was. I told him such promise was made to Arthur Devlin by Captain Hume at the surrender of said Devlin.

The above was declared by me upon oath before the Judges, and upon such declaration being made I desired Dr. Trevor should be called. I repeated the same before him upon oath, and desired that Dr. Trevor should be put to his oath, whereas he could in any respect contradict me. He declared upon his oath he believed I told the truth.

I now wish to know if such treatment is given to me and others who have surrendered to the government, on your faith, with your knowledge and concurrence. I am conscious it is not with your immediate knowledge or consent. I therefore, request your immediate enquiry into the nature of what I have herein related, and if you find upon minute enquiry that the above statement is true, I request immediate redress, agreeable to the implicit faith which I have placed in you.

I beg leave to remind you of the promises which you have made me, of your goodness, after my surrender, and hope you will by no means lose sight of them until you see them duly performed. I also return you my most sincere and grateful thanks for your kindness to me since the above period, and flatter myself with the assurance of a continuation of your protection and friendship.

I am, Honoured Sir,

Your most humble and obliged servant,

Michael Dwyer.

Number Two

**Kilmainham Gaol
January 9th 1805**

Honoured Sir,

At the time of my surrender the Government I had such implicit faith in your honour and veracity, as induced me not to have entertained the least doubt of seeing the conditions on which I had so surrendered faithfully observed and performed. On the contrary scarce any of them is performed. My Uncle Bryan Devlin and family were to have been restored to liberty, but to the poor man's irretrievable loss he, his son and daughter still are detained close prisoners. I have been promised some clothes, but these were not conditioned for; it was your goodness to promise them, and I hope for the performance of your promise. I shall say nothing further of any complaint until I shall have the honour of seeing and telling you thereof in person.

We are given to understand that a major part of the prisoners are ordered to be liberated, all I believe except those who are conditionally predisposed of. I also think it would be time to dispose of me, life is not by any means worth enjoying on my present terms, there would be no sort of utility to government in keeping me here for a long time and then suffering me to transport myself out of his Majesty's Dominions.

I therefore wish it to be done speedily and hope you will press that business for me on such sort as that I may be sent quickly, or otherwise that you would cause me to be again restored to liberty, which if I professed in such sort as to be under apprehensions, I would certainly by my future conduct render myself worthy. I also beg of you, at all events to cause my Uncle and his family to be restored to liberty as agreed upon at the time of my surrender.

I am Honourable Sir with respect,

Your most humble and obliged servant,

Arthur Devlin.

Number Three

Humewood
February 19th 1805

My Dear Sir,

There is scarcely a day passes that I am not tormented with letters or messages from those fellows in Kilmainham, who surrendered themselves to me – viz. Dwyer, Arthur Devlin and Hugh Byrne, complaining of ill treatment, of being almost naked, with various other complaints, and yesterday Dwyer's wife came here to tell me that she and her children had been turned out of the prison and that he was thrown into that part allocated for felons and put on the jail allowance and as she says without cause, which I am certain is not the fact.

But although I know there is no punishment too severe for them, yet it places me in a very awkward and unpleasant situation in this country to have these complaints made (however unfounded) that the terms I promised them to induce their surrender are not kept. It is now near fourteen months, I believe, since they surrendered. Is there any use in keeping them longer? If not, I must earnestly request that they may be sent off as soon as possible; for as long as they are kept in Kilmainham, I shall be tormented by them.

At the time they surrendered, you were in England. I told Mr. Wickham the terms I agreed to on their surrender which was that they should be sent off out of the Kingdom as soon as possible and that in the meantime they should not be ill treated in prison, that their relations who were confined merely on their accounts should be liberated, and that Dwyer's wife and children should be allowed to remain with him while in prison and sent along with him, and I assure you it cannot be of any service to this country, to have her at large here now. I therefore request that she may be confined again with her husband in Kilmainham, that is, if something very particular has not occurred to prevent it that I know nothing of at present. I enclose you some of letters they have sent me lately.

I am my Dear Sir
Yours most faithfully,
William Hoare Hume.

Number Four

Kilmainham Gaol
May 12th 1805

Sir,
As I don't know where to direct to your nephew, Mr. H. Hume Esq. and as you were pleased to say, that any terms which were made with me, you would see fulfilled, in his absence, I therefore call on you as a gentleman of Honour and Humanity to stand forth and save me from the effects of a flagrant breach of my conditions.

A very short time ago Dr. Trevor told me I should be sent away, and that not to America. I was alarmed and wrote to Mr. W. H. Hume twice but received no answer.

This day Dr. Trevor told me and the others who surrendered to Mr. Hume, to hold ourselves in readiness for that we should immediately be sent to Botany Bay, a ship being now ready. This communication, he declared, was by order of Government. Now Sir, my terms, which you well know, was to be sent to America, and my wife and children furnished with a comfortable passage along with me. But what is now attempted to be done? My solemn conditions are to be violated, the Sacred Honour of Mr. Hume is set at nought, and my wife and children are to be left without the smallest means of living or protection. This is such a terrible dereliction of everything which, even in uncivilized life, is held sacred that I know not what to do. The only thing which strikes me, is that you'll be so good as to exert your power on my behalf and that of the injured honour of your nephew.

May I request the honour of a visit from you as soon as possible and may I hope that I may not be the cause of attaching disgrace on the name of Hume, a family who hath heretofore been distinguished for their strict adherence to every principle of honour, as any breach of faith with me, will surely be published to the world.

I again humbly request a speedy answer, and the favour of a visit. Mr. W. Hume also said that I should not be removed without his acquainting my father. Your goodness will excuse my earnestness and attribute it to the unhappy circumstances which oppress.

Your very humble and obedient servant,
Michael Dwyer.

APPENDIX 6 COMMEMORATION

The memory of the events of 1798 has remained alive in the folk memory, both at national level and locally, within Dunlavin and its hinterland. This section records events during some of the main anniversary years.

50th Anniversary The fiftieth anniversary of the rising took place in 1848, but there was not much in the way of commemoration. There were many reasons for this. Firstly, the area was still in the throes of famine. West Wicklow suffered very badly during this time. [1] Secondly, the political activities of the Young Irelanders at this time meant that the authorities would take a very dim view of any type of 1798 commemoration. Thirdly, many people who lived through the events of 1798 were still alive, and remembrance might bring themselves and their families to the attention of the authorities; apart from the fact that only fifty years had passed meant that 1798 was, in a sense, an open wound.

100th Anniversary The centenary in 1898 was very different, however. The post-Parnell era of the 1890s was a time of resurgent nationalism in Ireland. Hopes of home rule, coupled with widespread cultural revival meant that the centenary of 1798 was a big event nationally, and Dunlavin and its hinterland was no exception as the following passages illustrate. The Leinster Leader of 21 May 1898 set the tone: [2]

> Nothing can ever make the Irishmen forgetful of the butchery and incendiarism that ushered in the Union, whose fruits the country has been reaping for the past hundred years in famine, over-taxation, agricultural and industrial decay; and the demonstrations during the next few weeks will disillusion those who think otherwise. We may be supine, we may be apathetic, we may quarrel amongst ourselves – but we are united in our recollection of the cruelties and the crimes, the sufferings and sacrifices which constitute the blackest and yet one of the most inspiring chapters in the history of our country. Next week and the succeeding weeks will find the National pulse throbbing vigorously and the National blood aflame, in a demonstration which will manifest both this remembrance, and a determination that nothing will satisfy Ireland in the future but a realisation of the ideals for which the men of '98 fought and died.

This local newspaper was unreservedly Nationalistic, and this tone was maintained in another article from the edition. [3]

> On Monday next – the anniversary of the first blow struck for Irish freedom in '98 – the centenary celebrations will be spiritedly initiated. Demonstrations and illuminations will take place in various districts throughout the country, and speech, music and procession will prove that the 'memory of the dead' is proudly cherished, and that the national sentiment and determination to carry out the struggle for Irish freedom until the long fought for victory is won, are as strong as ever, though temporarily obscured by apathy and indifference, the fruits of division and disappointed hopes. In many districts the celebrations will be heralded by meetings and displays of patriotic enthusiasm on Sunday. There will, for instance, be a great demonstration at Rathfarnham, and many branches in Kildare, Queen's, and other counties will meet for the purpose of completing or pushing forward the arrangements that they are making for giving adequate expression to the patriotism of their localities. We hope to see the Kildare branch leading the way in the work of organising memorial processions and public gatherings. It would be a discredit to the native county of Lord Edward Fitzgerald if the indifference displayed in some parts of it since the inception of the '98 movement was maintained during the coming month. Branches like those in Kildare and Kilcock, to mention a couple, have set a stirring example, and it is to be hoped that the action taken by the people in these districts, and not the neglect and indifference of other towns and villages, will be generally imitated in the county on Monday next and during the period over which the celebrations will extend.

News of events that were held locally appeared in the following week's edition. I have chosen two contrasting reports from towns within Dunlavin's extended hinterland: [4]

> **Naas** The one jarring note marring the general harmony and unanimity of the celebrations was struck here. The band paraded the streets, and a few houses were illuminated, but beyond that no interest was publicly taken in the demonstrations. The majority of the inhabitants, through sheer indifference or other reasons best known to themselves, abstained from joining in them. It is regrettable that a more patriotic feeling was not made manifest.

Obviously Naas was one area that had displayed indifference. Considering the ferocity of the battle of Naas in 1798, this was strange. The second report comes for Athy, and is much more

typical of the newspaper's reports for the local area on the day:
Athy On Monday evening last a torchlight procession took place
through the streets of Athy for the purpose of commemorating
the opening of the rebellion of 1798. The procession, which was
accompanied by one of the local bands, was of splendid
dimensions, and those taking part in it showed the greatest
spirit and enthusiasm. The Nationalists of the town had their
houses illuminated, and in this respect the desire to do honour
to the memory of the dead was universal. It would, perhaps, be
invidious to make distinctions, but the drapery establishment of
Mr Murphy, the licensed premises of Mr Knowles of the Square,
and Heffernan's hotel had a particularity striking effect, whilst
Mrs Fitzgerald had the windows of her house illuminated with
green candles. After the procession a public meeting, which was
addressed by Messrs P. Knowles and Timmons, was held in the
Square. Mr John Orford presided. Mr Knowles in coming forward
was received with great enthusiasm. He said, in the course of a
lengthy and instructive address, that in order to find the cause
of the '98 Rebellion they should go back to the period when
Grattan forced from an unwilling English Government the
establishment of an Irish Parliament and a limited National
freedom. This period, beginning in 1782 and extending to 1798,
was a bright and glorious one for the country, notwithstanding
the many drawbacks in her Parliamentary constitution – so
bright, glorious, and successful that on the testimony of most
disinterested and competent authorities, no country in the
annals of the world could show a parallel for the same space of
time [cheers]. This extraordinary prosperity – national and
commercial – aroused the envy of the English to such an extent
that they determined to undermine the Irish Government and
thereby rob the Irish people of their prosperity. To this end it was
necessary to decry Ireland and everything Irish. This they did
through the medium of the Press, which was utilised to the
greatest extent. The English and their agents were bent on
subverting the established order of things, and creating false
public opinion. They were unscrupulous as to their means and
courses. The secret service system was put in force, the
informers were unearthed, and persecutions and assassination
of the people carried on until a regime was imposed of such a
nature as to drive Irishmen of education and position to reflect,
in those extraordinarily circumstances, how best they would
throw off such a galling yoke [cheers]. The Irish leaders decided
that prompt and energetic steps should be taken to resist the
cruel and murderous onslaught that had been organised. They
claimed liberty for the Irish people without distinction of class or
creed. The society of United Irishmen was formed. It quickly
spread throughout the country, and large numbers joined its
ranks. It offered a fierce resistance to the Government, but the
English of the day knew that the force, fraud and numbers were

on their side, to their cost they subsequently learned that
honour, patriotism and chivalry were on the side of the Irish
[cheers]. Such qualities existed at the present day. It would be
altogether outside his [speaker's] range to deal locally with the
cause of Irish rebellion. They know on the one hand its sad
result, but they know also on the other that only for such
national upheavals had the demoralised and tyrannical Saxon
ever conceded any of their just demands [cheers]. Then they
should remember the days of '98 were days, by English law of
enforced ignorance. Education was at a very low ebb; steam,
telegraphy and electricity were not the practical factors they are
just now. In their time the resources of civilisation were in their
hands. They had wrung at length from an unwilling legislature a
measure of education very incomplete indeed. Their demands
were made known throughout the world, their opinions were
expressed and circulated. The public were informed and
enlightened as to their views and their wants, and it needed but
the memory of that moral power which was soon a factor to-day
throughout the world to bring about by a bloodless revolution
necessary reforms in their country. The aim of every Irishman of
whatever section should be to inculcate and foster that moral
force which formed and moulded the public opinion of a country,
which swayed and shaped the destinies of a race, which brought
the whole world within one compass and one limit. That was the
moral force that they called to their aid. Should they despond
and grow sluggish in their efforts? Should they lose heart, and
give up the struggle that they had carried on so long? (a voice –
'never') They should go on undaunted and undeterred and
resolved to achieve their hopes. They looked to the comfort with
hope and light hearts confident that their cause was just and
indestructible [cheers].

Mr. Timmons, a well known local Nationalist, also spoke. In the
course of a stirring address he advised the people to cherish the
traditions of the men of '98, to honour their memory and to
remember their unselfishness.

The proceedings then terminated, but the crowds continued to
parade the street until midnight singing 'The Boys of Wexford'.

Evidently, in that time of cultural revival, the language and
tone of the speakers was very republican, and any attempt at
political niceties was ignored. The 1890s was a time when
Gaelic organisations were spreading quickly at both national
and local level. Douglas Hyde's lecture The Necessity For
De-Anglicizing Ireland was delivered in 1892, and at local level
the most successful Gaelic organisation was undoubtedly the
Gaelic Athletic Association (G.A.A.). In Dunlavin a branch of the

G.A.A. (called Sons of St. Nicholas) was formed at a meeting held on 20 January 1890. [5] No doubt the existence of a G.A.A. club added to local interest in commemorating 1798 in Dunlavin.

As the end of May 1898 approached, attention in Dunlavin naturally centred on the massacre on the fairgreen. Like Athy, the commemoration took the form of a torch-lit procession. The procession retraced the last journey of the executed men, from the market house, via the fairgreen, to the cemetery at Tournant, where the men were buried. We have an eyewitness account of that procession. [6] The Rev. Samuel Russell McGee who was Rector of Dunlavin from 1894-1906 provided a detailed account on Tournant:

> During the rebellion of 1798 several rebels were captured and shot on the fairgreen just outside the town. They were interred at Tournant burial ground which is on a hill above the town. On the centenary of the rebellion, 1898, on a Sunday night, the town was illuminated with candles, which were placed two inside each pane of glass in most of the houses. Hundreds of candles were used and although after a while they started to do obeisance to each other, and some had to be extinguished for fear of setting the houses on fire, the effect was striking. Early that Sunday night a procession of torch bearers was formed which wended its way up the hill with their torches alight to the Tournant graveyard. It was a weird and impressive sight and partook more of a religious than a political character.

Another aspect of the 1798 centenary in Dunlavin concerned the refurbishment and extension of the Catholic church in the village. The 1890s, saw cultural and nationalistic revival and was also a great air of confidence evident in the Catholic Church at national level. The work on the church was to include stained glass windows to commemorate the Dunlavin massacre and Michael Dwyer's campaign. The mood at the meeting of parishioners was upbeat as the following extract shows: [7]

The Catholic Church at Dunlavin: Meeting of Parishioners

> A public meeting of the parishioners of Dunlavin Catholic Church was held on Sunday last for the purpose of collecting subscriptions towards the completion of repairs, which are at present being carried out by the Rev. John Maxwell, P.P. to the church, the condition of which some time ago was not only ruinous but dangerous to the congregation. Mr. Michael Roche, the contractor, has made a number of structural changes and additions, with the result that for all intents and purposes the

church will in a short time be as good as new. The old wooden gallery has been removed, new confessionals erected, the ceiling taken down and replaced, the wainscotting changed, the floor tiled, not to speak of other improvements which are yet to take place. The High Altar will be very considerably beautified by marble additions. A side altar to the memory of Canon Donovan, the late pastor and Canon Whittle are to be erected, and also stained glass windows in commemoration of Michael Dwyer and the United Irishmen, who were killed on Dunlavin Green in '98. The thanks of the parishioners are is no small manner due to the Rev. John Maxwell, P.P. for the painstaking manner in which he has acted in seeing to the improvement of the Church. The Cryhelp Brass Band played a session of sacred airs in front of the church before the meeting commenced.

After last Mass the Blessed Sacrament was removed from the Church, and the public meeting held. On the motion of Mr. Anthony Metcalfe, seconded by Mr. James Cunningham, the chair was taken by the Rev John Maxwell, P.P.

Amongst those present were Rev. John Healy, C.C., Joseph Dunne, Thos Metcalfe, Jas Cunningham, Anthony Metcalfe, John Kehoe, Mrs. Lawlor, John Hoxey, Mrs. Mooney, Jas Norton. Michl Griffin, Jos Kane, Jas Nolan, Mrs. Kelly, Miss Ennis, John Parke, Jos Deering, Mark Deering, John Ennis, J.P. William O'Brien, Miss Norton, Jas Kelly, Thos Roche, Thomas Grace, John Mullally, Tos Whelen, Mrs Coogan, Patk Cullen, Patk Neill, Edwd Roche, Michl Molloy, Stephen Nolan, Jas Synott, Henry Hoey, Jas Kane, Richard Doyle, Jas Roche, John Doyle, Wm Maher, John Hayden, John McDonald, James Gorman, Thos Jackson, Thos Kirwin, William Walsh, Mrs. Saunders, Patk Benson, Mrs. Sheridan, Hugh Daly, Chas Kavanagh, Mrs. Mary Reilly, Brian Molloy, John Byrne, John Smith Mrs. Theresa Leigh, Patrick Byrne, Mr. Byrne, Mrs. Byrne, Mrs. A. Nolan, John Brien, Jas Copeland, Mrs. Kate Byrne, Mrs. Ellen Rochford, John Halahan, Martin Roche, Mrs. McHugh, Jos Whittle, Segt Rattican, Jas Cashin, Wm Moore, Ed Wall, Mrs. McIntee, Thos Cunningham, Mrs. Keating, James Kelly, Jos Nolan, Ed Leigh, Jos Byrne, Head Const Fallon, Patk Esmond, Mrs. Toole, Mrs. Kenny, Sergeant Carroll, Constable Farrell, Mr & Mrs Ryder, Patrick Cunningham, Christopher Kelly, Patrick Byrne, Thomas Finley, Patk Holland, Thos Nolan, Catherine Bryan, Daniel Brady, Michl Murray, Jas Walsh, John Walsh, B. McDonald, Miss Rochford, Jas Gordon, Patk Byrne, Edward Rourke, Thomas Heally, Jas Byrne, John Dempsey, John Mackey, Jas Christy, Mrs. Boland, Jas Cleary, Andrew Fay, Patk Mooney, Kate Byrne, John Deegan, Wm Doyle, Edwd Nolan, Patrick Lalor, Philip Nolan, Myles Carroll, Jas Byrne, Michael Owens, Michl Davis, Thos Gaul, Mrs Corrigan, John Kavanagh, John Moore, Mark

Doyle, John McGurike, Eliza. Carroll, Jas Mulhall, P. Harvey, John Kelly, Patrick Foley, Michael Farrington, Laurence Owens, Mrs. Williams, Patk Flood, Miss Anne Harvey, Miss Julia Robinson, Miss Kate Donnell.

The Rev. Chairman said that when His Grace the Archbishop of Dublin appointed him pastor of this church in the beginning of January 1897, he was surprised and grieved when he came down to Dunlavin and saw such a miserable, poor and dangerous church. As he stated in his circular, it was nothing short of a disgrace to religion and altogether unfitted for Divine Worship. However, no fault in this matter had rested with the parishioners.

He had heard a great deal about the people of Dunlavin prior of his coming, and was told that he should be happy because he would be over the most practical Catholics in Ireland. He had a proof of this and was not disappointed, and it was a great consolation to him, in an undertaking of this kind, that he had such a good and generous people to deal with.

At the same time, it should not be for one moment imagined that he would undertake this very heavy work, were it not for the bequest from the late Canon Donovan, who left towards the building of a new church £1000. Unfortunately they had a difficulty about that. If the Canon had left £1000 towards the repairing of the Church of Dunlavin he (the chairman) would have had the money long since, but owing to the words 'new church' being mentioned in the bequest he had met with very great obstacles. The Archbishop of Dublin, who was one of the executors, told him that he could not use the money without the consent of the Chancellor of Charitable Bequests, but although the Rev. chairman had not yet received the £1000 he hoped to be able to get before the year expired. Unfortunately, in this matter there has been a good deal of law, and a number of legal forms had to be gone through, as lawyers would not allow such a big sum to pass through their fingers without taking many pounds out of it.

He had asked the Archbishop of Dublin when he last visited the parish what he could do for them, but the very pertinent query put by his Grace was 'What have you done for yourselves?' He (the Rev chairman) assured the Archbishop that from what he knew of the people of Dunlavin it would not be long until they would take action in this matter, and that they would do their duty more so perhaps than the people of any other parish would be found ready to do. He had been moved to take immediate action by the serious report which had been supplied to him on the condition of the church, by an architect whom he had got to examine it. The galleries were in a fearful state, being supported

by rotten beams, portion of the ceiling was also in a most
dilapidated condition, and the wonder was why some of the
parishioners had not been killed or maimed. Nothing remained
for him to do but to raise this £1000 in the banks on the
security of the parishioners of Dunlavin. He then entered into a
contract with Mr. Michael Roche, who undertook to thoroughly
renovate the church for the sum of £1300. He (Rev chairman) did
not let a half penny go out of the town, but had it all spent on
labour in Dunlavin, Protestant as well as Catholic getting a
share, and indeed, one of the principal men who repaired the
church was Mr. Waldron, a Protestant and a thoroughly good
workman into the bargain. In the event of not carrying out those
repairs, only one alternative remained and that was to build a
new church, which could not be erected at less than £10,000 or
£12,000. He informed the Archbishop, that he would rather give
up all hopes of getting the £1000 than set about building a new
church, because the people of Dunlavin would be unable to stand
the heavy expense which would accrue in erecting a new
building. The Rev. chairman, referring to the improvements
which had taken place in the church and to the new stainglass
windows which are to be erected said that Dunlavin was always
remarkable for its great spirit of nationality and it was scarcely
fair to allow the church to be completed without placing in it
some commemoration of the thirty six poor men who were shot
on the Green or of Michael Dwyer, who lived and was married in
Dunlavin Parish and was chased through it by Red Coats in '98.
Indeed before this thought occurred to him he was about to open
communications with parties in Australia to try and have the
remains of Michael Dwyer sent over to his native parish. He (the
Rev chairman) would have taken charge of them and have them
honoured as they deserved to be. However, he was too late. The
least that could be done was to erect one window to the memory
of Michael Dwyer and another to the memory of the thirty six
patriots who died for faith and fatherland. He calculated that he
would require about £1000 in addition to what Canon Donovan
left, he had avoided putting the people to any unnecessary
expense. The Rev. chairman concluded with an eloquent appeal
to the parishioners to contribute generously for the love of God
and His Virgin Mother.

Mr A. Metcalfe, J.P. proposed and Mr. T. Metcalfe seconded and it
was carried unanimously that the chairman's report as to the
expenditure on the church be adopted.

Mr. John Rochford then addressed a few words to the meeting
and remarked that in subscribing towards the renovation of that
historical old church they would be performing a noble work.
The parishioners owed three debts of gratitude. The first to God,
second to their late Pastor Canon Donovan and third to their

present worthy Parish Priest and by subscribing generously towards this fund, they would discharge these debts of gratitude. Mr. Jas Synott proposed, seconded by Mr. John Hoxey, that the subscription list be open.

The subscription list was then opened and every person named in the list above subscribed, from £30 given by Mr. Dunne down to 1s. Amongst those who were not present at the meeting the following subscribed: Messrs Edmund Sweetman, DL Longtown, Clane, Naas, James Molloy, Frances Street, Dublin, Philip Nolan, Mr McMullen, Patk Cunningham, the Bakery, Naas, M. McHayden, Cornelius Kelly, Seskin, Miss Catherine Whittle, Mrs. Walsh, Michael Kincella, Margaret Dunne, Mrs. Evans, B. McDonald. A sum of £400 in all was collected. The second chair was then taken by Mr. Anthony Metcalfe, J. P., after which a vote of thanks was moved to the chairman by Mr. Rochford, seconded by Mr. Cunningham, to which the Rev Father Maxwell suitably replied, and the proceedings then terminated.

The restoration and extension of the church was completed, and the present building bears a plaque with the date 1898 inscribed on it, above the main door. The centenary of the Dunlavin massacre was a significant local event, and well remembered and commemorated in a dignified way.

150th Anniversary The next main anniversary of the events of 1798 occurred in 1948, when the young Saorstát Éireann was evolving. The 1937 constitution, neutrality during World War Two, nationalistic teaching of history in the schools and other factors meant that local press reports were once again republican in tone regarding events in Dunlavin and its hinterland to mark the 150th anniversary of 1798. Events in the town of Naas certainly contrasted with what had happened in 1898, as this report shows: [8] The full report is included here to provide the reader with the original primary source. However, the author does not share the sentiments contained in the report and in Fr. Burbage's oration!

The 150th anniversary of the Battle of Naas on the night of the 23/24th May 1798, was commemorated at Naas on Sunday, when a huge gathering assembled in the town to pay tribute to brave Michael Reynolds and his comrades who intrepidly attacked the entrenched yeomen in Naas an put them to flight on that memorable date afterwards retiring from the town.

Glorious sunshine favoured the event and thousands of people lined the thoroughfare in the flag-bedecked Main Street as the parade led by Ballyshannon Pipers' Band marched from the assemblage point on the Fair Green to the Town Hall, where a memorial plaque to Michael Reynolds and his fellow insurgents was unveiled. Mr. Jack Delaney was Chief Marshal of the Parade which included contingents of the Old I.R.A. from Kilcullen, Naas, Droichead Nua, Athgarvan, Suncroft, Ballyshannon, Kildare, Straffan, Mainham, Kill, Ardclough and other centres. Mr. P. Carroll, Naas, was in command. A large contingent of the F.C.A. colour party consisted of Lieut. Wm. Byrne, Lieut. G. Robinson and Lieut. E. Kinsella, with Parade Sergeant Major P. Brennan. The Ex-L.D.F. and Ex-L.S.F. from Naas and district were commanded by former officers D. L. Jos. King, Adjutant T. Harvey and Intelligence Officer T. Hayden.

Other organisations taking part in the parade were former members of Cumann na mBan, the Naas Hurling Team, captained by Mr. P. Murphy, the Naas Boy Scouts, Naas Unit of the Order of Malta, men and women, school boys and outside bodies, and the general public.

There was a deeply impressive scene as with the full parade assembled in front of the Town Hall. Very Rev. P. J. Doyle unveiled the memorial plaque to the '98 patriots.

Three volleys rang out breaking the stillness which had descended over the town and F.C.A. Bugler Noel Murphy sounded the Last Post. As the Reveille followed the National Flag which was half-masted was raised and dipped by Mr. P. Carroll, Vice-Chairman of the County Kildare Committee of the Old I.R.A. The Firing Party which was favourably commented upon for its discipline and precision was drawn from the Kilcullen Branch of the Old I.R.A under Mr. Paddy Quinn.

Prior to the unveiling ceremony Mr. M. J. O'Donoghue, Vice-Chairman of the Naas Urban Council, in introducing Father Doyle, said that their beloved parish priest was well-known for his kindly acts not only by the people of Kildare, but numerous people all over Leinster. The entire parade then proceeded to the top of the town and re-assembled on their return around a platform in Market Square where an oration was delivered by Very Rev. Thomas Burbage, P.P. V.F. Mountmellick.

The Oration
Very Reverend Father Burbage said: Michael Reynolds, whose memory we honour today was one of the valiant band who 150 years ago dedicated themselves to the cause of Ireland's Freedom, and to the promotion of goodwill and understanding among all Irishmen. He was one of those who believed that when

all other means of rescuing the nation from slavery and degradation had been used in vain, that recourse to armed force was justifiable. Those men were confirmed in this belief by the fact that the invaders had driven the mass of their victims to such a state of desperation that revolt had every prospect of success.

For generations before 1798, England pursued a deliberate unwavering policy of fermenting disunion among all classes in Ireland. They encouraged religious strife between Catholics, Protestants and Presbyterians and ill-feeling between landlords and tenants. Even children were set against their parents. There was method in this criminal procedure. English rulers realised that internal dissension in Ireland facilitated their alien rule.

England was warmly seconded by this policy by the possessors of the confiscated estates and their hangers-on who feared that if by any chance the people came together and used their strength, they (the planters) would lose their ill-gotten goods.

The United Irishmen
This policy was disastrous for the country as a whole. It was aimed primarily at Catholics, but discerning Protestants came to realise that it would eventually cause the ruin of themselves as well as of their Catholic fellow countrymen. It made the rectification of almost any public grievance practically impossible and left the country seething with injustices and discontent. In 1791, twenty distinguished Protestants came together and planned to meet the situation inaugurating a body that would include Irishmen of all creed and classes, united for the promotion of their common interests, and specifically for the reform of a very corrupt Parliament and for the emancipation of Catholics. This body was known as the United Irish Society. It spread rapidly. It reached a membership of 500,000 in a very short time. This was the last thing on earth that England wanted. Though the Society was legal and constitutional, steps were taken at once to stamp it out. As early as 1792, less than a year after its inception by means of packed juries, heavy fines and long terms of imprisonment were being inflicted on leading members for the crime of criticising the corrupt constitution of Parliament. Later a savage campaign of terrorism was let loose on the general defenceless population. A lustful alien soldiery was quartered and billeted among the homes of the people with permission and encouragement to flog, pitch-cap, and press-gang and drive the people by every means into an insurrection that it was expected could easily be suppressed. Reacting to the Government's measures the Society changed its character and began arming its members. Arms of one kind or another were supplied to as many as 300,000 men, of whom 100,000 were

resident in the northern counties, showing clearly that there was nothing sectarian about the movement.

It is interesting to note that this County (Kildare) was so highly organised, that it had over 60,000 enrolled. This was largely due to the residence here of Lord Edward Fitzgerald. The British nearly overshot their mark, for if the other counties had risen and fought with the same determination and tenacity as did Kildare and Wexford there would have been an end to British rule in Ireland. Failure was not due to want of members on the part of the insurgents, neither was it due to the inferior quality of their arms, primitive as they were. It was due to want of thorough preparation, and above all to a system of spying and informing organised by the British Secret Service, and operations in the highest ranks of the insurgents and in other unsuspected quarters.

This enabled the British to effect unexpected arrests of leaders, and to anticipate military actions, as they were kept informed well beforehand of important military moves that were decided upon.

Thus the plans of the insurgents were thrown into utter confusion, and they were rendered incapable of using their strength. The men of 1916-21 were much more successful in their handling of the British Secret Service. It is never too late to learn.

The Signal
The Insurrection was fixed for the 23rd May 1798. The signal was to be simultaneous stopping of the mail coaches that left Dublin General Post Office daily for Belfast, Cork, Athlone and Limerick. That stoppage was duly carried out. On the 23rd May the mail coaches were seized and burnt at Santry, Naas, Lucan and the Curragh and the rising began. At the commemoration meetings being held during the past couple of months in different parts of the country you have heard the story of the fighting at Prosperous, Clane, Kilcock, Maynooth, Rathangan, Timahoe, Monasterevan, and so on. The attack on Naas was made on the 24th of May by a body of insurgents led by Michael Reynolds, whose memory you honour today. He was a young farmer from the neighbourhood of Johnstown. He was previously active in organising the county and held the rank of Colonel. The town was garrisoned by the Armagh Militia, part of a regiment of Dragoons, the Ancient Britons (a Welsh regiment) and Yeomanry, and was warned beforehand of the impending insurgent attack.

Fell at Hacketstown

Michael Reynolds led three attacks which were pressed with great courage and determination. But finally, discipline and superior armament prevailed and the insurgents were forced to retire with a loss of 140 men. On the withdrawal of the insurgents the British took revenge on the town by what is described by Father O'Hanlon, the historian, as disgraceful military executions and excesses. In other words by the butchery of those in the town who sympathised or were suspected of sympathising with United Irishmen. Michael Reynolds and his men later fell back on Wicklow. He himself fell during the attack on Hacketstown. Fighting in Kildare ceased with the surrender made at Sallins on the 21st July.

Parallels with Present

The Insurrection of 1798, and other such movements that followed in its track are not to be judged in retrospect as isolated and unconnected events, and pronounced on according to the immediate military victories or defeats. The end of the first and second world wars atoned and compensated for colossal initial defeats by an ultimate victory on the part of one of the belligerents, known as the Allies. So, too, in the case of Ireland. The movements of 1798, 1848 and 1916-21, are to be viewed as parts of a whole not yet completed, where the inspiration and knowledge of what is needed for success is drawn from the valour self-sacrifice and methods of those who first faced the foe. In other words in the great campaign for freedom there are lessons to be learned and applied. Things that are found worthy of imitation and also things carefully to be avoided. So we find justification in our day for the scorn and contempt deservedly poured on the Knaves and Slaves unworthy of the name of Irish men who hang their heads in shame at the mention of those brave men who kindled that blaze that does not die, but lives on in the hearts of the people, and will eventually destroy alien rule in our land. Without the Tones and Fitzgeralds, McCrackens and Russels and men like Michael Reynolds in 1798 who faced the foe despite the odds, there would have been no 1916-21 and without '21 no onward march which the people of Ireland will take good care will not cease, till every trace of slavery and subjection to alien rule and influence has been blotted out.

The merit of men like Michael Reynolds lies in the fact that they had vision and faith in their countrymen and foresaw the effect of their actions.

They proved that it is possible to raise up this dominant race, no matter how trampled under foot in mud and blood – possible to bind them together for their mutual protection to inspire them with self-reliance and a striking power of which even powerful enemies must take account. They showed too, that in this land, those who strive for freedom have never cause to despair for Ireland, given the opportunity, can always raise up men who will take the glorious risk of leading the way to victory, in spite of difficulty and danger.

I would strongly urge the young men of Kildare to make themselves thoroughly acquainted with the lives of the young leaders of '98, '48 and 1916-21.

The object to which these men dedicated themselves, and for which so many of them gave their lives, has been through the inspiration of their example, carried far on the way to success. This object should be as dear to the men of today as it was to them. Don't forget that there is still grave and urgent work to be done. Work requiring foresight, determination and self-reliance – needing too, the energy, enthusiasm and leadership of the young generation. Nowhere is the inspiration for this work more surely to be found that in the patriotic cycle which starts with 1798, with its splendid vision of national union of hearts and hands – with the sun of freedom shining brightly on a peaceful, prosperous, happy and united people.

Example of Leader
Irishmen reading the lives of those young leaders will be astounded at their intellectual and moral stature. They will wonder at the meanness, depravity and malice of enemies who have striven to discredit them, and to brand them as brainless, crazy fools. These young men stood head and shoulders over their compeers in the professions to which they belonged and which they in many cases sacrificed together with liberty and life for the sake of the country they loved. Study the lives of Tone, Emmet, Fitzgerald, of McCracken, Russel and Orr, of Davis, Duffy, Mitchel and Meagher, of Pearse and half a hundred of others. In no nation on earth will you find such thrilling examples of devotion to the truth and justice, nowhere such hatred of oppression, unqualified spirit of sacrifice, unconquerable love of country.

If you seek an antidote to the poisons of this age, to self-seeking, selfishness, hypocrisy, sham and shoneenism, you will find it in the story of their aspirations and achievements.

If there is any body of men more than another to whom I recommend this study it is to those who have taken on themselves the profession of arms, whether in the National Army or Local Defence and have sworn to defend their country's flag even at the sacrifice of their lives. Ireland will be glad to know, and to feel that these men are in spirit and conviction, and not merely in outward form, descendants of the heros of '98, Ireland's real defence in every hour of danger. See that your county and branch libraries, as well as libraries at the Curragh and other garrisons in the county are fully stocked with these works and that the thoughtful study of them is encouraged. But if the study of the leaders of '98 is of importance, no less worthy of consideration are certain serious events that provided a setting for the revolt, at the time.

England's difficulties at the end of the 18th century forced the concession of a native government, just as England's international difficulties contributed to the victory of 1921.

Hereditary Enemies
But England in 1782 took the precaution of placing more than three-fourths of the power of government in the hands of hereditary enemies of the people. These were a group of a hundred families, closely related by blood and marriage and social position, an infamous traitorous group that disbanded and disarmed the National Army at the first opportunity and garrisoned the country with foreign troops. Then when the way was clear and safe they sold the country for bribes into more soul-destroying slavery than it had been delivered from only two decades before. This narration has an unpleasant resemblance to things that claim our attention in our land today. Our National Army has not been disbanded but foreign troops are on our soil. Our native government is intact, but a foreign satellite State has been established in the invaded part of our country. This hired British garrison disguised as Irishmen, for the discrediting of our people, displays the same antiquated policy of disunion that was practised by their paymasters in the penal times. Sectarian strife is formed, mutual distrust generated among citizens, civil and religious rights are denied to those who call themselves Irishmen and act as such. This whole situation is not merely irritating to the county, it is a danger as we know from the past – a danger not merely to be noted and commented on, but to be actively resisted and dealt with without delay.

No other nation in the world would be asked to tolerate such a disturbing condition of things in their midst. France, Holland, Belgium, Luxemburg, even Russia whose territories are no longer invaded, demand additional security against the possible revival of German power.

Is it unreasonable that Ireland should at least be freed from the invasion of a power that has treated our people, not merely in ages past, but up to our own day, with a savage brutality, that has no parallel in the history of civilised States? This position created and maintained in six of our counties is a pestilence that is contaminating and poisoning the economic, industrial, social and political life of the whole country. It is an act so hostile, that it constitutes England the only serious and real active enemy we have in the world. There should be no mincing of words about that. Attempts of English spokesmen to evade full and unqualified responsibility in this matter are an exhibition of fraud and make-believe that is beneath contempt and should be a warning to all those who have any dealing with them. There are many conceivable ways in which an approach may be made to the righting of this infamous injustice imposed on our people. If we have the spirit, vision and determination of the men of '98 – the men we honour in this commemoration – with the opportunity we have, a successful way will soon be found of ending this gross outrage against the dignity and safety of the nation.

Conclusion
At the conclusion, Mr. O'Donovan who presided thanked the various bodies and individuals, who had co-operated so whole heatedly in making the Commemoration the success that it was. He conveyed his particular thanks to Father Burbage for coming there at great inconvenience to himself to deliver the oration. They were all aware of Father Burbage's great National record, and his work for Ireland, which had endeared him to the hearts of young and old in every county in Ireland.

Mr. O'Donoghue also complimented the energetic committee headed by Mr. Padraigh Crowley, for their splendid work in the organisation of the Commemoration and the townspeople for their co-operation in adorning the town. The people of Kildare should feel proud of their record in 1798. They were the first county to throw aloft the banner of rebellion and they were the last country to surrender, and then only on honourable terms. They had fought valiantly and courageously throughout the struggle and even in other countries they had lent a helping hand to banish the oppressors from their land. He hoped that the lesson of '98 would not be forgotten and that the deeds and exploits of those heroes would be enshrined in their hearts, and that the ideals for which they fought would ever be a beacon light for generations to come.

Also on the platform were Very Rev. P. J. Doyle, P.P., Very Rev. E. Crampton, P.P., Kill, Rev. C. Phelan, C.C., Rev. G. Brophy, C.C., Naas; An Tánaiste, Mr. William Norton T.D., Messrs T. Harris, T.D and G. Sweetman, T.D.; Colonel Collins Powell, Commandant Weddick; Senator Michael Smyth, Mr. James Dunne, Kill; Mrs. Higgins, U.D.C., Messrs L. McGarr U.D.C.; J. Taylor P.C.; John Monohan, J. P. Whyte, Town Clerk, Naas.

A letter of apology regretting inability to attend was read from

Rev. Irwin Lucan, one of the patrons of the Commemoration.

Commemorations in Naas had certainly changed between 1898 and 1948. If most of the primary sources extant from 1798 had a Loyalist bias, there is no doubt that the Republican rhetoric of the commemoration ceremonies of 1948 (and, indeed, 1898) contained in this chapter are strongly biased towards green, rather than orange, tendencies. There are many examples of blatant republican propaganda; but, of course, the political climate of 1948 was very different to the present day situation. The year 1948 saw commemorative events in West Wicklow too. One of the biggest of these was held in Baltinglass, and it reflected the fact that the violence in the West Wicklow area lasted for quite a while after the year 1798 itself. The massacre on Dunlavin green was recalled as possibly the most significant event to happen in West Wicklow during the crucial period in late May 1798. The insurgent activities of Michael Dwyer, whose prolonged but ultimately futile resistance outlasted that of the other rebel leaders was also remembered in Baltinglass. The speech given by Mr. J. Everett makes reference to local folk memory. Everett stated: "Here in Co. Wicklow local history is not forgotten and it is remembered not with bitterness, but with pride." Certainly the local folk memory in West Wicklow and in the village of Dunlavin regarding the massacre is very strong. The report of the 1948 event in Baltinglass read as follows: [9]

Tattoo at Baltinglass – '98 Commemoration Ceremony

A spectacle reminiscent of the scenes witnessed during the Military Tattoo in Dublin some years ago was staged in Baltinglass on Sunday night. This was part of the '98 commemoration and was the first in the country to take the form of a Tattoo.

The tattoo was a succession of scenes based on the life of Michael Dwyer during his insurgent campaign in Wicklow. The programme was arranged and conducted by the Carlow Battalion of the F.C.A. aided by units from Baltinglass and surrounding towns and under the supervision of Army officers of the Eastern Command.

Four scenes were presented –

1. The massacre at Dunlavin. This scene opened at the

residence of Col. Saunders of Saunders Grove, when he was accused by a Yeoman Captain of harbouring rebels. Saunders protested, but when proof was forthcoming, 19 of his men are marched away to a summary court-martial and brought before a firing squad on Dunlavin Green. The order is to execute in groups of five, and finding that one group has only four men, the spy, Hawkins, who had already given information leading to the arrests, is forcibly compelled to take his place in the group of four to make up the five, and was executed with them.

2. The second scene portrayed the marriage of Michael Dwyer to Mary Doyle. The ceremony was performed by Father James Murphy in the presence of his insurgent comrades.

3. The siege of the cottage at Derrynamuck. This was the most striking and most spectacular scene of the night, depicting as it did, the most outstanding incident in Michael Dwyer's career. A replica of the cottage at Derrynamuck was erected on the arena and the whole scene of the ambush as it is known to every schoolboy was realistically enacted.

4. The surrender to Colonel Hume. Here Dwyer is first seen reading a poster which offered attractive terms for his surrender. His wife urges him to accept. He sends a messenger to Col. Hume at Humewood Castle, and he is heard making his surrender to the Colonel and seen handing him his arms, and finally being escorted to Dublin under heavy escort.

The scenes were portrayed with a reality and precision that seemed hardly possible, considering the short time at the disposal of those in charge and reflected great credit on all concerned.

Two 22,000 watt. A.A. Search lights in charge of Capt. Banahan were used to give a moonlight effect to scenes. Numerous flood lights in charge of Lieut. Seward, lit the arena, while a battery of five loud speakers relayed the commentary to the huge gathering, who were able to follow each scene with ease.

The day began by a Church parade and Military Mass at St. Joseph's Baltinglass, which was followed during the day by band parades, displays of modern drill and precision marching by units of the F.C.A. local G.A.A. clubs, school children etc.

A local choir ably accompanied by Mrs. Ben Farrell, gave a selection between the scenes of Irish songs, which were very much appreciated.

Mr. J. Everett, Minister for Posts and Telegraphs, said – I have already had the honour of speaking at a '98 Commemoration in County Wicklow, when the cottage from which Michael Dwyer made his memorable escape was handed over to the keeping of the people of Ireland, as a previous reminder of their ceaseless struggle for freedom. It was an honour which, as a Wicklow man, I felt very deeply and I feel it all the more, therefore, that I should have the privilege of speaking here today.

The proud record of our history has been faithfully preserved by our writers and historians and is there for all to read who wish to learn. But the libraries are not within the reach of everyone (please God someday they will be) and even if they were, it would be a sorry day for us if an interest in history were confined to the scholar and student.

It is a glorious thing and an encouragement to all who have the love of Ireland in their hearts, to know that here in County Wicklow and in many other parts of the country, the historical traditions live in the minds of the people of the land, and are so strong that out of them can grow the enthusiasm that has made the organisation of this magnificent commemoration possible.

I have helped to organise many things in my time, and I know well what planning and patience it has taken to organise this commemoration. I know it has meant many months of quiet work undertaken in addition to all the cares and worries which every one of us carries these days. It has called for a spirit of co-operation on a very wide scale. You will not mis-understand me if I say it is that spirit which is the important thing almost more so than the object to which it is directed.

One of the tragedies of our time is the decline of local spirit and local pride. We had begun to fear that people only realised their love for their own locality when they had travelled far from it, but the '98 Commemorations have done much to re-assure us. Here in County Wicklow we have all the evidence that anyone could demand to prove that local history is not forgotten and that it is remembered, not with bitterness, but with pride.

Thank, God, we have travelled far along the road on which Michael Dwyer and his followers set out. Their glorious deeds seemed at the time to end only in hopelessness and ruin, but they were part of the chain of national struggle, and others came after them to link their work with that of new generations, so that we can now look back along an unbroken line of patriotic effort, leading up to Easter Week and beyond it, to the final struggle in arms which achieved, not full independence, but, at least, some foundation on which it it could be built by peaceful methods.

Our efforts have not yet been crowned with complete success, nor will they until we see an Ireland undivided by an artificial and unnatural barrier, with every Irishman – North and South – thinking himself as one of a strong, if small, island people, whose only boundary is the blue sea around our shores. Smallness doesn't mean helplessness or weakness. One man, by his way of life can inspire many, and one small nation, by its Christian example, may well be an influence to turn the world to the only true principles on which peace can stand.

Present at Reception and Dinner
Those present at reception and dinner were – James Everett, T.D. Minister for Posts and Telegraphs; G.O.C. Hugo Mac Neill, Lieut. Russell, A.D.C. to the G.O.C.; Comdt. Cosgrave, Comdt. Blake, H. C. Doyle, M.I.A.A., Baltinglass, Chairman of local committee; F. Lanigan, State Solicitor, Carlow and Mrs Lanigan; Capt. Banahan, Lieut. Seward, Lieut. Morgan, O/C, Portlaoighise F.C.A.; O/C Abbeyleix F.C.A.; Tom Fleming, Shillelagh; Comdt. G. O'Doherty, Lieut. Sean Doyle, Richard L. Barron, N.T.; F. Glynn, N.T.; Peadar O'Reilly and party, and Press representatives.

In Dunlavin itself, a monument was erected to at the fairgreen to mark the 150th anniversary of the massacre. A campaign was set in motion that resulted in a Celtic cross type structure being unveiled amidst a banner-carrying but sombre crowd. The monument was made of Wicklow granite, and blessed by Fr. S. Burke C.F. No doubt there was some republican rhetoric at the unveiling ceremony, but equally doubtless, such rhetoric rang rather hollow. The event in Dunlavin was not a battle but a massacre; and a massacre constitutes a tragedy in everyone's language.

200th Anniversary Fifty years later, the bicentenary of the massacre in 1998 was a significant event in Dunlavin village. Firstly, the Roman Catholic church was refurbished and a plaque erected in the porch to commemorate the executions which took place outside. Secondly, a book about the massacre was published in March of that year. Thirdly, Sinn Fein held a commemoration ceremony on 17 May. Led by a lone piper, a parade that included a fifty-strong contingent from north-east Dublin marched from the market house to the fairgreen. Mr. Gerry O'Neill called on Mr. Derek Sweetman [who had been recently released from the H-Blocks] to lay a wreath. Piper Michael Foy played a lament. Cllr. Christy Burke, a late replacement for the injured Cllr. Larry O'Toole, then spoke. He was followed by Mr. Micheal Mac Donncha, who delivered the main oration, before those in attendance dispersed.

Undoubtedly the largest commemoration, however, was held at the newly restored monument on the following Sunday, 24 May 1998. The names of thirty six victims had been inscribed on the plinth of the monument and a great crowd turned out for the rededication ceremony. A new commemorative stone was also visible on the fairgreen just behind the original monument. Master of Ceremonies Mr. Jim Whittle opened the event by welcoming everybody on behalf of Ms. Maura Greene, Chairperson of Dunlavin Tidy Towns Committee. Ms. Joan Kavanagh of the Wicklow '98 Committee and County Manager Mr. Blaise Treacy were the guest speakers at the event. There were appropriate readings by Ms. Caroline Deegan and Mr. Robert Barrett and Mr. Dudley Kirwan, a descendant of two brothers who had been executed on the fateful day, laid a wreath. Representatives of the Roman Catholic, Church of Ireland, Baptist and Quaker communities said prayers, before the crowd, led by a contingent of pike men, walked from the monument to Tournant graveyard. An ecumenical liturgy, based on the themes of forgiveness, reconciliation and peace, was held at Tournant, where a new commemorative wall plaque was in evidence. The site of the mass grave had also been marked with a new standing stone 'peace pillar' and the crowd was invited to ring the 'peace bell' before leaving after the ceremony. The most mysterious event to happen on that day though was the very high wind – almost a mini-hurricane – that blew up for a few minutes during the religious ceremony. The phenomenon was not noticed in any part of the surrounding area, not even in the adjacent village of Dunlavin!

On 14 June 1998 a pageant was presented in Derrynamuck to commemorate Michael Dwyer's escape from the cottage there. The three-act pageant was written by Mrs. Poppy Bolton, directed by Mr. Aidan Conron and produced by Mr. Frank Moynihan. The cast included Messrs. Leo Bowder, George Finlay, Sean Byrne, Luke Griffin, Ernest Mackey, Bill Walshe, John Spain and Edward Allen, Ms. Siobhan Kearney and Ms. Nicola Conron. Large crowds attended on a glorious June day. Act one showed Michael Dwyer relaxing among friends, act two concentrated on a meeting of William Hume of Humewood and Captain McDonald of the Scottish Highlanders and act three re-enacted Dwyer's famous escape. This pageant was repeated in front of an even bigger crowd in February 1999, the actual bicentenary of the escape. Before the year 1998 had finished – on 31 December to be precise – three more monuments were unveiled in West Wicklow. One was at Dwyer's Brook near Lacken to commemorate the decapitation of a rebel scout at that spot. The other two monuments commemorated Christopher Byrne, William Burke and Oliver Hoyle. These men were killed in a house in Knocknadroose in 1801. One plaque was unveiled at the house and the other at the gate to the churchyard in Hollywood, where the men were buried.

The next large-scale commemorative event in the region was the erection of a statue of Michael Dwyer in his native Glen of Imaal. Harry Murphy and his family donated the site for the new statue. A committee was formed to mark the bicentenary of the end of Dwyer's military campaign in December 1803. The committee members were:

> Chairperson: Tommy Cullen M.C.C.
> Vice Chairperson: Pat Doran M.C.C.
> Secretary: Finbarr Coyle.
> Treasurer: Harry Murphy.
> P.R.O.: Bill Walshe.
> Artistic Advisor: Eve Carroll.
> Fundraising Officer: Jim Keogh.
> Local Advisor: Seán Byrne.
> Historical Advisor: Chris Lawlor.
> Special Appreciation was also given to the late Jim Rogers for his input.

The people involved in the erection of the statue were:

> Sculptor: Paddy Roe.
> Draughtsman: Vincent Cronin.
> Contractor: Pat O'Neill and the 'Parnell Construction' crew.
> Stonemason: Jack Corcoran and his team.

A new book about Dwyer's life was published in advance of the unveiling, which took place on 14 December 2003. On that day, another large crowd assembled for the historic event, which was attended by An Taoiseach Bertie Ahern, the Australian Ambassador, two government ministers, local TDs and councillors. Before unveiling the statue, the Taoiseach spoke about Michael Dwyer. He said: 'It is very satisfying to see the fruits of these efforts and to see local communities involved in such a positive way in remembering and commemorating our past. All of these events ... were seminal to the establishment of republicanism, based on the principles of freedom, equality and social justice, as the radical force behind the birth of our nation.'

Other speakers on the day included the Australian Ambassador Dr. John Herron, Brigadier General Pat O'Sullivan, County Manager Eddie Sheehy, and Mr. Martin Miley, who recited T.D. Sullivan's 'Ballad of Michael Dwyer'. Groups in attendance included the Army Number One Band, two pipe bands, units of pike people from Imaal, Wicklow, Monagear, Wexford and other places, members of the Michael Dwyer G.A.A. club from Belfast and many local organisations. On the same day a stone monument to Dwyer was unveiled in Kiltegan.

The final commemorative events to be mentioned in this work occurred in 2006 ... on the other side of the world. That year was the bicentenary of Michael Dwyer's arrival in Australia. In that year the author of the present work travelled to Australia and during that trip commemorated Michael Dwyer in both Sydney and Melbourne. On 29 July in Sydney, I spoke about Dwyer on the radio show Ireland Calling presented by Vince Murray. On 1 August in Melbourne, I gave a lecture on Dwyer in the University of Melbourne. The full text of that paper is given in appendix 7.

NOTES

1: For a brief account of conditions in and around Dunlavin during the famine, see Chris Lawlor, Ecclesiastical – and Secular – Views of the Wicklow-Kildare region during the years of the great famine and in its immediate aftermath, in the Fifteenth Dunlavin Festival of Arts Brochure p.53-63 (1997).

2: Leinster Leader, 21 May 1898, Editorial.

3: Leinster Leader, 21 May 1898, The '98 Celebrations.

4: Leinster Leader, 28 May 1898, The Celebrations.

5: Jim Whittle, (editor): Sons of St. Nicholas – a history of Dunlavin G.A.A. Club. p.4 (Published by Dunlavin G.A.A. Club, 1984).

6: Fr. Patrick Finn, (quoting the Rev. Samuel Russell McGee) in The View from the Mountains, in Dunlavin, Donard, Davidstown, Parish Link, p.1, Vol. 3, No. 5, (October 1997).

7: Leinster Leader, 24 September 1898, The Catholic Church at Dunlavin; Meeting of the parishioners.

8: Leinster Leader, 9 October 1948, Naas Patriots Remembered – Impressive '98 Commemoration Ceremonies.

9: Leinster Leader, 25 September 1948, Tattoo at Baltinglass '98 Commemoration Ceremony.

APPENDIX 7 MICHAEL DWYER, THE WICKLOW CHIEF

Paper delivered at the University of Melbourne on 1 August 2006 by Chris Lawlor

Let me begin by thanking you for allowing me to deliver this paper here in the beautiful surroundings of Newman College in the University of Melbourne. I am very honoured to be here to mark the bicentenary of the arrival of Michael Dwyer in Australia with this talk, which, as you will know, is part of the University's prestigious series of Irish Studies Seminars. I am especially grateful to Dr Elizabeth Malcolm and Mr Philip Bull as they have organised this seminar on the life and significance of Michael Dwyer, the man known as the 'Wicklow Chief', a man, indeed, whose exploits have almost assumed the proportions of myth in his native county.

The mythic quality of Michael Dwyer is something that I have grown up with in West Wicklow. The name of Michael Dwyer was 'up there with the best of them'. A 19th century traditional ballad called The Three Flowers compares Dwyer with Wolfe Tone and Robert Emmet. This ballad is merely one example of how Dwyer, who was not a major United Irish leader before the 1798 rebellion (although he worked his way up the chain of command somewhat during the conflict) was posthumously elevated to a status of leadership which he did not enjoy during his lifetime. Dwyer probably never saw Wolfe Tone, let alone met him. They moved in different circles. Unlike many of the leading figures within the United Irish organisation, Dwyer did not come from a well-to-do background. While planning the abortive rising of 1803, Emmet and Dwyer met only twice. Yet the guerrilla leader of a tiny band of freedom fighters in the Wicklow Mountains is mentioned as an equal in the same breath as Tone, the 'Father of Irish Republicanism' and Emmet, the 'Darling of Erin'. In the folklore of Ireland, the myth of Michael Dwyer has transcended his own time and place. No doubt Dwyer, the politically aware freedom fighter, would have been pleased. The legend lives on. This talk will attempt to separate legend from fact ... though an account of the facts of Dwyer's life makes it easy to see how the legend developed!

Michael Dwyer was born in the Glen of Imaal in 1772. Making a living, especially from farming was difficult in this remote glen, deep in the Wicklow Mountains. Nevertheless, Michael Dwyer was the son of a small tenant farmer and he grew up

among the people of this glen. The Dwyers were not rich –
Michael's parents, John and Mary, were ordinary people. His
father, John Dwyer had married Mary Byrne of Cullentragh.
Michael was their eldest son. The family moved from the
townland of Camara to the townland of Eadstown in 1784, when
Michael was about twelve years old. Eadstown was not quite as
remote as Camara, but it was still situated well within the Glen
of Imaal. The Dwyers were Roman Catholic, so Michael was
educated at a hedge school. His teacher, Peter Burr, was a
remarkable figure. He was a graduate of the strictly protestant
Trinity College, Dublin, but he was also a progressive thinker,
who kept up with political changes at the time. Burr made sure
that Michael Dwyer and his other pupils also knew about these
changes.

And what changes they were! The late seventeenth century
witnessed the American Revolution and French Revolution.
Both of these events brought about huge changes and
established two independent republics. The American War of
Independence threatened the very concepts of Empire and
British 'superiority' in an age of imperialism. The loss of the
American colonies was the first real blow suffered by the British
Empire, and it cut deeply. The colonies were gone, but at least
they were three thousand miles away. The French Revolution
did not affect Britain as directly as the American one, in that
they lost no land as a result of it. However, in its own way, the
French revolution had an even more profound effect on British
Loyalists because it threatened the very concept of Monarchy.
Europe's Ancien Regime and the idea of the Divine Right of
Monarchs were swept aside. The French were guilty of possibly
the worst possible crime in Loyalist eyes – regicide. After all,
who were Loyalists loyal to, if not the Monarch?

The establishment of the United Irishmen in Belfast in 1791
fuelled Loyalist fears. Now Ireland, the island on Britain's
doorstep, was showing separatist tendencies. In the Glen of
Imaal, Peter Burr was among the first to join the new
organisation of United Irishmen. Burr's action probably
influenced his old pupil, who became even more politically
aware as new ideas infiltrated the Glen. Michael Dwyer also
joined the United Irishmen in 1797.

At this stage, the government moved to quell the United
Irishmen. Terror was employed as a tactic and this terror spread
through Ulster and into Leinster during late 1797 and early
1798. A new part time force, the yeoman, was founded in 1797

to assist the militia and regular army in tackling the United Irish threat. A reign of terror swept through Leinster and into County Wicklow. The United Irishmen were strong in Wicklow, where they had 14,000 sworn members. The United Irishmen's second strongest Leinster county was Kildare with 11,919 members.

Michael Dwyer lived in an area of Wicklow close to the Kildare border. The Glen of Imaal is in Dunlavin parish and Dunlavin village was a place that Dwyer visited often. The Roman Catholic parish was centred on Dunlavin, and Dwyer's family worshipped there. Dunlavin was also the local market town, so as farmers the Dwyer family also had reason to attend Dunlavin's markets and fairs. Dunlavin held a pivotal position between the principal towns of Kildare and West Wicklow, such as Naas, Kilcullen, Blessington and Baltinglass.

In 1798, Dunlavin was also a garrison town for West Wicklow. The West Wicklow area saw harsh methods employed in the hunt for United Irishmen. The flogging triangle was used, as was half-hanging. Arrests of United Irish suspects followed. Dunlavin market house became a temporary jail. A kinsman of Michael Dwyer, John Dwyer of Seskin, was arrested in April 1798. His house in Imaal was burned and he was incarcerated in Dunlavin. Michael Dwyer was also wanted by the authorities, so he left his home to lie low in the remote wilderness area at the head of the Glen of Imaal.

While Dwyer was evading the authorities, the rebellion broke out in West Wicklow (and Kildare). On the opening day of the rebellion, 24 May 1798, a horrendous massacre of prisoners occurred in Dunlavin. The authorities had good information from spies, such as John Smith, who had learned that many Dunlavin yeomen were also sworn United Irishmen. The Dunlavin yeomanry was divided into Dunlavin cavalry corps, which was led by William Ryves of Rathsallagh and the infantry corps, which was led by Morley Saunders of Saundersgrove. Another spy, Joe Hawkins, had uncovered a plot to kill Morley Saunders. On Monday 21 May 1798 Corporal James Dunn of the Saundersgrove corps had been arrested. On Tuesday 22nd May eighteen more of Saunders's men were arrested on the parade ground, and prisoners from Narraghmore and elsewhere joined local suspects in Dunlavin market house.

On the morning of the 24th, with rumours of rebel victories sweeping through a tense and volatile Dunlavin, many of the prisoners were paraded through the town – and 36 of them were shot at the corner of the fair green beside the Roman Catholic chapel. The sectarian nature of the massacre was overtly displayed. The wounded were finished off by pistol shots in the ear, but one man, David Prendergast, feigned death and was rescued. Some prisoners were also hanged at the village market house. The exact number is unclear, but between five and eleven men seem to have been hanged. State terror had reached its zenith in the Dunlavin massacre.

The effects of the Dunlavin massacre were far reaching. News of the massacre was one factor that prompted Fr John Murphy to rebel and so the Wexford rebellion commenced. News of the massacre also had a profound effect on Michael Dwyer. Dwyer still lying low in the remote Glen of Imaal when the news reached him, but after Dunlavin, Dwyer went to Wexford, where he joined the rebels. At this stage, Dwyer was a captain in the United Irishmen. He was not, however, a principal leader. There is no record of his movements or journey to Wexford ... this in itself indicated that he was not as yet very well known. Once in County Wexford, Dwyer joined the United army of North Wexford. The North Wexford campaign eventually led the rebels across the border into Wicklow, and the town of Arklow was to be the scene of the next battle. Dwyer's bravery was noted at the Battle of Arklow. Despite the courage shown by Dwyer and others, this battle was a major defeat for the rebels, who had to retreat into Wexford once again.

Following an action at Kilcavan Hill, Dwyer and his comrades reached Vinegar Hill on the 20th June. This was the eve of what was to prove to be the decisive government victory of the campaign in the southeast. Vinegar Hill was another major defeat for the insurgents, and marked the beginning of the end of the rising. On the 21st June, the rebel forces broke and the main body retreated towards Wexford town. Dwyer, however, did not go with them. Instead, he retreated northwards, rejoining some of his comrades on the way. They spent that night at Peppard's Castle and reached the sacked settlement of Aughrim on the 24th June. The survivors of Vinegar Hill began to regroup. Their commander, Garret Byrne of Ballymanus, now decided to attack on Hacketstown, just over the Carlow border on the 25th June.

At Hacketstown Michael Dwyer was given his first significant command as he led one of the rebel flanking parties. However, a determined loyalist resistance meant that the attackers' losses were high as the defenders picked them off from within stone buildings. Solid resistance from well-armed forces within well-fortified positions amply demonstrated that, without cannon, the rebels could not hope to take such positions. Once again, Dwyer's courage was noted at Hacketstown. With two brothers named Laffan (Laphen) from Kilmuckridge, he managed to climb the barracks wall using scaling ladders. Despite this gallant effort, the barracks proved too tough a nut to crack and the rebels eventually had to withdraw.

The tide of war had firmly turned in favour of the government forces. Retreat into the fastnesses of the Wicklow Mountains was now the only sensible option for the beleaguered rebel forces, but Michael Dwyer could scarcely have imagined just how long his resistance would last in these fastnesses as he and his comrades trekked towards Glenmalure in the first week of July 1798.

For a while, Dwyer defended the secluded valley at this time and he was referred to as 'the Governor of Glenmalure'. However, Dwyer evacuated Glenmalure with the remainder of the insurgents on the 6th August and on the next day they arrived in the Glen of Imaal. Dwyer was home! The Glen of Imaal was geographically remote and the community within it was a close-knit one, which meant that Dwyer had many friends ready to shelter him locally. Even some elements of the yeomanry in this area were prepared to harbour Dwyer. Here, in Imaal he also had an extended web of kinship on which he could rely.

Such support and shelter influenced Dwyer's decision not to avail of a protection, which was offered to him in August. He feared becoming the target of a Loyalist reprisal attack. A protection might be all very well, but with the memory of the Dunlavin massacre and other incidents fresh in Dwyer's mind, no doubt he may have felt that such a protection might not be worth the paper that it was written on.

Dwyer considered the option of taking a protection, but ignored it and September saw him involved in the Battle of Keadeen. Dwyer and his men had decided to continue the fight. This battle was the first is a series of indecisive skirmishes, which harried and harassed the Crown forces. In fact, this was the beginning of a guerrilla campaign in the Wicklow Mountains that was on a par with the mountain campaign waged by the Austrian Andreas Hofer against Napoleon in the Alps.

Dwyer, who realised that pitched battles had been disastrous, was probably the first Irish rebel leader to employ such 'hit and run tactics' and both Michael Collins and Dan Breen cited Dwyer as an inspiration for their own guerrilla campaigns during the War of Independence, 120 years or so later. While small-scale operations were Dwyer's principal modus operandi during the protracted guerrilla campaign, there was always the element of hitting out against the crown forces. Dwyer's operations were of necessity small-scale due to the dearth of numbers within his following. Moreover, any larger scale operations would have attracted the attention of the authorities and the very nature of guerrilla warfare involves small bands that hit both hard and fast before moving on rapidly. Such a campaign suited Dwyer, who was on home territory and who was a fieldcraft expert with finely-honed survival skills.

As the campaign progressed Dwyer became a household name. He was actually far better known than many of the now more famous United Irishmen whose roles were re-appraised during the post-famine era. Dwyer's exploits were well known during his own lifetime and news of his daring escapades only served to fuel the growth of his legend. He became a Romantic figure, regarded as a criminal by the state, but considered a hero and champion by the people who sheltered him. A 'social bandit' in the mould of Robin Hood, Michael Dwyer was idealised and turned into a myth who supposedly never killed but in self-defence or just revenge. The reality was however, that Dwyer was ruthless when he needed to be. Children, women, invalids – Dwyer either shot them or had them shot if he thought they posed a threat or would inform on him. So while affection for Dwyer was one factor in the aid given to Dwyer by the local populace, fear was definitely another. Of course, had Dwyer not had such a ruthless streak, it is probable that he would not have survived so long.

Dwyer's guerrilla campaign continued into 1799. There is no doubt that many of Michael Dwyer's exploits were hair-raising – the real stuff of which ballads were made. Narrow escapes such as the evasion of detection by assuming the disguise of a beggar man and boldly passing by the soldiers who were seeking him or lying across the rafters of Mangan's house while the yeomen searched the building at ground level rank right up there with the legendary Robin Hood's entry into a hostile Nottingham in the garb of a butcher or his hiding in the branches of a tree as the sheriff's men passed beneath!

Dwyer's most famous exploit during his guerrilla campaign was probably also his narrowest escape. This occurred at the cottage of Miley Connell in Derrynamuck (also referred to as Dernamuck and Doire na Muc) on the night of 15 February 1799.

For once, Dwyer's lookout system had failed to alert him of approaching danger. Information received from a spy had led the military to the very door of Dwyer's refuge. Connell's cottage was the third in a clachan of three, situated at the end of an isolated boreen. The rebel occupants of the other two cottages had already been taken.

Ned Lennon and Thomas Clerk surrendered at Hoxey's house and Wat McDonnell (McDaniel), Patrick Toole, John Ashe, John Mickle, Hugh Byrne and Darby Dunn were captured at the home of the Toole family. The military, a detachment of Scottish Highlanders led by Captain Roderick McDonald, surrounded Connell's cottage and called on the men inside – Michael Dwyer, Sam McAllister, Patrick Costello and John Savage – to surrender.

They refused and Costello and Savage were killed in the ensuing battle of Derrynamuck. Sam McAllister also lost his life, which he sacrificed in order to give Dwyer himself a chance to escape. Dwyer emerged from the cottage barefoot and in his underclothes before he burst through the Scottish line and ran to freedom. The whole sense of the dramatic was enhanced because this event happened in the middle of a very cold winter with deep snow covering the ground. During his flight he was lucky to slip on an icy patch as the bullets from a second volley whizzed past overhead. Dwyer was the only member of the rebel band to escape that night. The others were all either killed or captured.

Following his escape from Derrynamuck, Dwyer made for the house of Thaddeus Dwyer, who was a brother of the John Dwyer shot on Dunlavin green, and then went into hiding again. It is said that it took six weeks or so for his feet to recover after his barefoot flight. The prisoners taken at Derrynamuck were taken to Baltinglass, court-martialled and executed (except for Hugh Byrne who turned Kings Evidence).

Dwyer's mountain campaign of guerrilla warfare would continue long after his escape from Derrynamuck in February 1799. Indeed, when Lord Cornwallis stated in a letter of 13 July 1798, 'Our war is reduced to a predatory system in the mountains of Wicklow and the bogs of Kildare' he surely could not have foreseen just how long Michael Dwyer and his followers would continue to hold out in the Wicklow mountains. Dwyer was involved in many dangerous escapades, near misses and scary moments.

Tales such as the 'sea whistle' incident, Dwyer's shooting of the disabled informer 'Danny the Bowl', Dwyer's narrow escape by impersonating the mad Augustus Fitzgerald, the escape from Rathdangan chapel and many more have come down through the generations. However, this talk cannot record all of Dwyer's perilous incidents! News of such exploits endeared him to the public at large both during his lifetime and after his death, and ensured that he became the subject of many ballads.

These ballads were vital because they ingrained Dwyer and his memory into popular culture. As noted already, Dwyer is synonymous with Wicklow in the minds of many people. He is also synonymous with the United Irish leadership. The fact that he was not one of the principal leaders during the main action of the rebellion in Wexford has been obscured by a 19th century revision of his role. The romantic account of his resistance written by John Thomas Campion and the numerous ballads about his time in the Wicklow Mountains have helped to etch the figure of Michael Dwyer into folk-memory far and wide. Dwyer's legend had been growing throughout his guerrilla campaign and posthumous literary works would later elevate Dwyer to hero status.

His prolonged resistance in the Wicklow Mountains had touched a communal nerve. Dwyer was more than an outlaw, more than a rebel, more than a guerrilla leader to many people. He was a symbol of hope at a time and in a place of oppression. As he continued to elude capture, that symbol became brighter and the hope, instead of being dashed, grew in the breasts of an admiring public. Dwyer was a cause célebre in his day. To Republicans who had tasted defeat in the main rebellion, Dwyer's continued defiance burned like an inspirational beacon. As long as there was any hope, however slight, of another revolution or another French invasion, Dwyer would remain in his mountain lair and await developments.

However, as the years passed, hope of such developments faded. By 1803, the Treaty of Amiens of the previous year, though short-lived, had shattered any remaining hope of French intervention in Ireland. In July of that year, Robert Emmet's attempted revolution had petered out. Meanwhile the net was tightening on Dwyer and his followers. The completion of the Military Road through the mountains was a major boost to the Crown forces. This was possibly the first purpose-built road in Ireland – the purpose being to capture Dwyer and his band. Military barracks were occupied at strategic points along this road. There were garrisons stationed at Leitrim, Glencree,

Seven Churches (Glendalough), Glenmalure and Aughavanna.
This new reality considerably hindered Dwyer's capacity for
movement within the heart of the mountains. Coupled with this
was the fact that the military had unleashed a campaign of
arrests against known or suspected friends and relations of
Dwyer.

This strained Dwyer's kinship network almost to breaking
point. The situation was very bleak for the remnants of Dwyer's
pitifully small force as the winter of 1803 drew in. Without the
kinship contacts, there was a lack of safe houses. Caves and
other outdoor places of refuge such as abandoned mine
workings were not suitable during a winter when snow lay
several feet deep on the mountains. In this season cold, damp
and dreary conditions awaited the Dwyer faction as they faced
into their sixth winter 'on the run'.

With the changed political situation in France, the debacle
that was Emmet's abortive rising, the large garrisons stationed
along the new Military Road, a renewed military campaign
against him which began on the 10th December and the absence
of many of the arrested kin, Dwyer's thoughts turned to ending
his guerrilla campaign and the drawing up of terms which would
allow him to lay down his arms.

Dwyer made overtures via his wife to the liberal landlord and
MP, William Hume of Humewood. The commander of the
military, General Beresford, wanted Dwyer to surrender 'upon
the mercy of government' (i.e. unconditionally) but Hume, while
informing Dwyer that the actual surrender would have to be
unconditional, certainly gave some assurances to Mary Dwyer.
The exact nature of these assurances, or at least of Hume's
ability to honour them, is unclear.

Certainly Dwyer's life was to be spared and safe passage to
America for four of his leading followers and himself was
possibly agreed upon. Dwyer may have been led to believe that
he would obtain a full pardon on surrendering himself.
Whatever the truth of the situation, there is no doubt that the
United Irish Captain Michael Dwyer laid down his arms on what
he believed were his own terms when he walked though the
gates of Humewood and into the custody of the Yeoman Captain
and M.P. for County Wicklow, William Hoare Hume, on 14
December 1803, thus bringing to an end the brilliant guerrilla
campaign which had elevated him to the status of myth.

However, once the authorities had their man, they did not
adhere to the terms that had been outlined by Dwyer. Dwyer

wanted to be shipped to the fledgling United States of America. Instead, he was brought to Dublin under armed escort and imprisoned in Kilmainham Gaol. Michael Dwyer remained a prisoner in Kilmainham from December 1803 to August 1805, as did some of his men.

Dwyer and his followers were committed to Kilmainham on a charge of high treason. As state prisoners, they were not always satisfied with their treatment there. Dwyer had a long-running battle with the sadistic gaol doctor, Dr Edward Trevor. Eventually Dwyer's fate was decided upon and Dwyer found out that he was bound for the penal colony of Australia.

Michael Dwyer's captivity in Ireland finished in August 1805, when, in company with his wife Mary, his cousin Hugh 'Vesty' Byrne, Byrne's wife Rachael and their children, Arthur Devlin, Martin Burke and John Mernagh, the leader from the Glen of Imaal boarded the Tellicherry at Cobh, bound for Botany Bay.

The voyage on the Tellicherry took Dwyer and his comrades across vast, undreamt of expanses of ocean but it finally ended when the ship arrived at the entrance to Port Jackson on St. Valentine's Day 1806. Despite initial confusion regarding the Wicklow rebels, they were each given a hundred acres of land at Cabramatta. The Dwyer group may have travelled to Australia on a convict ship, but they went as free men and it seemed that a new and peaceful life awaited them in the Southern hemisphere.

However, when William Bligh (famous, or rather infamous, for his role during the affair of the 'Mutiny on the Bounty') succeeded Gidley King as Governor of New South Wales later in 1806, the peaceable new lives of Dwyer and his comrades were threatened. Bligh was paranoid about the possibility of an uprising in the colony and, considering their background, he perceived the Wicklow settlers as a huge threat.

Dwyer was arrested as a possible ringleader of a rebellion that had not taken place and kept in solitary confinement on board the H.M.S. Porpoise. Following an elaborate show trial, Dwyer was found guilty of 'conspiracy in order to raise a rebellion' and in May 1807 he was sent to the convict depot on Norfolk Island.

Dwyer was once again a prisoner, just as he had been in Kilmainham. He was moved from Norfolk Island to Van Dieman's Land in January 1808. However, moves to oust Governor Bligh were afoot in Sydney and following the so-called 'Rum Rebellion' he was removed from office. With the departure of Bligh, Michael Dwyer and his companions were pardoned and released from captivity.

Under the more enlightened Governor Lachlan Macquarie, on 25 August 1810, Dwyer was appointed as a constable at George's River. By 1819 Dwyer owned six hundred and twenty acres and the solid expansion of his land holding was further proof of his acumen and ability. In May 1820 Dwyer was appointed Chief Constable of Liverpool. Dwyer now served the King that he had rebelled against, but in a place where, by doing so, he could make a difference and help fellow Irishmen and their families.

However, Dwyer had also invested in a tavern called the Harrow Inn. This was perhaps not a good move on the part of a man who was well known to have a fondness for alcohol. The public house brought financial problems and Dwyer was removed from his position as chief constable due to misconduct. To boost his finances, Dwyer had illegally set land belonging to a woman named Ann Stroud. On Christmas Eve 1822 he was found guilty of 'having broken the colonial regulations' and was fined £20. More serious however, he lost his spirit licence and was unable to pay his creditors. Many of his possessions and some of his lands were sold, and in 1824 he was incarcerated in the debtors' prison in Sydney.

He was released in May 1825, but was in poor health when he returned to one of his few possessions that had not been sold – his house at Cabramatta. Weak and suffering from dysentery, he lived only another three months and the 'legend' died on 23 August 1825.

Or did it? The death of Michael Dwyer in Australia only strengthened the legend of the wronged leader who was shamefully exiled by a deceitful establishment. It was now certain that this 'Exile from Erin' was never to return. Dwyer's acceptance of the positions of constable and later chief constable was either kept hidden or worked into the myth by portraying Dwyer as a dispenser of justice for other Irish exiles. Dwyer had been so well known during his guerrilla campaign and at the time of his transportation against his negotiated terms of surrender that he had achieved celebrity status. In those pre mass media days, the press had made him into a superstar. The longevity and romantic nature of his mountain war had captured the imagination.

Posthumously also, he became a valuable symbol – an icon – for Nationalists to aspire to and for Nationalist historians to incorporate into their corpus of literature. Although his guerrilla campaign was always peripheral to the bigger picture, the never-say-die attitude that it embodied was inspirational to a Nationalist Ireland that was crying out for heroes in the wake of the disheartening defeats of 1798.

On 14 December 2003, Taoiseach Bertie Ahern unveiled a statue of Michael Dwyer in his native Glen of Imaal. This is part of a process of remembrance. It is important to remember. This is not to say that Dwyer and his followers should become role models ... but remembrance helps us to understand them, their motives and their sacrifice. With Dwyer we remember a man of the people – the son of a small tenant farmer. Dwyer was also a man of action and was personally involved in many battles. With Dwyer, we remember what was, not what might have been.

Here he differs from Emmet, Tone and Fitzgerald, who were all visionaries and who came from a privileged background. These visionaries did not have the practical survival skills of Dwyer, who held out for over five years and was excellent in the field. He was much more than a mere bandit and always had a United Irish agenda – Burr had taught him well! The visionaries were either executed or died in gaol. As a realist, Dwyer knew that his best – and only – option was Australia. The fact that he did not die for his cause does not belittle him. His mountain war gave inspiration and hope at a hard time and he became an icon to post famine nineteenth century nationalists.

However, his later life was written out of 19th and early 20th century histories and there was a tendency not to mention anything about his life in Australia. Perhaps this is wrong, especially as Michael Dwyer spent twenty of his fifty-three years in Australia. Following his death on 23 August 1825, Michael Dwyer was buried in Devonshire Street Cemetery, but in 1898 his remains were re-interred in Waverly Cemetery. A crowd of over 200,000 attended the re-interment and his memorial stone is the largest of all the monuments over any Irish patriot, and still the highest headstone in Sydney. However, Dwyer's life in Australia is not the reason that he is a significant figure in Irish history. He is significant, rather, for his campaign of 1798-1803; a campaign that also inspired later Irish rebels. Without such men, we might not enjoy the freedom that we do today, and we do well to remember them and study the times in which they lived. Thank you very much.

APPENDIX 8 THE ANCIENT BRITONS

Much has been written about the atrocities perpetrated by the Ancient Briton [1] regiment during the 1798 period. The Ancient Britons were a regular cavalry regiment. They were raised in 1794 by Sir Watkin Williams Wynn, the fifth Baronet Wynn of Wynnstay, Ruabon, Wrexham in Wales. The name 'Ancient Britons' was chosen because it was a politically correct title for the Welsh. The idea behind the name was to emphasise Britishness, rather than Englishness [or Welshness]. This type of thinking allowed both the Scots and even the bilingual Welsh to participate in Hanoverian Britain.

Therefore when Wynn raised his cavalry regiment he chose a name to match his pretensions. His regiment is the Welsh regiment! The new regiment would help to bolster troop numbers in mainland Britain, which found itself with a shortage of such troops at this time. In 1794 Ireland had a separate army and was technically (if not actually) independent of Horseguards.

The Britons were a fencibles regiment. This meant that, by a special act of parliament, they were forbidden to serve outside the United Kingdom unless they volunteered for such service. In this they differed from the regular forces. Also, unlike regulars, fencibles were 'duration only' formations. Hence the fencible regiments were short lived and were disbanded between March and September 1800, following negotiations for the Treaty of Luneville.

Despite only being hereditary knights, the Wynns were the powers of their day in North Wales. Originally Welsh gentry who consolidated land through local marriage, they then married into the English landed gentry and became Anglo-Welsh. Thereafter the Wynns grew wealthier and ever more British, although they never wholly lost their north Welsh credentials.

The fifth Baronet Wynn, Sir Watkin (1772-1840) inherited a temporarily straitened estate then in the care of his Grenville uncles, one whom became the Marquis of Buckingham, and another a cabinet member in the government of William Pitt. The Wynns presided over landed wealth, mines, interests in industrial development and held valuable political offices.

Although their full political impact is unclear, they held at least half a dozen seats in Westminster. Spanning both sides of the Welsh Marches, the Wynn family served as mayors of

Chester, Oswestry and Shrewsbury and provided several Lord
Lieutenants. From 1796 till his death in 1840 Sir Watkin held
the seat for Denbigh.

Interestingly, the regiment he raised in 1794 is not known outside of Ireland because Wynn's burgeoning military career and
the regiment's reputation were blighted by their precipitant
flight from Arklow following Tuberneering. Ireland was not a
glorious campaign for which battle honours were given or
reputations made.

The terror tactics employed by the regiment in East Wicklow
have been well documented. They were also stationed in Naas,
and from there some of their number were posted to Ballymore
Eustace. They carried out the executions there before moving
on to Dunlavin on the morning of the massacre. An incident
which happened on the way to Dunlavin was recorded as
follows: [2]

> May 24th 1798: Twelve insurgents were shot on the green of
> Ballymore Eustace. These were commanded by Horan, a
> protestant. Next day **[the timing is confusing here, but if the
> Ballymore executions happened at about 4 a.m. and the
> soldiers left Ballymore at about 6.30 a.m., it is possible that
> the phrase refers to the morning of the twenty fourth, as the
> Ballymore executions were perceived as happening on the
> night of the twenty third]** the military marched to Dunlavin and
> passing through Lemonstown halted at the house of one
> McDonald, a farmer, (one Fox, a miller of Hollywood, having given
> secret information concerning his (McDonald's) sons).
> McDonald, his wife and sons Kit, John, Harry and Tom were at
> dinner. When the troops rushed into the house the sons were
> taken into the barn before the door and one of them was
> compelled to put a burning turf into the thatch of the house, and
> while doing so his hand was shot off by one of the Ancient
> Britons. In vain the aged father protested his and his sons'
> innocence, and produced a written protection given to him by
> Captain William Ryves of Rathsallagh. Notwithstanding, two of
> his sons, Kit and Tom, were put on their knees. The father knelt
> down then to deprecate mercy or shoot him also. They were shot
> down in the presence of their parents. Harry and John escaped
> in the confusion concealed by the smoke of the burning
> homestead but being perceived they were chased to the recess of
> [Sluwgad?] Church Mountain, escaping unhurt amid volleys of
> bullets from the pursuers. Their aged parents concealed the
> bodies of the others until the following Sunday when they buried
> them in sacks before daybreak in the churchyard of Hollywood.

Once in Dunlavin, the Ancient Britons carried out the executions there. Dunlavin was the only known incident where the regiment participated in a military execution. The Ancient Britons shot the captives under express orders. In many other cases the military shot, sabred and killed people at will. The killing of the McDonalds was one of hundreds, if not thousands of such incidents.

The Britons remained in Dunlavin at least until early June [3] and the death of one member of the regiment there was recorded thus: [4]

> Nicholas Ryder of Crehelp, while working on Friarhill, was attacked by an Ancient Briton who came with Councillor Fisher of Merginstown, whose house then was burned a few days before. Ryder came on quickly with them but in a narrow lane made a prod of the dung fork at the mounted soldier and unhorsed him, thrusting its prong into his bowels. Fisher begged his life and got away, as also the soldier, who died in Dunlavin from his wounds. Ryder then, desperately wounded; escaped to the valley of Crehelp where some women concealed him in clamps of turf for three weeks until his wounds were healed and [he] escaped. After the rebellion he was taken and imprisoned for two years in Dublin's Marshalsea prison.

However, the loss of this soldier was not reflected in the regimental pay return, which was signed off in Cork in March 1799. Hence it was clearly drawn up after the period it covered. On the one hand, this fact meant that the pay return was less likely to contain errors, as it was not compiled under the stresses of active service. On the other hand though, the time lapse meant that events such as the probable loss of Paymaster Burganey's papers and those of several other slain officers, actually made the document more susceptible to errors. The pay return could be wrong on names (enlisting under false names being common enough) but in cases of death and desertion such documents were meticulous. Neither dead men nor deserters drew pay and allowances! This is a case where local records and tradition says one thing and the regiment's pay records another. The pay records may contain errors, but the above extract may also be erroneous and Nicholas Ryder killed a member of a different regiment, perhaps with a similar uniform, and the dead soldier was wrongly recorded as an Ancient Briton. Either way, the Britons left Dunlavin shortly afterwards.

The regiment was later involved in the Battle of Ballyellis on 30 June 1798, where the regiment suffered about thirty dead. These were painful losses, but not the devastating defeat their rebel enemies thought they had inflicted. One regimental anecdote concerned Lieutenant Colonel Richard Puleston, and their narrow escape at Ballyellis. At that time, Wynn had left the regiment under the operational command of Puleston.

On the day of the ambush Richard Puleston was riding a black mare called 'Priestess'. The horse was a highly-prized hunter, which had been given to Puleston by his new wife Emma Corbet. Priestess was killed by the rebels at Ballyellis, but Puleston was saved by his servant Thomas Crane who warded off a blow and rushed his master a new mount enabling him to make a desperate escape to Carnew. The horse had one of its ears lopped off as a memento mori by the rebels, but the ear was somehow recovered by Crown forces and became a Puleston family relic, now alas mislaid! Ballyellis was not the regiment's finest hour, but at least Puleston had a story to tell!

Following the Wexford campaign, the regiment cropped up again in the mountains outside Dublin in October 1798 chasing Michael Dwyer. They went back to Kildare sometime in late 1798. They appeared in Mary Leadbeater's diary in January 1799, accidentally shooting someone in a barn. In March-April 1799 some troopers were involved in courts martial trying locals for trying to swear members into the United Irishmen, which was then a capital offence. In July 1799 the regiment volunteered to serve anywhere in the world but were not taken up on their generous offer! They were transferred back to Britain in November 1799. Once back in North Wales they were finally disbanded at Wrexham on 3 April 1800.

Whether unjustly censured after Arklow or not, Wynn never got round to commissioning a history of his first and finest regiment. After it was disbanded in 1800, he kept the regimental papers (aside from pay records), but they are now lost. They may have been burned in the Wynnstay house fire of 1858. The books recorded the day to day running of any regiment. In their absence it is difficult to build up a picture of the Ancient Britons. Certainly a good proportion were Welsh and some were drawn from across the English border in Cheshire and Shropshire. However, it is difficult to distinguish individuals with common first and second names, so it has not been possible to track soldiers from one pay record (the only surviving documents) to the next. There is no way of knowing whether the seven Jones, five Williams, four Pritchards, and the many Owens and other common Welsh surnames in every pay list came from the Welsh or the English side of the border. Similarly, one cannot say whether the Welsh were Welsh-speaking or bilingual from day one. Once the regiment reached Ireland, there could have been Catholics or Irishmen in the ranks. As a regimental community, they did not remain stagnant but changed over time and location.

Following the regiment's disbandment in 1800, its former members largely disappeared from sight. Only forty two are traceable because they went on to serve in the regular army and lived long enough to be discharged. However, such a small sample is unrepresentative. The regiment existed for nearly six years. In that period its strength varied from four hundred and fifty in late 1795 to around three hundred in 1800. A half dozen or so died or deserted each year. Some were discharged, usually for medical reasons. So potentially two thousand or so men could have been through the ranks.

Despite this, there are very few tangible reminders of the regiment's existence. Their part in the Dunlavin massacre means that the 1798 monument in the village is one. There are also a handful of graves across Wales and Shropshire. More unusual links include a charity running a girls' school in Middlesex, and a foxhunt in north Wales! Baronet Wynn and the present girls' school can be linked through the Loyal and Honourable Society of Ancient Britons. That society was a London based club for pro-Hanoverian Welsh worthies, which was founded on St David's day 1715. It sponsored a charity school for the education of the Welsh poor. The school continues to exist today as a registered UK charity, albeit now educating girls only. Sir Watkin Wynn was the society's president in the 1790s and donated funds and a bust of himself to the school. The society gave Wynn the name of his regiment. The foxhunt is the Wynnstay hunt. Despite the Wynn family selling Wynnstay after World War Two, the hunt survives and is still patronised by the current Baronet Wynn.

NOTES

1: I am indebted to Mr. Paul Haycock, a military historian from Wigton, Cumbria for sharing his knowledge of the Ancient Briton Regiment. His input was invaluable.

2: Shearman Papers XVII, quoted in Chris Lawlor, Dunlavin Green Revisited, in Dunlavin-Donard-Davidstown Parish Link, Vol. IV, No. 3, November 1998, p. 6-7.

3: N.A.I. 620/38/23.

4: Shearman Papers XVII, quoted in Lawlor, op cit.

APPENDIX 9 THE JUDGE BY CHRIS LAWLOR [1]

Dunlavin Market House, 21st May 1798: He was in pain. All other feelings subsided as the pain took over. The harsh iron blade ripped the skin from under his right arm and once again he had reason to curse the bridle hooks that Thomas Egan, the local blacksmith, had put on to his pike heads. The bridle hook continued to bite and to pull him upwards. His right shoulder was probably dislocated, but the pain couldn't get any worse.

After what seemed an eternity, the bridle hook was slowly lowered and he reverted to his normal position. Normal? Trussed up like a chicken and tied to this triangle – it was hardly normal. The voices of his tormentors began to seep through to his battered ears as the pain eased a bit. 'How do you like that Dunn?' 'Is that how you'd use those pikes on us?' 'Where's Erin go Bragh now, you treacherous bastard?'

'Erin go Bragh'. His mind flitted back to his first introduction to that phrase. It had been in a whiskey shop in Hollywood, after a hard day's labour in the fields. He was hot and sticky and he had decided to quench his thirst in Patrick Burke's shebeen before he went home. There was a small man with a strange, harsh accent in the whiskey shop. What was his name now – Mac-something? Magarr? McGennis? No, McCabe, that was it – McCabe. McCabe was talking about strange, wonderful things – the Declaration of the Rights of Man, Liberty, Equality, Fraternity – and Erin go Bragh.

He was in pain again. As the razor sharp blade of the knife – his own bloody knife that he had often used to skin rabbits – was inserted violently under his big toenail, all other thoughts were blotted out. His big toe became his universe. He tried to cry out 'No', but his mouth would not form the word. Instead a strange sound, half groan, half gasp, emerged. His toenail was almost off, and his tormentors were pulling it backwards, away from the toe itself. 'Oh God, Oh God'.

Slowly the pain subsided, to become bearably unbearable once more. The guards cut him down from the triangle and he fell in a heap. His pride brought him slowly to his feet again and he stood shakily, swaying like a leaf. Thoughts flitted through his mind again. He was in the mountains, at an isolated cottage. It was a moonlit night and he was excited. McCabe had told him that he would meet 'Captain Fearnaught' here. The cabin door opened, and in the dim light he could see the captain – a small man who, even in the dim light, seemed to have the sign of drink on him. Nevertheless he repeated the words of the oath after the captain. Strange words, about things he had never heard of, but the ideas behind it all seemed to be right. He didn't know what 'Land Reform' really meant for one thing – and here in this wild place, somewhere between Humewood and Avondale, he had even reflected that it would take a hundred years for anyone to organise the tenants to look for this so-called land reform!

He was in pain again. Worse than before, if that were possible. Choking, his neck, his throat, his very being. Stomach heaving, head spinning: 'My God', he thought dimly, 'They're hanging me'. But just as consciousness seemed to be fading away, his feet – his sore, sore feet – touched the ground. The cruel rope loosened and a fist smashed into his face. He dropped to the ground, gasping for breath amid the phlegm and the vomit. He was heaved back up to the triangle. Voices began to break through again: 'Who else'? 'Who are they'? 'Kill Captain Saunders, would you'?

His mind wandered again – away from the stern blocks of granite and the cold dome above him. He could see blue skies – and a real hooley both inside and outside the long stone cottage that was to be his new home. Mary was there – his Mary now – with her wide smile and warm heart. She hadn't liked the midnight meetings that he went to. He had tried to placate her, but she had said that these wild ideas would only lead to trouble. He hadn't listened – why hadn't he listened? Mary had become his bride yesterday. Fr. Travers had told him about another meeting tonight, but he would miss that one. Fr. Travers could go on his own – he wasn't a newly wed!

Suddenly his mind returned to the present. The captain that had just walked in was a stranger to him. A gentleman, no doubt. One could see that at a glance. The captain spoke to his tormentors 'Anything'? It was a question. 'Nothing Sir', 'Nothing yet Sir' they replied. The captain began to converse with the men in low tones.

He was remembering again, good news, happy news. Mary wasn't sure, but she thought ... He remembered thinking that a little boy would be nice to carry on the name and to work the small bit of ground. A girl – well, she'd be welcome too, no doubt, even if more expensive to marry off later! As long as Mary would be alright – Oh God!

Suddenly he was back in the present again, his face smarting from a hard blow delivered by the soft hand of the gentleman captain. 'Who are the others'? 'Who else is involved Dunn'? Slowly he shook his head. The officer nodded to the men and he was tied to the triangle again. Terror shot through his pain-racked body as the red-hot brazier was carried in on long metal handles. One of his tormentors had a sheep-iron in his hand. He struggled, but he could barely move an inch. The triangle was effective!

The officer was speaking again. 'I'll ask you one last time, you croppy bastard, before the boys here pay a visit to your wife – who are the others'? The man with the branding iron stood behind the officer, but even the terror that he inspired had paled into insignificance. The officer, the gentleman, had mentioned Mary. His Mary; their child? The terrible pain was replaced by a weakness – an all-embracing weakness. He slumped, in so far as one in his position could slump, on the triangle. The names began to come. An incoherent babble at first, but one of his tormentors had his ear close to the bruised and battered mouth and he repeated the names to the officer.

Once he had started, he couldn't stop and the names rolled off his swollen tongue. Eighteen, twenty of them – he'd lost count. Tears came for the first time during his ordeal as he named his colleagues. He vaguely hoped that they'd fare better than he had if they were imprisoned in this dreary place. The weakness was overpowering now. 'At least' he thought, 'they'll hardly fare any worse'! Relief mingled with shame as the weakness advanced through his whole being. Vaguely he heard the door close and he sensed that he was alone. Alone – and weak. Another thought flitted through his mind. 'They'll brand me anyway – an informer! In a hundred, two hundred years from now, there'll be hard men swilling pints of porter and cursing the informer. My God, history is a harsh judge'! Weakness. 'Eloi, Eloi, lamma sabacthani'? But consciousness was gone.

NOTE

This short story is the only work of fiction based on the events surrounding the Dunlavin massacre. The story won first prize in its category in the 2001 Dunlavin Festival of Arts.

APPENDIX 9 CHRIS LAWLOR INTERVIEWED

Robert Allen's interview with Chris Lawlor on the occasion of his visit to the Irish Centre, Hammersmith, London, on 6 March 2004 to speak about his book In search of Michael Dwyer.

RA What is the relevance of Michael Dwyer to modern Irish society?

CL A difficult question to start with ... I will leave it till the end, when the answer may be read in the light of the other answers that I have given.

RA How much does the myth about Michael Dwyer matter to the legend?

CL The myth and the reality of Dwyer are often not quite the same. However, what is important here is people's perceptions of Dwyer. The myth ensured that Dwyer was perceived as a Nationalist/Republican hero. Dwyer attained some qualities that were almost superhuman. However, the myth was no accident. Many ordinary people identified with Dwyer, the son of a small tenant farmer, much more readily than they could identify with rich, powerful and influential leaders such as Tone, Fitzgerald or Emmet. They were viewed as being on a pedestal, separated by social class, rank, status, wealth and sometimes, it has to be said, religion from the ordinary populace. Dwyer, on the other hand, was one of their own This fact was not lost on the post-famine revisionists, people like Fr. Kavanagh, who wrote the popular history of 1798. Kavanagh's writing should be viewed as part of the wider post-famine Catholic Devotional Revolution, a movement which forged closer links between Irish Catholicism and Irish Nationalism. Thus the myth of Dwyer was carefully cultivated, the noble Catholic peasant who tried to change an unjust system and who remained undefeated, only laying down arms on his own terms, and who was then shamefully treated by the representatives of that system. References to his later life in Australia were totally wiped out ... indeed, Campion's book has Dwyer dying in 1805 instead of 1825, and Campion's book was the authority on Dwyer for over half a century. The myth of Dwyer was further accentuated by the many romantic poems and ballads written about him. In a peculiarly oral tradition, an important part of the Irish psyche, Dwyer's legend lived and grew. Also, very importantly, the inclusion of The Ballad of Michael Dwyer by T. D. Sullivan in the primary school curriculum once the Irish Free State was founded meant that many generations of impressionable youngsters were exposed to the romantic tale of Dwyer and his daring deeds. Thus, the legend continued to grow and the perception of Dwyer as a superhuman hero, escaping from the cottage in Derrynamuck to continue the noble fight, was ingrained into the minds of generations of Irish children nationwide. Dwyer's status as a major icon was ensured and it was the perception rather than the reality that was now important.

RA I also ask this because Dwyer's deeds have taken on a character of their own comparable to those of the mythical legends like Medb, Cuchulain, etc. Does this tell us that we need the mythical figure as well as the living legend?

CL I am not sure, but can offer some opinions. The first important point is that we have to differentiate Dwyer from purely fictional figures. He did exist and many of his deeds are recorded. In fact, his escapades are so numerous and so daring that in many cases the reality matches, if not surpasses, the myth. Truth was stranger than fiction! However, there is more than this to the growth of the myth. As already mentioned. Dwyer's lowly origins meant that he was perceived to be one of our own by many ordinary people. He was master of the mountains and controlled his area of operations almost totally. Thus the idea of the romantic outlaw, wronged and fighting to right that wrong, becomes part of the myth.

The parallels with the English Robin Hood saga are obvious. Even some of the stories are similar. Dwyer hides overhead while soldiers search below for him; Dwyer disguises himself to evade capture; Dwyer shows his skill as a marksman; Dwyer proves himself a noble enemy by allowing certain prisoners to walk; surely the stuff of legend. However, I liken Dwyer not so much to Robin Hood as to two other famous freedom fighters, both of whom operated in the Alps. These are Switzerland's William Tell and Austria's Andreas Hofer. The legendary Tell has become a major tourist attraction and is commemorated in many Swiss towns and villages. Hofer's huge statue overlooks the ski-jump in Innsbruck and his image is found all over the Tyrol. Yet the legendary Dwyer was not commemorated in stone in his native place until 2003. In other countries, these national icons, who were also local heroes operating in mountainous areas, are widely celebrated and commemorated with pride. They have a mythical status of their own. Yet, in Ireland, there is a shying away from such commemorations and in the absence of official events, the unofficial versions – i.e. the myth rather than the reality – takes over. This is why it is the job of the historian to delve and to inform. If Dwyer and similar figures are left in an information and commemoration vacuum, the myth will be the only version of his life that is related. Similarly, the myth will only be celebrated and commemorated by an Irish Republican minority element and this is wrong. Dwyer was a man of the people, and his memory belongs to all of the people. However, if his life is not studied and if the official channels do not recognise him (and others like him) then there is certainly a need for the mythical figure to be held up as an icon.

RA Michael Dwyer clearly means a lot to the people of West Wicklow and to republicans of various hues but do you believe he has a place in the national psyche in the same manner as others who were involved in the struggle for freedom?

CL Referring to my answer to question two above ... also – and very importantly – the inclusion of Sullivan's ballad in the primary school curriculum meant that Dwyer's status as a major icon was ensured and it was the perception rather than the reality that was now important. I think it is true to say that Dwyer had a place in the hearts and minds of many people of the older generation. However, when the ballad was removed from the school texts and when the teaching of history (rightly) became less biased, particularly after the outbreak of the Northern Troubles post-1969, Dwyer, with many other Republican figures, moved from their centre-stage position. Now that historians are starting to revise the revisionism of the past thirty years or so, I think that figures such as Dwyer are starting to emerge from the shadows again. The bicentenary of 1798-1803 has rekindled interest in the period generally and a large corpus of new work has been published recently. Lives of major leaders such as Fitzgerald and Emmet have been published, and some general histories of the rebellion have also been produced. However, it is very interesting to see books such as Women of '98 – women's history has long been neglected and Fellowship of Freedom – the study of history through artefacts dating from the time or made in commemoration of the event is also a neglected area of Irish historiography. The great difference in the bicentenary corpus of work however, is the plethora of books taking a local area as the focus of their studies. There is a strong feeling of locality and an increasing awareness of local history nowadays, and using this sense of place to investigate what happened in our area at a particular time – e.g. 1798-1803 – is a very important part of the process of finding out where we came from and why we are the people we are today. My own study on Dwyer fits into this category, but there is also a local history of national events and the story must place Dwyer firmly within the bigger national picture, in which he was for a time a leading character.

RA Are people neutral about Michael Dwyer and the rest of the 1797-1803 leaders because it is so long ago, while tempers still tend to fray over the 1916-22 leaders?

CL There is a lot of truth in the inference included in the question, but I think there is also more to it than the mere passage of more time. I think that we must look at outcomes here. There is no doubt that everyone loves, praises and has sympathy for the heroic failure. Thus the efforts of the Great O'Neill some years before the Flight of the Earls, the efforts of the United Irishmen in 1798-1803, the efforts of the Young Irelanders in 1848 and the efforts of the Fenians in 1867 are all held in high esteem. They are all variously viewed as romantic, heroic, futile, courageous, hopeless, patriotic and pathetic (i.e. inducing pathos). They were all 'fine efforts' and everything from 'the informer' to 'the weather' has been put forward as a reason for their failure.

However, in the cold hard light of day, that's what they all were, failures, and they changed nothing. The period 1916-22 was different. It had a definite outcome and one that involved major changes. Viewed alone, the 1916 Rising could be viewed as another failure, but, and even the wording of the question confirms this, it was (or it became) the first part of a wider, longer revolutionary movement. The treaty and all that went with it divided the country at the time, so it is no surprise that it should still be so and that some tempers still tend to fray.

In my own paternal family, for example, my grandfather Pat and his brother Ned were in the Free State Army, while their other brothers, John and Arthur were anti-treaty. Hence the outcome of the 1916-22 period had a direct effect on my family, in a way that the outcome of 1798-1803 could not have had. Now, if we multiply the experience of my family by the many other affected families, we begin to get a picture of how the divisions of the treaty etc. diffused into every local area, every parish, every townland and nearly every household in the country. Had the period 1916-22 produced another failure with no change as its outcome, it would probably be viewed in the same way as the list of failed attempts above! We could hardly argue over Collins and Dev if both had been executed in Kilmainham; then they would have 'died for Ireland' and joined the martyrs and the ranks of myth!

RA Why did Michael Dwyer achieve legendary status; was he clever or lucky or both?

CL He was good! Yes he was lucky, yes he was clever, and the whole idea of his being a man of the people added to his legend, but first and foremost, he was good. By 'good' I mean he was good in the military sense A few quotes from the book might be relevant.

Admittedly, Dwyer had shown conspicuous bravery during engagements with these crown forces such as those at Arklow, Hacketstown and Ballyellis. He had been given his own command and had stayed in the field even after the demise of Holt's contingent. Holt had laid down his arms in November 1798, but Dwyer continued his resistance until he gave himself up, on terms of his own choosing, in December 1803. In total, Dwyer continued his fight against the authorities for over five and a half years. The longevity of his campaign was staggering and his feat becomes all the more amazing when one considers the huge weight of odds stacked against him.

At the outset, it is important to clarify that Dwyer was not a mere criminal or bandit. From late 1798 onwards banditry and minor raids could continue as long as there were small numbers of unreconciled or outlawed rebels but this in itself could not he considered as insurrectionary warfare. However. Michael Dwyer had been a captain of the United Irish force. His family background was also entwined within the United Irish organisation. Many of his kinfolk had been deeply involved in the movement; for example John Dwyer of Seskin had been a baronial delegate.

Michael Dwyer's leadership qualities were noticed during the Wexford campaign and he had his own command from the time of the second battle of Hacketstown onwards. Hence Dwyer had a mandate for his actions from within the organisation to winch he belonged.

Dwyer's operations were of necessity small-scale; small bands that hit both hard and fast before moving on rapidly. Such a campaign suited Dwyer, who was on home territory and whose fieldcraft and survival skills were of the highest order.

The whole idea of being on home territory is vital here. The situation was very simple; whoever came looking for Dwyer in the mountains stood a good chance of being killed. Dwyer was ruthless; he once shot three deserters of the Meath militia who had come to join him because he was unsure and suspected their motivation. He once killed a twelve-year-old boy because he had informed on some of his comrades. Dwyer ruled his upland bastion with an iron hand. Yes, he had kin in the area; yes, he had many sympathisers; yes he was well supported in his own place, but woe betide anyone who crossed him! Perhaps such actions seem repellent today – but we must judge them by the standards of the time rather than by today's standards. And the time was tough; it was 'kill or be killed' and such actions were part of the reason why Dwyer survived so long and achieved the legendary status that he did. Now ... back to where we started ...

RA What is the relevance of Michael Dwyer to modern Irish society?

CL When I lecture on Dwyer, I try to finish by addressing this whole area. Here are some of the points that I make:

• Without Dwyer, and people like him, we would not enjoy the democracy and the freedoms we have in Ireland today.

• Dwyer operated at a time when Irish Nationalism was on its knees. The bloody events of 1798 and its aftermath were a horrendous blow to the National cause. Just when all seemed lost, a beacon of hope appeared in Wicklow. Dwyer and his band gave back a sense of pride and self-respect to all whose hopes had been dashed so devastatingly.

• It is important to commemorate and remember Dwyer et al as it helps us to understand how we got to where we are now. However, understanding their motives and their sacrifice does not mean that we have to use these men as role models.

• Dwyer was a man of action; we remember what he actually did, not what he wanted to do or might have done. Here he differs significantly from Tone and Emmet. Dwyer carried on the struggle on the ground – he was at the cutting edge (literally at times!)

• Dwyer was much more than a bandit; he always had a United Irish agenda. The United Irishmen were part of a wider Trans-Atlantic phenomenon; a democratic upsurge against Colonialism and Monarchy. Dwyer was a Republican, i.e. he believed that leaders should be elected and the idea of people being subjects of a monarchy was anathema to him. Today in Ireland, the basis of our democracy is built on the model espoused by Dwyer and the United Irishmen.

• Dwyer fought for his beliefs, for as long as possible, but his practical nature meant that he made terms and laid down his arms. He chose life over death; surely this fact in no way belittles his heroism? As a realist, his best option was America; but it turned out that his only option was Australia.

• In Australia, Dwyer and others left a legacy of many generations of families who have upheld Dwyer's own principles and who have helped to shape the modern nation of Australia, where the rights of the individual and the place of human freedom is recognised by the state. The close links that exist between Australia and Ireland today can be traced back through the history of Dwyer and many others like him, who re-built their lives from scratch in Australia.

• Back in Ireland, Dwyer's campaign inspired later generations of freedom fighters. Michael Collins and Dan Breen both held Dwyer's guerrilla campaign in high esteem and modelled some of their military actions on his. Indeed, it was guerrilla warfare that made the War of Independence of 1919-21 different in its outcome and that eventually led to the establishment of the new state. Dwyer was one of the first to see the value of such warfare, thus blazing a trail for the people who eventually established the Irish Free State.

GENERAL WORKS

Thomas Pakenham: The Year of Liberty, London, 1972

Frank MacDermot: Tone and his times, Tralee, 1969

Patrick C. Power: The Courts Martial of 1798, Carlow, 1997

Sean Cronin and Richard Roche: Freedom the Wolfe Tone Way, Tralee, 1973

Michael Kenny: The 1798 Rebellion: Photographs and memorabilia from the National Museum of Ireland, Dublin, 1996

Kevin Whelan: Fellowship of Freedom: The United Irishmen and 1798, Cork, 1998

Daniel Gahon: The People's Rising: Wexford 1798, Dublin, 1995

R.R. Madden: Literary Remains of the United Irishmen of 1798 and selections from other popular lyrics of their times, Dublin, 1887

Sean McMahon: Robert Emmet, Cork, 2001

William Fitzpatrick: The Sham Squire and the Informers of 1798, Dublin, 1866

Richard Musgrave: Memoirs of different rebellions in Ireland, Dublin, 1801

WORKS ON THE WICKLOW-KILDARE-CARLOW AREA

Myles V. Ronan (editor): Insurgent Wicklow 1798, Dublin, 1948

Chris Lawlor: The Massacre on Dunlavin Green – A Story of the 1798 Rebellion, Naas, 1998

Ruán O'Donnell: The Rebellion in Wicklow 1798, Dublin, 1998

Chris Lawlor: Dunlavin Green Revisited, in Dunlavin-Donard-Davidstown Parish Link, Vol. IV, No. 3, November 1998

Deirdre Heaney: Land and Life in the Glen of Imaal 1830-1901, Unpublished B.A. Thesis, N.U.I. Maynooth, 1983

Ruán O Donnell: Exploring Wicklow's Rebel Past 1798-1803, Wicklow, 1998.

L.M. Cullen: Politics and Rebellion – Wicklow in the 1790s, in Ken Hannigan and William Nolan (eds), Wicklow: History and Society, Dublin, 1994

Pat Power: The Battle of Arklow, in Wicklow Historical Society Journal, Vol. 2, No. 4, May 1998

Chris Lawlor: Unfinished Business, in Dunlavin-Donard-Davidstown Parish Link, Vol.V, No. 1, July 1999

Patrick O'Byrne: West Wicklow, in Souvenir Guide and Programme of the Imaal Bazaar and Fete, Leinster Leader Ltd. Naas, 1926

Samuel Russell McGee: Dunlavin, County Wicklow – A Retrospect, Dublin, 1935

Claude Chavasse: The Story of Baltinglass, Kilkenny Journal Ltd., 1970

Ruán O'Donnell: Aftermath: Post-Rebellion Insurgency in Wicklow 1799-1803, Dublin, 1999

Chris Lawlor: Canon Frederick Donovan's Dunlavin 1884-1896: A West Wicklow Village in the Late Nineteenth Century, Dublin, 2000

Chris Lawlor: Loose Ends from the Dunlavin Area 1797-1803, in Dunlavin Festival of Arts Brochure, XVIII, Naas, 2000

Ruán O'Donnell, Ultra-Loyalism in Wicklow: The case of the Dunlavin massacre, in Wicklow Historical Society Journal, Vol. 2, No. 4, May 1998

Chris Lawlor: From Wicklow to Woomera – Wicklow's Criminal Australian Connections, in Dunlavin Festival of Arts Brochure, XVI, Dunlavin, 1998

Wicklow County Council: Wicklow commemorating 1798-1998: Calendar of Events, Wicklow, 1998

Carlow County Council/Carlow Urban District Council: Carlow '98 Bicentenary Commemoration 1798-1998: Schedule of Events, Carlow, 1998

Robert Duffy: One hundred years too soon: Hacketstown and 1798, Hacketstown Community Council, 1998

Ruán O'Donnell: The Rebellion of 1798 in County Wicklow, in Ken Hannigan and William Nolan (editors.), Wicklow: History and Society, Dublin, 1994

Pat Power: People of Wicklow 1798, Dun Laoghaire, 1999

Robert Fraser: General view of the agriculture and mineralogy present state and circumstances of the County Wicklow with observations on the means of their improvement drawn up for the consideration of the Dublin Society, Dublin, 1801

Thomas Radcliff: A report of the agriculture and livestock of the County of Wicklow prepared under the direction of The Farming Society of Ireland, Dublin, 1812

Noel Bergin: Kilcullen in 1798, Naas, 1998

Brendan Farrelly and Michael Moore: Massacre at Gibbet Rath 1798, Naas, 1998

Peadar Mac Suibhne: Kildare in '98, Naas, 1978

Mario Corrigan: All that delirium of the brave, Naas, 1998

Liam Chambers: Rebellion in Kildare 1790-1803, Dublin, 1998

Dermot James and Seamas O'Maitiu: The Wicklow world of Elizabeth Smith 1840-1850, Dublin, 1996

WORKS ON DWYER

Charles Dickson: The life of Michael Dwyer with some account of his companions, Dublin, 1944

Thomas Bartlett: Masters of the mountains: the insurgent careers of Joseph Holt and Michael Dwyer, County Wicklow, 1798-1803, in Ken Hannigan and William Nolan (eds.), Wicklow: History and Society, Dublin, 1994

John Thomas Campion: Michael Dwyer or the insurgent captain of the Wicklow Mountains: A tale of the rising in 1798, Glasgow, 1869 (also Gill, Dublin, 1910)

Elaine Hoxey and Caoimhin de Lion: Michael Dwyer – Battle of Doire na Muc, Donard, 1988

Kieran Sheedy: Upon the mercy of government, Dublin, 1988

Kieran Sheedy: The Tellicherry Five, Dublin, 1997

Paul Gorry: The Family of Michael Dwyer, in Journal of the West Wicklow Historical Society, I, 1983-1984.

Con Costello: Michael Dwyer in Captivity, in Journal of the West Wicklow Historical Society, II, 1985/1986.

Chris Lawlor: In search of Michael Dwyer, Naas, 2003

Joe Whittle SDB: Michael Dwyer of 1798: the day the quiet sow saved his bacon, in Dunlavin Festival of Arts Brochure, XVI, Dunlavin, 2003

WEB PAGES

There are many web pages with a Dwyer connection. The following is just a small selection.

http://www.dwyerclan.com/Three_Flowers.htm
http://members.tripod.com/granitefields/new_page_3.htm
http://www.local.ie/general/history/1798/biog.shtml
http://www.bartleby.com/224/0922.html
http://www.linuxlots.com/~dunne/ireland/Michael_Dwyer.html
http://www.iol.ie/~walshpa/mdwyer.html
http://www.waverley.nsw.gov.au/library/about/historical/cm_wlk_6.htm
http://omega.cc.umb.edu/~irish/october_1998.htm
http://members.ozemail.com.au/~slaven01/mckeon/dwyer.html

MANUSCRIPTS, DOCUMENTS AND NEWSPAPERS

National Archives, Bishop Street, Dublin, The Rebellion Papers
National Archives, Bishop Street, Dublin, State of the Country Papers
National Archives, Bishop Street, Dublin, Wicklow Gaol Register
Russell Library, N.U.I. Maynooth, The Shearman Papers, VII and XVII
Trinity College Library, Special Collections, The White Collection
Trinity College Library, Special Collections, The 1641 Depositions (Wicklow)
National Library, Kildare Street, Dublin, The Cullen Papers
The Freeman's Journal
The Press
The Leinster Leader
The Wicklow People

ORAL TRADITION

I am indebted to the people of my own place, West Wicklow, both living and dead, for the way in which they have kept the tradition of the Dunlavin massacre and Michael Dwyer alive over time. I extend my sincere thanks to each and every one of them.

smallworld publishing - books

SMALL WORLD Our Story – The Rossport 5
TRADE PAPERBACK
by Mark Garavan
Published January 2007
€12.50/£11.95

SMALL HISTORY The Longest Rebellion: The Dunavin Massacre, Michael Dwyer and West Wicklow 1798
TRADE PAPERBACK
by Chris Lawlor
Published October 2007
€12.99/£11.95

SMALL FICTION Freeborn Travelle
TRADE PAPERBACK
by Grattan Puxon
Published October 2007
€12.99/£11.95

SMALL FICTION Birds, Booze and Bulldozers
HARDBACK
by Peter Styles
Published November 2007
€21.99 (Republic of Ireland only)/£19.99

SMALL FOOD The Small Breakfast Book
TRADE PAPERBACK
by Anne Addicott
Published May 2008
€9.99/£11.95

SMALL LIVES Mackerel and Potatoes
TRADE PAPERBACK
by Robert Allen
Published June 2008
€12.99/£11.95

SMALL WORLD Birds of Prey: How the Doves brought down the Hawks
TRADE PAPERBACK
by CD Stelzer, Giovanna Baistrocchi and Robert Allen
Published July 2008
€12.99/£11.95

SMALL SPORT Roy Keane: A Sunderland Season
TRADE PAPERBACK
by Graeme Anderson
Published July 2008
€12.99/£11.95

SMALL WORLD Zapatista Spring
TRADE PAPERBACK
by Ramor Ryan
Published August 2008
€9.99/£11.95

SMALL FOOD Small Herbs
TRADE PAPERBACK
by Anne Addicott
Published September 2008
€9.99/£11.95

SMALL FOOD Small Spices
TRADE PAPERBACK
by Anne Addicott
Published September 2008
€9.99/£11.95

SMALL TRAVEL Swiss Postcards
TRADE PAPERBACK
by Allan Robinson
Published September 2008
€19.99/£15.95

SMALL LIVES Baburin's Dilemma
TRADE PAPERBACK
by Michael Wagstaff
Published November 2008
€12.99/£11.95

SMALL FICTION Jam Sandwiches - A Diary
HARDBACK
by Carina Jeisy
Published November 2008
€21.99 (Republic of Ireland only)

SMALL WORLD MEDIA

titles can be ordered from

www.smallworldmedia.ie

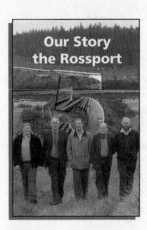

Our Story by the Rossport 5

introduced by Mark Garavan

Published: **January 2007**

Price: **€12.50 / £11.95**

Available: **Ireland, Britain and Europe**

Market: **Community, Cultural & Current Affairs**

ISBN: **978 0 9554634 0 2**

Binding: **Paper**

Extent: **208pp, 140 x 210 mm**

STOP PRESS

Rossport activist Willie Corduff is one of the winners of a prestigious global award, the Goldman Environmental Prize. Announced every April to coincide with Earth Day, Goldman winners are selected by an international jury from confidential nominations submitted by a worldwide group of environmental organisations and individuals. More information: http://www.goldmanprize.org/

The truth by the men in their own words

For the first time the Rossport Five talk directly about their experiences confronting the might of Shell Oil.

There are vivid descriptions of the sense of siege felt in the small village of Rossport as the enormous Corrib gas project was being prepared and developed. The men and their wives describe their frantic efforts to prevent Shell entering their lands.

In moving language, they detail their isolation and fear as Shell applied concerted pressure on them to consent to their project. This culminated in Shell's decision to seek to commit the men to prison indefinitely.

The book provides vivid first-time accounts of their prison experiences, how these ordinary citizens endured the efforts by the State and the multi-national to force them to abandon their opposition.

The men outline the wave of support which reached them in prison and made them more steadfast in their determination to defend the health and safety of their families and communities. Finally, they describe how these experiences have affected them personally. This dramatic account offers a series of telling insights into contemporary Ireland.

 small world media

Trade Orders (Ireland): Easons, Argosy, Small World Distribution
Trade Orders (Britain, Europe, North America): Gazelle Book Services, Active, Small World Distribution
Individual Orders: www.smallworldmedia.ie
Small World Media: 2 Great Strand Street, Dublin 1, Ireland 00 353 (0) 87 955 1504

BOOK INFORMATION

Birds, Booze & Bulldozers

a novel by Peter Styles

Published: **November 2007**

Price: **£19.99 (Britain, Europe & North America)/**
€21.99 (Ireland)

Available: **Ireland, Britain, Europe & North America**

Market: **Fiction**

ISBN: **978-0-9554634-5-7**

Binding: **Cloth**

Extent: **288pp, 140 x 210 mm**

Can you save the planet with a bicycle lock?

Maybe.

Birds, Booze & Bulldozers is the inside story of Britain's environmental direct action movement – the most effective political counter-culture of the 1990s.

More at home with a ball at his feet and a pint in hand, Lester Stype is drawn into becoming an activist to help save the downland of his youth.

The action follows Lester and his fellow 'dozer divers up cranes, down bunkers and through long, cold winters in an attempt to stand up for what we stand upon.

A motley band of protestors trying to find the balance between protecting life and having one, as their actions change policy, society and ultimately themselves.

Youthful passion clashes against the colossal power of big business and the state over issues as diverse as live animal exports, rainforest timber and the arms trade.

However, trying to defeat a £23 billion government road programme is a vegan picnic compared to dealing with heartbreak and hangovers.

Peter Styles was a full-time environmental activist for much of the 1990s. Deeply involved in a variety of campaigns, he was one of the first to be charged under the 1994 Criminal Justice Act and was jailed for his part in the Newbury bypass protests. He then spent several years covering the movement for the underground and mainstream press. Now living in Brighton, he has kept penury at bay with subsequent careers as a journalist, lecturer and comedy writer.

 small world media

Trade Orders (Ireland): Easons, Argosy, Small World Distribution
Trade Orders (Britain, Europe, North America): Gazelle Book Services, Active, Small World Distribution
Individual Orders: www.smallworldmedia.ie
Small World Media: 2 Great Strand Street, Dublin 1, Ireland 00 353 (0) 87 955 1504

Published: **October 2007**
Price: **€12.99 / £11.95**
Available for Sale: **Ireland, Britain, Europe**
Market: **Fiction (trade paperback)**
ISBN: **978-0-9554634-1-9**
Binding: **Paper**
Extent: **224pp, 140 x 210 mm**

Free Born Traveller

A NOVEL BY GRATTAN PUXON

The nuns call Denise Hanley 'the lame duck'. Her live-in boyfriend, Steve Aiken, has been proclaimed a communist by the Archbishop of Dublin.

Steve arrived in Dublin on the run from the British Army. It is a turbulent time. An IRA splinter group is letting off bombs during a ceasefire, while the country's travellers are massing on illegal encampments at Cherry Orchard near Palmerstown.

Based on actual events during the 1960s, this remarkable story – about a young English couple who take up with the tinkers of Ireland, get mixed up in IRA politics and find themselves personae non gratae with the Irish State – can now finally be told.

Handicapped Denise starts a makeshift school for the travellers, only to see it burned down by Dublin Corporation. A series of brutal evictions follow, causing the death of an infant. The travellers make their final stand at Cherry Orchard. The school is rebuilt and Larry Ward, the King of the Tinkers, joins the camp in time for the showdown.

For Steve and Denise imprisonment, betrayal and fear await.

Grattan Puxon joined the travellers on the outskirts of Dublin in 1962. Returning to England five years later, he founded the Gypsy Council. In 1971 he organised the first World Romani Congress, serving as its general secretary. After long sojourns in Eastern Europe and in the United States of America, Puxon came back to his native Essex in 1993 to find travellers under siege. He is the co-author of *Destiny of Europe's Gypsies*, documenting Nazi genocide, as well as many articles on the Romani movement.

 small world media

Trade Orders (Ireland): Easons, Argosy, Small World Distribution
Trade Orders (Britain, Europe, North America): Gazelle Book Services, Active, Small World Distribution
Individual Orders: www.smallworldmedia.ie
Small World Media: 2 Great Strand Street, Dublin 1, Ireland 00 353 (0) 87 955 1504